THE LEGACY OF THE NIZAMS

Under the auspices of

H.E.H. THE NIZAM'S URDU TRUST

HYDERABAD

Published by

VANI PRAKASHAN

New Delhi-110002

Phone : 3273167, 3275710 • Fax : 3275710

e-mail : vani_prakashan@yahoo.com

vani_prakashan@mantraonline.com

THE LEGACY OF THE NIZAMS

Translated and Compiled from Source Material

Translated by
Dr. Sheela Raj

Edited by
Prof. Satyanaraian Singh

ISBN 81-7055-164-1

Published by
Vani Prakashan
21-A, Daryaganj, New Delhi-110002

First Edition : 2002

Price : 195/-

Printed by
Nagri Printers, Delhi-110032

THE LEGACY OF THE NIZAMS
translated by Dr. Sheela Raj
edited by Prof. Satyanaraian Singh

CONTENTS

Preface xi
Foreword xv
Introduction xix

PART – I
The Asaf Jahi Kings

Chapter I : The Deccan: Background 3
Chapter II : Nizam-ul-Mulk Asaf Jah-I 14
'The Will' – A great testament on the kings' duties and concerns
Nizam Ali Khan – Asaf Jah II
Sikander Jah – Asaf Jah – III
Chapter III : Nasirul Daula – Asaf Jah-IV 33
Sir Salar Jung – I
Chapter IV : Afzal-ud-Daula – Asaf Jah – V 39
Chapter V : Mir Mahbub Ali Khan – Asaf Jah VI 46
Chapter VI : Mir Osman Ali Khan – Asaf Jah VII 61
(Executive Council)
Chapter VII : Symbols of Sovereignty 87

PART – II
Civilisation and Culture of Hyderabad

Chapter VIII : Civilisation and Culture 97
Chapter IX : Mode of Living 100

Chapter X	:	Performing Arts	113
Chapter XI	:	Urs, Fairs and Moharrum	126
Chapter XII	:	Lullabies and Hymns	135
Chapter XIII	:	Games and Sports	148

PART – III

Zauq-e-Sukhun

(Literary Taste in the Deccan)

Chapter XIV	:	The Poetry of Nizam VI and Nizam VII	167
Chapter XV	:	Dagh – Amir Minai – Jaleel, Amjad Faani – Qateel and others	180
Chapter XVI	:	Maqdoom, Nazr, Maikash, Sikander Ali Wajd	192
		Deccani (Dahkhani) poets lady Poets	

PART – IV

Archaeology Monuments

Chapter XVII	:	Salarjung Museum	209
Chapter XVIII	:	The background of Archaeology in Deccan	219
Chapter XIX	:	Ajanta–Ellora–Kailash Temple	227
Chapter XX	:	Islamic Buildings Mosques, domes and Palaces Forts and Tombs	232
Chapter XXI	:	Historical Monuments of Hyderabad Charminar – Mecca Masjid – Darushifa – Toli Masjid	241

PART – V

Association of Celebrated Personalities with Hyderabad

Chapter XXII : Association of celebrated personalities With Hyderabad 251

(A) *Expert Administrators*

(B) *Eminent Scholars, Professors and Poets*

(C) *Journalist, Politicians, Engineers and Doctors*

Chapter XXIII : Hyderabad's Cultural traditions: Some Commendations. 271

Chapter XXIV : A bunch of poetic tributes to Hyderabad 280

Bibliography 299

DEDICATION

Dedicated to Prince Muffakham Jah Bahadur for maintaining the Nizams' legacy of serving noble causes.

PREFACE

The Asaf Jahi dynasty ruled over the State of Hyderabad, which was not only the largest, but also the foremost in status and prosperity. In addition to its wealth, Hyderabad had been in the past a great seat of culture and learning.

Turning back to the pages of history, one will find that Hyderabad in the 19th century was not only economically and educationally backward but its crippled finances, chaos and confusion, retarded the all-round development of the State. The untiring efforts of gifted rulers and administrators put the State on the right track. Initially, the pace of development was slow. The closing years of the nineteenth century witnessed a vast transformation in socio-economic and cultural fields. Gradually with the introduction of new trends in administration, the erstwhile State of Hyderabad became one of the best administered Princely States in India.

During the last fifty years considerable historical and research work has been done concerning the erstwhile State of Hyderabad. The writing of history is not an easy task as it requires a deep insight into the march of events. However, some of the writers in recent times did not portray the real character and ethos of the State, as they did not have the biased knowledge of the Persian and Urdu languages and had a biased mind. It is the responsibility of a true historian to record facts free from prejudice and bias as historical works are a part of the national heritage for the present and future generations.

Taking into consideration the above mentioned facts I have added new dimensions to my translation. I have tried to unearth and add material in many areas where additional information is needed. The additions are made in true perspective and in the interest of the general reader. My aim has been to highlight the theme of Hindu-Muslim unity, which existed in the Hyderabad State for centuries and show how the Nizams maintained it. In my attempt to show the togetherness of the various communities which inhabited the State, I thought it befitting to show how this was done in the years gone by in the State of Hyderabad. I have consulted many papers and books and tried to balance the views expressed in the original version by presenting it in an unbiased manner. Mamlakat-e-Asafia is a good source material and reference book on the history of the Asaf Jahs amongst the other books on the subject. The author has particularly dealt with all the administrative departments and socio-economic developments which took place in the State.

The major feature of the reign of Mir Osman Ali Khan Nizam VII, was the re-organisation of finances, re-classification of heads of revenue and expenditure and streamlining of all departments of administration.

The Hyderabad Government promoted a policy of progressive development in the fields of agriculture, revenue, public works, industries, trade and commerce, medical, care veterinary, planning and transport among others. In the source, which has been consulted of the State, Mir Osman Ali Khan emerges as an enlightened ruler, a shrewd diplomat and a capable administrator. Though he was the richest man in the world, he disliked the gaudy pageantry of Princely India. He led a simple life and his simplicity set an example to others. His simple life was such that it could be followed by others as has rightly been said by Raja Narsing Raj in his speech on the occasion of the Silver Jubilee celebration of the rule of Mir Osman Ali Khan.

"The respect won by our renowned Master is not because he is the king of an independent State but because of his deeds and actions. He not only established his authority in the hearts of his relatives, dependents and hereditary servants but he ruled over millions of hearts in and outside India. It is easy to become a sovereign but it is very difficult to become the ruler of action. Only those fortunate and exalted personalities become men of action for whom god has a special graciousness. The fountain of learning which is known the world over as "Osmania University" is only because of the laudable qualities of our Master Osman Ali Khan, which were apparent like broad day-light. Prevention of extravagance, check and unresonable and unnecessary expenses on festivals, simplicity in the conduct of life, all these are the consequences of the deeds of this holy personality. Today the Deccan, following his footsteps, saved itself from becoming dependent on others. Now, where are those personalities who made themselves the model of simplicity, inspite of having affluence, for the sake of their people, children relatives and nobles. It is quite impossible to present such an example now".

In this context about the simplicity of his Master, Raja Narsing Raj quoted the shloka of the third chapter in Bhagvad Gita, which is as follows:

Yadadacarati Sresthasta Adevetaro Janah
Sa Yatpramanam Kurte Lokastadanuvarte

According Lord Krishna whatever is done by eminent persons other men to do it, the world follows that which he makes as his standard.

The translation of the book entitled Mamlakat-e-Asafia into English was a gigantic yet pleasant task. H.E.H. The Nizam's Urdu Trust had entrusted me with the translation of the volumes which has been successfully completed, though it took more than three years to do it satisfactorily.

I am thankful to Prince Muffakham Jah, Chairman, H.E.H. The Nizam's Urdu Trust for having entrusted me with the task of translation of such an informative and useful book. Hence in view of its importance and usefulness, its publication is of great interest as it is a complete and comprehensive history of the Asaf Jahi rule.

I am thankful to Mr. Abdul Mahmood, Secretary, H.E.H. The Nizam's Urdu Trust and the staff of the Trust for their kind co-operation.

I could not have accomplished this work but for the constant encouragement and co-operation extended by my husband, Narayan Raj.

–Dr. Sheela Raj

FOREWORD

The erst-while Hyderabad State was the largest among the Indian States and was as large as France and Turkey. It occupied a unique position having its own currency, post and railways. During the benevolent rule of Asaf Jahi kings the State made remarkable progress and was ahead of the British Indian provinces in many respects, particularly in the sphere of education. By far the most important legacy left by the Nizams is that under their rule a composite culture evolved and flourished based on tolerance, justice and brotherhood. The founder of the dynasty Asaf Jah I laid the foundation of a pluralistic and secular society as defined in his will or testament. The successive Nizams nurtured the ideals of secularism without distinction of caste, creed or community. Hindus, Muslims, Parsis, Sikhs, Christians all participated in the governance of the State and enriched the common culture which came to be known as "Hyderabadi culture". In fact, Hyderabad State became a shining example of good governance based on tolerance secularism and equal opportunities for all. There was no concept of majority or minority. Hindus and Muslims shared power and were proud of the cultural heritage which they all shared.

A number of books have appeared in Persian and Urdu on the Asaf Jahi Dominions written by historians and interllectuals of the sub-continent. However, there is hardly any book which highlights the distinctive role of Hyderabad as a symbol of culture and secularism. Recently an authoritative book has been published covering all aspects of Hyderabad culture and the salient features of governance. It was decided to translate the valuable material from Urdu to English in order to make it available to the larger section of the English knowing public.

Dr. Sheela Raj an eminent scholar translated this book in English and Prof. Satyanarayana Singh, Retired Head of the Department of English, Osmania University has edited and abridged this translation. Both these scholars have taken pains to project the ideas with force and clarity.

H.E.H. The Nizam's Urdu Trust has published many books in Urdu on different topics. This is the first book in English which is being published with the collaboration of M/s Vani Prakashan, New Delhi. The main idea and aim in publishing the book is to acquaint the present generation with the secular ideas of the State which gave equal opportunities to every religion, caste and community to live in peace and harmony. When the Hindu rulers were in power they gave equal importance to Muslims and when the Muslims came to power they too gave important positions to Hindus and non-Muslims. There was complete harmony among the citizens in all walks of life who shared a common culture, customs, traditions and rituals. It was Nizam-ul-Mulk Asafjah, the first Nizam, who established his Government in Deccan which ruled with honour, dignity and glory for 200 years enjoying the faith and confidence of all classes of people. H.E.H. The Nizam's Urdu Trust feels happy and proud to present this book based on historical data culled from various sources.

In conclusion, it is my bounden duty to record my sincere thanks and gratitude to Prince Muffakham Jah Bahadur for his valuable advice and for providing financial assistance to get this book published in English to reach a wider audience. My thanks are due to Dr. Sheela Raj for translating the book from Urdu to English and Prof.

Satyanarayana Singh for editing and abridging it. I offer my sincere thanks to Mr. Arun Maheshwari, M.D. M/s Vani Prakashan, New Delhi for having agreed to publish this book and print it within a short time. I must not forget to thank our Trustees Dr. Ali Mohammed Khusro, Mr. M.A. Hadi, Dr. Jafar Nizam and Prof. Lakshmi Reddy for their valuable suggestions and advice from time to time in enriching the contents of this book. The Urdu Trust is deeply grateful to the Trustees of H.E.H. The Nizami's Charitable Trust for providing financial assistance from time to time for completing the project.

This project was started under the supervision of my predecessor, Mr. Abdul Mahmood and he strove hard for its successful completion. I offer my sincere thanks to him.

Last but not least, my sincere thanks are due to those institutions and persons who came forward to provide the requisite information and gave full co-operation at various stages of printing of this book.

Iqbal Muzaffar Ahmed,
Secretary,
H.E.H. The Nizam's Urdu Trust.

INTRODUCTION

The present study is neither a historical assessment of the Asaf Jahi dynasty nor a critique of the Nizam's political alignments. It steers clear of controversial issues without passing value judgements on the Nizams' policies and style of governance. The main compulsion behind such a study on the legacy of the Nizams is to cherish those things that are worthy of remembrance and to treasure such memories of the Asaf Jahi era that will leave an abiding and wholesome impact on posterity.

The book is the result of the combined efforts of mostly the alumni of the Osmania University who take pride in the finer aspects of the legacy of the Nizams' rule in Hyderabad, where, historically speaking, different Indian languages, communities and religions not only co-existed peacefully but interacted with one another for mutual enrichment and helped evolve a composite culture that has since become the distinguishing feature of our national identity.

The study seeks among other things to highlight, the following contours in the history of the Deccan:

1. The Nizams displayed great statesmanship and foresight in bringing the administration closer to the people and implementing welfare measures for the benefit of the people.
2. The secular credentials of the Nizams were in line with the great traditions established by the Qutub

Shahi Kings. No historian has blamed the Asaf Jahis for religious intolerance and discrimination. The State was not an Islamic polity in the sense of being a theocracy. There was no official religion of the State. Hindus, Muslims, Parsis and Christians lived in perfect amity and participated with ardour and enthusiasm in each other's festivals such as Ramazan, Moharram, Dushera, Holi, Deepavali, Nowroz and Christmas. The Hindus held the highest positions of power and responsibility in the administration of the State. There is no government order or policy decision or record to show that a member of any community was deprived of a position in Government on the basis of religion.

Religion, as commonly understood and practised, served to forge the bonds of unity and fraternity among people of differing faiths. Religion had not become a byword for bigotry to breed communalism and sectarianism causing ill-will between the communities. Tolerance and respect of all religions was the hall-mark of Deccani culture. The Hyderabadis were liberal and cosmopolitan in their orientation and outlook. The ethical values that made them respect the worth and dignity of a human being irrespective of class, community, race or religion were the mainsprings of the Deccani ethos for centuries.

3. The chapter on civilization and culture attempts to clarify the factors that constitute the Hyderabadi way of life such as their mode of living, their conduct and behaviour, manner of speaking, food and dress. The two important things that determine the quality of a people's culture are firstly, the general standard of living and secondly, the force of tradition. Extreme poverty or affluence exerts, in the final analysis, a negative impact on human psyche. Extreme disparity in living conditions breeds in the poor discontent,

anger and rebellion. Excessive opulence in the wealthy leads to arrogance, greed and exploitation. Hyderabad under the Nizams, by and large, enjoyed peace and material well-being. Economic hardship and political instability harm and hamper the progress of civilization and culture. Fortunately the era of peace and prosperity under the Nizams generated an aesthetic and moral resurgence in the field of fine arts and philanthropy. The Asaf Jahis carried forward the tradition of a benign monarchy which was benevolent and people-oriented, not autocratic or anti-people, and which worked for their all-round welfare, progress and prosperity. It is a recognized fact that backing by life-affirming traditions improves the quality of life. Wealth is spent on organising social gatherings, in designing the architecture of buildings, in preparing appetising delicacies and in patronising poets and artists.

The feudal structure of society was not without redeeming graces.

The social scenario unfolded an attitude of generosity, averse to meanness, arrogance, and narrow mindedness, which permeated all classes of society. In line with this tradition there is a measure of nobility and decency in Hyderabadis which abhors crudity and foolishness. The observance of basic courtesies is integral to their behavioural pattern irrespective of class, position or community.

4. It is not correct to suggest that the Nizam who as conferred the title of "Faithful Ally" was an unqualified admirer or an unquestioning loyalist of the British rule. Whatever be the compulsions or constraints of political expediency in befriending the British, the Nizams from Nasir-ud-Dowla to Mir Osman Ali Khan nourished a dislike, or even anger at the glaring manifestation of the arrogance of British power. The signing of the

Subsidiary Alliance in 1798 by Nizam Ali Khan (Nizam-II) resulted in the stationing of British troops in Hyderabad, and the imposition of a British resident marked an erosion of sovereignty. All these came to a head in the Berar question which exposed the colonising tendency of the British when they rejected the Nizam's claim on Berar and attempted to belittle him by proudly asserting their paramountcy.

Another facet of the colonial attitude was the callous indifference of the British to the tragic plight of Orissa where the floods ravaged the State and lakhs of people lost their lives. At the instance of Afzal-ud-dowla, Nizam-V, Prime Minister Sir Salar Jung wrote a historic letter to Sir John Lawrence arraigning the Government of British India in these words:-

"The British authorities should not forget that it is because of the Hyderabad Government that the British could establish and maintain their rule in India. Being responsible for the welfare of British India they cannot escape responsibility to cope with the situation. They will be well advised to handover the province of Orissa to the management of Hyderabad as Hyderabad cannot remain silent while lakhs are dying in Orissa".

The letter, if any thing, reveals the Nizam's patriotic concerns as also his anti-colonial bias, his distrust of the British and his anxiety concerning the sufferings of fellow Indians.

5. The study underscores in particular the achievement of the first and the seventh Nizam. Nizamul Mulk-I the founder of the Dominion expounded the basic concerns and duties of the kind in his 'Will' – which is rated as an important and epoch making political document. This historic testament consisting of 17 clauses was an unfailing source of inspiration and guidance to the successive kings who at the time

of accession solemnly swore that they would adhere to the clauses of the 'Will' which in effect could be termed as the directive principles of the State concerning politics, administration and inter-religious harmony.

Mir Osman Ali Khan the Seventh and the last Nizam was a humanist and a dervish in royal robes. He was extremely frugal in his personal life but was munificent in serving the noble causes of education, health and religion. He took a pioneering step in making the judiciary independent of the executive and initiated the democratic process by introducing the principle of functional representation in the legislature.

An outstanding and, in many ways, a unique contribution of the last Nizam is in the sphere of education. As a pioneer in educational reforms he promulgated a law that education be free. By far the most memorable achievement was the establishment of the Osmania University – the only University in the whole of India to have an Indian language, Urdu, as its medium of instruction at the graduate and post-graduate levels in the faculties of arts, social sciences, law, science & technology, engineering and agriculture. Sir Rabindranath Tagore celebrated the event as a fulfilment of a long-felt need to free the people from the shackles of a foreign language.

6. The Nizams aspired to make their kingdom an independent polity and strove to build a self-reliant economy. All through the history of the Asaf Jahs, one thing that stands out prominently is the ruling passion of the Nizams to have a strong, self-supporting and autonomous kingdom. Their sense of royalty and dignity made them abhor all forms of subservience and subordination.

   Although Nizam-ul-Mulk-I, as Subedar of the Deccan, did not choose to declare his independence from the Mughal Empire, he could not tolerate any interference from Delhi in the internal affairs of Deccan. He administered the Deccan in his capacity as Subedar like an independent ruler. He was loyal to Emperor Aurangzeb but disliked his successor Mohammed Shah Rangeela for his frivolous ways and incompetent administration, and resented his autocratic attitude towards the Deccan.

The successors of Nizamul-Mulk-I following in his footsteps zealously guarded their freedom and preserved their sovereign identity. Unlike any other State, the Nizam had his own currency, postal system, railways, bus services, police army and an efficient civil service which are essential components of an independent state.

When the British left the country and India won her independence, the Nizam-VII faced a predicament when Majlis-e-Ittehadul Muslemin, an extremist Muslim organisation urged upon the Nizam to break free from the Indian Union and declare independence, ignoring the geo-political realities of the State. After the Police Action he adjusted himself admirably as the first Rajpramukh and dismissed the ill-advised movement as a temporary aberration in a State which for centuries had been an example of communal peace and harmony.

In retrospect, the Nizam's penchant for autonomy and economic self-reliance could well be interpreted to presage the present day demand of the States for greater autonomy and devolution of powers.

The Centre-State relations for the past 50 years after independence have been constantly under review. The Sarkaria Commission's recommendations have endorsed a larger measure of autonomy to the States and decentralisation of powers particularly on the financial side, so that the States could be free to plan and mobilise their resources and utilise the income for developmental schemes within the State. In essence, it is the enunciation of the federal principle which empowers the States to rule themselves by making them economically viable and self-supporting.

The study has been divided into four parts:

Part – I : After recounting briefly history of the Deccan, this part deals with the contribution of the Asaf Jahi kings to the many sided development of Hyderabad, in particular, the achievements of Nizamul-Mulk, the First and Mir Osman Ali Khan the Seventh Nizam.

Part – II : This Part analyses the factors that consitute the essence of Hyderabadi culture under the Nizams - the peoples' way of living, language, food and dress and the widespread prosperity and peace which improved the quality of life resulting in the development of performing arts like dance, music, painting, calligraphy, the culture of social interaction, designing the architecture of the buildings, food delicacies and celebration of fairs and festivals & composing of lullabies and hymns.

Part III – deals with the efflorescence of poetry containing the poetical works of Mir Osman Ali Khan, Faani, Amjad, Maqdoom and a host of others who had migrated to Hyderabad from Delhi and Lucknow.

This Section has also an independent chapter on the museum named after the legendary art connoisseur Sir Salarjung. The Salarjung Museum, a marvellous one-man collection is the biggest in Asia and a major centre of tourist attraction in Hyderabad.

Part – IV : deals with archeology and describes ancient historical monuments, domes, mosques, palaces, forts and museums. The Department of Archeology earned national reputation for its style of functioning and professional expertise and excellence.

The last section deals briefly with the eminent

personalities from Hyderabad and outside who contributed to the multi-faceted development of Hyderabad in different spheres of activity.

The other chapter in this section i.e. Part-V consists of commendations and tributes by outstanding statemen and poets concerning the beauty of Hyderabad City, its unique culture and the directive principles of State policy first outlined by the great Nizamul-Mulk in his historic testament. These tenets included genuine secularism, justice and measures to ensure the welfare of the people and prosperity in every field of endeavour which were scrupulously followed by the Asafia dynasty and, in particular, by His Exalted Highness Mir Osman Ali Khan.

It should be noted that although Hyderabad was governed by a Muslim ruler, it was never an Islamic or theocratic State. There was equal respect for all religions and, according to Mr.Mohammed Ali Jinnah's remarks in 1916, Hyderabad set an example worthy of emulation to the rest of India.

—Prof. Satyanaraian Singh

PART – I

THE ASAF JAHI KINGS

CHAPTER – I

THE DECCAN: BACKGROUND

The civilization of Deccan and its different aspects are historically important and of enduring value. The land of the Deccan is separated from the Northern India by two mountain ranges, Vhindhyachal and Satpura and by two rivers namely, the Narmada and the Tapti. These luxuriant mountains and green valleys form a beautiful setting to the Deccani region.

The foundation of the Deccani civilization was laid before the advent of Christ. The Dravidians settled down on the plains of the Deccan after escaping from the Aryan invaders and made the Deccan as their motherland. Gradually, with the passage of time, capital cities were established in Pattan, Badami and Kalyani. The Chalukyan rulers in Badami and Kalyani achieved orderly progress by virtue of their strong and efficient administration. This is the glorious period during which the magnificent workmanship in painting and sculpture was inscribed in the caves of Ajanta and Ellora.

At the end of the thirteenth century, the Muslim and the Khilji invaders came to the Deccan. The Muslims arrived at the beginning of the medieval period. They brought with them modern concepts and new dimensions of social life. The learned Sufis organised congregations and leading personalities like Shaik Siraj Junaid, Mulla Ishaq Shirhindi, Mulla Aleem Uddin Tabrazi, Hakim Nasar uddin Shirazi and above all Hazrath Amir Khusro were invited. The actual organisation of the Deccan was accomplished at the hands of Amiran-i-Sadah, (nobles of Sadah) who were men of ambition and faith. They were Turks of respectable families and were assigned different management wards in the villages to maintain a strict check on the administration of the Deccan. There were 100 villages in each ward, which were known as Sadi. The Turkish administrative officers who were appointed for these wards were known as Amiran-i-Sadah, or nobles of Sadah. Their alliance against the Delhi Empire and efforts for the establishment of an independent empire in the Deccan were nothing less than a miracle. These nobles of Sadah selected Zafar Khan, who was the descendent of the ancient king of Iran, Bahman, son of Isfandyar. Zafar Khan with his splendid past credentials ascended the royal throne with the title of Allauddin. The coronation ceremony was performed on Friday. This heralded the famous Bahamani kingdom in the Deccan known for its many splendoured achievements. The real grandeur of the Bahamani kingdom was evident in Gulbargah and Bidar. The greatness of the Bahamani kingdom was two-fold with the dazzle of the 'Takht-i-Firoza' (name of the throne of Khusrow), which was studded with numerous jewels. When the 'Takht Mahal' of Ahmed Shah Ware Vagnabu in Bidar was completed, Shaik Azari praised it in the most eloquent words.

The rulers of the Bahamani kingdom were remarkable for their wisdom and statesmanship of a high order. These rulers introduced modern methods in the administrative machinery. They were foremost in establishing peace and united the people of the Deccan into a political entity. It was nothing short of a miracle that the Bahamani kingdom established the Deccani nationality. Significantly, the people of the Deccan affirmed and asserted themselves as 'Deccani'.

The impact was so deep that even after the decline of the kingdom, the name was remembered for decades and the Bahamani currency continued in circulation.

After the fall of the Bahamani kingdom, when five kingdoms were established on its ruins, a new chapter was opened in the Deccani civilization. Streams of knowledge and learning began to flow. The Nizam Shahi family of Ahmednagar was the chief architect of the new resurgence. Hussain Nizam Shah, who was the illustrious ruler of this family, established his leadership in the Deccan. He was acknowledged as a leader by other kingdoms. When Chand Bibi, the daughter of Hussain Nizam Shah married Ali Adil Shah I, ruler of Bijapur, the inter-dominion relationship became strong and cordial. The Sholapur district of Ahmednagar was given as dowry to the bride. The renowned historian Mohammed Qasmi Farishta, accompanied the palanquin of the bride from Ahmednagar to Bijapur. When Mughals invaded the Deccan, Chand Bibi, the heroine of Deccan, stood with a sword in her hand to protect her ancestral kingdom and fought courageously against her enemies. She never bowed down in her entire life before the Mughal invaders. The Mughal General praised her courage and was forced to accept her demands. She was awarded the title of 'Chand Sultana'. After her death Malik Amber carried on the fight. This faithful General maintained the traditions of the heroine and fought courageously against the Mughal invaders. His fight against the Imperial Forces constitutes a sensational event of history. The cultural services of Malik Amber are comparatively higher than his achievements as a warrior. His systematic administration and settlement of land revenue deserve special mention. His capital enjoyed a high degree of civil amenities. He constructed canals. Mirza Sadiq Asfhani, a Mughal officer who visited the Deccan was highly impressed with the civic amenities and wrote thus:

"Shahr Ambar Nasim Mush Sarisht

Ab o burdabru-e-bihisht"

"The morning breeze of the city like Amber and its water have taken away the primacy and glory of paradise."

The rise of Bijapur and Golconda is a golden chapter in the history of the Deccan. These kingdoms were centres of knowledge and learning. Science and literature were vigorously promoted. The mausoleum of Bijapur and the Farah Bagh of Ahmednagar revive glorious memories of these kingdoms. It is a famous saying in the Deccan that after seeing the beautiful imposing buildings, Shah Jahan drew up his plan for the Taj Mahal. These kingdoms were proud of the fact that with their rise, Persian literature and the Deccani language achieved extraordinary eminence. Mullah Zahuri wrote 'She nasr Zahuri' and Mohd. Qasim Farishta compiled a detailed 'History of the Deccan' which is held to be an authoritative book on the entire Deccan and mirrored the richness of its life. Under the patronage of the Deccan rulers outstanding books on prose and poetry were written. The 'Subras' and 'Qutub Mushtari' of Wajhi, 'Tutinama' of Ghawwasi', 'Phoolban' of Ibn Nishati, and 'Ali Nama' of Mullah Nusrati are the masterpieces of the Deccan language. Mohd. Quli Qutub Shah the founder of Hyderabad city was also a great poet. In his Kulliyat (the collection of poems) there are hundreds of verses in every genre of poetry.

The construction of the city of Hyderabad in 1000 H reveals the flawless culture of the Qutub Shahi rulers. The foundation of this city was laid at a revolutionary period, when the first Alif of the Hijri era of thousand years was completed and the second Alif was about to begin. There was much excitement and exhilaration in the Islamic world. Muslims in every country looked forward to the birth of great thinkers and reformers, who would emancipate the world from its besetting evils and bring about enlightenment and progress. Mohd. Quli Qutub Shah the founder of the city of Hyderabad was aware of these ideas. He spent his entire energy and devoted his time and thought to make Hyderabad a picturesque and memorable city.

Significantly, the construction of the city was done according to a special map that conformed to the best principles of town planning. Straight roads were laid and on both sides of the roads similar types of buildings were constructed. Besides, all the necessities of civic life were provided. For the supply of water, canals were constructed. A number of gardens were laid to give the city a look of greenery and freshness. Arrangements were made for the treatment of the sick. A big hospital was constructed in the eastern part of the city, which was known as Dar-ul-Shifa. It was a spacious two-storeyed building with well qualified and experienced physicians and surgeons who provided treatment. Boarding and lodging arrangements were made for the sick.

The newborn city was very dear to Mohd. Quli Qutub Shah. Hence, he prayed for the progress of his city in the court of Supreme Being:-

"Mera Shahr Logan se mamur kar ya Sami."

"Oh God let my city be filled with people like fish in the sea."

His prayers were not ineffectual. Indeed, Hyderabad city prospered and progressed in every period. The Mughal historians, who saw this city praised the city more than its founder. Even though they were the residents of monarchical cities like Delhi and Agra which were renowned for their magnificence, they placed Hyderabad in the forefront of all other cities. The noted historian Farishta has recorded that as far as its beauty and cleanliness is concerned "there is no other city in the whole of India like the city of Hyderabad either in the East, West, North or South." Khafi Khan wrote thus: "In reviewing the vastness of the city, elegance and climate, charming beauty, greenery and its productivity, my words fail me even if I take an aerial view". Mohd. Saqi wrote "It is a land of heaven and a place of relaxation which imparts comfort to the body and tranquility to the soul. Its population is larger than I imagined, the buildings are tall, and more extensive than I thought. There is plenty of moisture in the air, and the flowing springs and greenery of gardens, added to its charm. One is inclined to believe that the flowers and greenery are as pure as water and as colourful as emerald and ruby."

Maulana Hali wrote:-

Sahn-e-gulshan mein kisi kam ko aye koi
Jayega booye reyaheen se muattar hokar
Hyderbad bhi yek bagh hai masha Allah
Hai jahan faiz ke darwaze kushada sab par

"If anybody enters the garden for work he will certainly return with the aroma and fragrance of flowers. Hyderabad is indeed a garden city, its doors of prosperity are open to all.

Allama Iqbal Says:

"Noor ke zarron se qudrat ne banayee ye zamin
Ainah tapke Deccan I khak agar paye fishar"

"Nature has created this earth with the particles of divine light: the atmosphere of the Deccan radiates light and shines like a mirror."

The decline of Qutub Shahi kingdom was marred by tragic events. The eight-month long siege of Golconda witnessed strong self-defence, courageous confrontation with the enemy and unstinted loyalty of the people of the fort. The dignified stand of Abul Hasan Qutub Shah and unshakable loyalty of Abdul Razzakh Lari stand out unparalleled. A disloyal Afghan opened the gates and allowed the Mughal soldiers to enter the fort. Abul Hasan faced the confronation with great fortitude and dignity.

The establishment of the Asafia kingdom in the eighteenth century is a great landmark in the history of the Deccan. When the Mughal Empire was about to collapse, Nizamul Mulk Asaf Jah took the reins of the Deccan. In his capacity as Diwan of Mughal Empire, the policies and schemes which Nizamul Mulk framed to bolster the falling empire were not upheld due to the insensibility and slackness of the Mughal Emperor. The insolence of the Mughal Darbar proved to be the last straw. In disgust, Nizam-ul-Mulk bade farewell to Delhi and arrived in the Deccan. His move was nothing short of a divine blessing. Had it not been for his timely arrival, Maratha invasions would have continued and the region would have disintegrated into pieces, and the territorial integrity of Deccan jeopardised.

Nizam-ul-Mulk was the scion of a respectable family of Turkistan. His predecessors, Khwaja Abid and Ghaziuddin Khan Firoz Jung, acquired great honours during the reign of Shah Jahan and Aurangzeb. Nizam-ul-Mulk inherited the honours and commanded great respect. He was endowed with high perception and sagacity and was a good administrator well acquainted with the rules of governance.

After the battle of Shakar Kheda in 1724, he ascended the throne. After taking over the reins of office, he streamlined political affairs and administered with efficiency all the departments of the Government. Military and non-military Departments were revamped. The relations between the Central and State Governments were good. Efficient officials were appointed. Lala Mansaram, Peshkar and Musavi Khan'Jurrat' were his trusted officers. He used to call Musvi Khan 'Jurrat' his Abdul Fazal. He was firmly committed to the welfare of the people. Religious tolerance was one of the guiding principles of his administration. He respected the rights of the people and believed in justice and saw to it that there was not the least suspicion of injustice. His vast kingdom, which extended from Vindyachal to Madurai became a region with various sections of people who lived in perfect harmony and peace without distinction of caste or creed. Nizam-ul-Mulk was a learned man and was endowed with the zeal to promote education. Students were encouraged with the award of scholarships. He was a poet too. His diwan is memorable in Deccani literature.

His political sagacity came to the force when even on his death bed, he explained his bequest to his successor, Nasir Jung.

After the death of Nizam-ul-Mulk, his eight successors never deviated from the time-honoured customs and traditions. The reign of each successor was not only marked by the tradition of religious tolerance and welfare of the people but was also noted for the expansion of educational services. Importance was given to historiography and historiographers were paid generously. In the nineteenth century educational activities gained momentum. The contribution of the nobles of Paigah towards the promotion of education was boundless. Fakhruddin Khan Shamsul Umara became very famous for his foresight and vision. The enlightened Nawab spent millions of rupees for the promotion of arts and sciences. In fact, Hyderabad blossomed with learning.

First and foremost, he made translation his main objective. Books published on arts and the sciences in Europe and America were translated into Urdu. He engaged many translators for his work. A printing press was setup for the publication of these translations. It was the first printing press in Hyderabad. The collection of these translations published in six volumes is known as "Sitah Shamsiya". This collection is dedicated to Fakhruddin Khan Shamsul Umara and stands as a great memorial to his dedication and devotion to literature. Another landmark in education was the establishment of a school, known as "Madrasa Fakhria", which attracted many students who were encouraged in their studies by monetary help. Those students of the State who passed out from the school spread enlightenment among the people of the State and promoted ethical and cultural values.

The successors of Nawab Fakhruddin Khan were extremely fond of education and moral values. The generosity of Hyderabad towards the promotion of every facet of education was not confined only to the Dominion but extended to the rest of India. Hyderabad's contribution to Indian educational institutions is a memorable chapter in the literary history of Hyderabad. Aligarh University was given lakhs of rupees. The illustrious, nobles of Hyderabad Asman Jah and Viquar-ul-Umara, were true representatives of Hyderabad in this respect and valuable grants were given to the University. Asman Jah granted pension to Maulana Hali. Hali thanked him for his valued services in these couplets:-

"Ae bashir daulat o din naib shah-I-Deccan
Hai mukmmat-I-Deccan ka zat par teri madar
Mujh pe farmaya hai jo lutf-o-karm sarkar ne
Shukr is kar nahin sakta ada main zinhar"

"O' viceregrent of the king of the Deccan, a haven of prosperity and faith. You are the keystone of Deccani arch. I can never express fully my thanks for the favours and generosity shown to me."

At the end of the nineteenth century there were administrative reforms which became necessary. In 1869, when Maghfirat Makan Afzal Ud Daula died, the entire administrative machinery fell into the hands of Salar Jung. This prudent Minister organised the entire administration of the State. The British Indian principles of administration were included in the reforms. Amila or the Executive and Judiciary were set up on the British lines. The ancient land revenue system, which was defective, was changed. Taluqdars and Tahsildars were appointed and were held responsible for maintaining law and order and for collection of revenue. The judicial system too was reorganised. In place of the ancient court Darul Khaza, a High Court and subordinate courts were established.

In 1884 when Ghufran Makan Mahbub Ali Khan reigned the kingdom, there was progress and prosperity in the entire State. He was a pattern of excellence in affability and virtue. He ruled with love and affection and was passionately devoted to his subjects. He never tolerated any hardships of his subjects. Whenever his subjects suffered, he became restless. He considered Hindus and Muslims as his two eyes.

In 1908, when there were floods in Hyderabad and half of the city was washed out, Ghufran-I-Makan opened the gates of his palaces for the flood-affected destitutes and food was distributed straight from the royal kitchen to the flood affected victims. The love and affection of Ghufran-I-Makan had tremendous impact on his subjects to such an extent that people belonging to all castes and communities considered him as their Wali (Saint Avtar or incarnation of the deity). During his reign, there was no discrimination of caste and class. It is a well established fact of history of Hyderabad that Hindu subjects used to affix their names with the name of Mahbub (beloved) Badshah (king). In their names 'Mahbub' was included, namely Mahbub Raj, Mahbub Karan, and Mahbub Narayan. There is nothing like that in the entire history of Asia.

In 1911, when Ghufran-I-Makan passed away, his son, Mir Osman Ali Khan ascended the throne. His reign, which lasted for 38 years, is one of the longest in the Asaf Jahi dynasty. It is a happy coincidence that this period commenced when science and technology had made great advances in the realm of knowledge. The great discoveries fascinated the world. The ruler of the State and the heads of administration kept pace with these revolutionary changes. There was sustained progress in all branches of learning and science and all out efforts were made to modernise the Dominion. In 1919, the Osmania University was established. This newly established University, boosted arts and sciences, and the literature which was confined in foreign languages was translated into Urdu. Thus the new generation was more idealistic and with the educational progress and administrative changes the State rapidly advanced in both intellectual and artistic fields. Unfortunately, world events brought in their wake many difficulties which the State had to face. Two wars were fought in Europe and this hampered progress in the State. Neverthless under the wise stewardship or the ruler the State made all-round progress even in those difficult and turbulent times. In 1948, when the British left India, the Asaf Jahi Dominion entered a new era of democratic polity with the integration of Hyderabad into the Indian Union.

CHAPTER II

MAGHFIRAT MAAB NIZAM-UL-MULK

MIR. QAMRUDDIN KHAN –ASAF JAH-I
FOUNDER OF THE ASAFIA KINGDOM

Nizamul Mulk Asaf Jah-I was a farsighted statesman. He was the founder and architect of the Hyderabad Dominions and an epitome of all that is best and finest in the Asaf Jahi rule. He was a God-fearing man who had the wisdom and courage to chastise and chasten a tyrant like Nadirshah, and an accomplished warrior who could defeat the evil designs of powerful and scheming chieftains. Nizamul Mulk in his 'Will' left a historic testament laying down the directive principles of State policy to be followed by successive kings after him.

On the suggestion of Emperor Aurangzeb Alamgir, Ghaziuddin Firoz Jung got married to Sayeedunnisa Begum daughter of Allama Saadullah Khan, the Prime Minister of Shah Jehan. She delivered a male child on August 11th, 1671. Mir Qamaruddin was the name suggested by Aurangzeb Alamgir. The chronogram according to the Hijri date of birth is 'Nekbaqt' i.e. 1082 H i.e. 1671 A.D. At the age of six, he was awarded a mansab of four hundred zat by the king. On attaining maturity he was admitted to the royal palace. At the age of twenty, in 1690, the king conferred on him the title of Chin Killich Khan (small sword) and a mansab of four thousand.

In 1697, he was sent on an important mission to tackle the Marathas. He was given an important post in the Criminal Court of Bijapur in 1700. After two years, he was made Subedar of Bijapur and Karnataka. He became a commandant of the military of Karnataka in 1704. During the siege of Wakankhed, in 1705, the embattled men fired cannons from the ramparts of the fort. A cannon ball released with tremendous force wounded a leg of Killich Khan's horse. The horse collapsed. When the Emperor heard the news he sent to him a Persian horse with gold ornaments and accompaniments. On conquering the Fort, Aurangzeb honoured him with an enamelled sword and his personal elephant.

Besides, he gave him an emerald ring, on which the name of 'Chin Killich Khan Bahadur' was engraved. In 1706, with a mansab of 5,000 zat he was reappointed Subedar of Bijapur. Aurangzeb died in 1707 at Ahmednagar and, according to his will, his body was brought to Khuldabad. Chin Killich Khan reached Khuldabad from Bijapur and buried the Emperor with his own hands.

After the death of Aurangzeb, a war of succession broke out among his sons. Chin Killich Khan kept aloof. A battle was fought between Prince Azam and Prince Mouzam near Agra in which Azam was killed. Mouzam ascended the throne and assumed the title of 'Shah Alam, Bahadur Shah-I'. Bahadur Shah bestowed the title of 'Khan-I-Dauran Bahadur Khan' on Chin Killich Khan offering him Subedari of Oudh and Foujdari of Lucknow. Bahadur Shah, however, disliked the family of Chin Killich Khan. The style of the functioning of his court was completely different from that of Aurangzeb. Chin Killich Khan was not happy with the royal favours, but continued with his post, though aggrieved. At last, on a Saturday, he appeared in the court and submitted his resignation to the king. A proverb would have it:

'Haich afat na rasad gosha tanhaira' (No hardship is greater than the recess of loneliness). He opted for retirement in Delhi. Dressed like a poor man he spent his time in the company of scholars and saints.

Mohammed Shah Rangeela with the help of Sadaath brothers ascended the throne. The Sadaath brothers were the defacto masters and had the craft and cruelty to eliminate their opponents. Mohammed Shah was given to the pleasures of the flesh and the lure of wine and women. Better known as 'Mohammed Shah Rangeela', the life-style of the King suited the Sadaath brothers and their ambitions. They conspired to liquidate the principled Nizamul Mulk. Nizamul Mulk was farsighted and wise statesman who desired to free the wayward King from the clutches of the Sadaath brothers. He finally succeeded in killing the crafty manipulater Sadaath Baroh.

The Central Government was relieved forever from the mischief of Sadaath. The King contrary to his promise appointed Mohd. Amin Khan, his relative, to the post of Prime Minister, which naturally displeased Nizam-ul-Mulk. Later, Mohammad Shah himself wrote a letter to Nizam-ul-Mulk offering him the Ministry but being a self respecting person he did not accept the offer. He thought that in case he accepted the offer Mohd. Amin Khan would be deprived of the Ministry. He was satisfied with the post of Subedar.

Historians are of the opinion that Mohd. Amin died within three months. At that time, Nizam-ul-Mulk was in Talikota; The King invited him to hold the post of the Ministry. On January 28, 1722, Nizamul-Mulk reached Delhi and took charge as the Prime Minister. The court of the King, at that time, became the arena of avaricious, corrupt and mean-minded men. The open merry-making and profligate ways of Mohd. Shah were the talk of the town. The people rightly dubbed him as: "Mohd. Shah Rangela".

The loyal Nizam-ul-Mulk, soon after assuming the

ministerial post, strove hard to organise the Court and tone up the adminstration. Mohammad Shah resented any interference in his personal affairs. His companions opposed Nizam-ul-Mulk. In the event of his absence from the royal Darbar, they imitated his mannerisms and dress. They remarked in jest "Nizam-ul-Mulk looks like a monkey in the outdated Darbari dress". When Nizam-ul-Mulk was informed of what was going on behind his back, he remarked:

"If the King has reached such depths, the day is not far off, when monkeys will dance on the ramparts of the Red Fort."

His words came true and what he said actually happened.

Nizamul Mulk had a sound psychological insight into the minds of the King and the chief courtiers. He could easily sense palace intrigues and conspiracies, against the Empire and was able to counter them effectively by his adroit planning and strategy. He was himself a faithful servant of the Emperor capable of staking his all for the integrity and progress of the Empire. He had great organisational powers and a staunch loyalist following.

Mohammed Shah was not favourably disposed towards Nizamul Mulk and appointed Mubariz Khan as the Subedar of the Deccan. This official was as flippant and pleasure loving as the King himself. Nizam-ul-Mulk had no faith in the King.

On October 11, 1724, Nizam-ul-Mulk fought a fierce battle with Mubariz Khan at Shakarkheda. Heaps of bodies piled up. Mubriz Khan was also killed. This decisive war had great significance in the history of the Deccan. For all practical purposes, this was the first sign of independence of the Asafia dynasty. Accordingly, the date of the laying of the foundation of Asafia kingdom was decided as 23rd Muharram 1137 – 11th October 1724.

The efforts of Nizam-ul-Mulk to protect the Deccan

province from political disorder and destruction and to declare his independence were very timely and statesman-like. The King was excessively addicted to pleasure. His court consisted of corrupt and immoral men. The Treasury was bankrupt. The unruly activities of the Marathas were beyond control.

Nizamul Mulk awarded gifts and honours, conferred titles and mansabs to those who participated in the battles. He organised the administration on a proper footing. The battle of Shakarkheda marked the establishment of Nizam-ul-Mulk's hereditary rule in the Deccan. In January 1725, Nizamul Mulk went to Hyderabad and made it his new capital.

While doing so he was probably guided by two considerations. Hyderabad was much farther from the Maratha capital than Aurangabad where he could plan his secret military strategies to confront his powerful rivals, the Marathas. Secondly, he could conveniently approach Karnataka over which Nizam-ul-Mulk wanted to tighten his grip.

TITLE OF ASAF JAH

Nizam-ul-Mulk's successive victories became a cause of anxiety to Mohd. Shah. After the victory of Shakarkheda and the death of Mubariz Khan, the King conferred on him the title of Asaf Jah and permitted him to stay back in the Deccan as long as he wished. Whenever, he so desired he could visit Delhi in the capacity of a vakil (Ambassador). All this was done to win the heart of Nizam-ul-Mulk.

Nizam-ul-Mulk on this occasion never deviated from the norms of integrity and loyalty. In order to give an assurance of good faith, he sent his petition expressing his faith and sincerity. He neither displayed royal affluence nor assumed titles and did not enforce a new currency.

He kept in mind his faithful adherence to the Emperor and continued with the administration of the Deccan province in his capacity as a Subedar like an independent ruler.

The Central Government at Delhi was then losing its power and becoming weak. The unfortunate shadow of the Maratha designs for the expansion of their rule towards the environs of Agra made Mohd. Shah Rangeela sit up and take notice of the alarming situation. He sensed that his very throne and crown were in danger. He sent a Farman to Nizam-ul-Mulk asking him to come to Delhi and take stock of the situation. In these circumstances, finding no other way of safety in Delhi, Nizam-ul-Mulk appointed his third son, Nasir Jung, his deputy, to enable him to carry out the orders of the Sultan. He reached Delhi on July 13, 1737.

HISTORICAL RECEPTION AT DELHI

It is said that the reception of Nizam-ul-Mulk Asaf Jah by the Mughal emperor was organised on a grand scale in view of his loyalty and sincere services. Not a single Subedar was accorded such a grand reception. Qamaruddin Khan, Wazair ul Mumalik was sent by the King to welcome Nizam-ul-Mulk when still 55 miles away from Delhi. As Nizam-ul-Mulk Asaf Jah approached Delhi, the King expressed his great eagerness to meet him. He sent numerous presents and made grants. When his cavalcade entered the borders of Delhi, brushing aside ancient traditions and royal etiquette, the kettle drums were sounded. When he entered the capital to the resounding sound of shahnais and trumpets, the entire city was out in large numbers to have a glimpse of him. Fazal Ali Khan chronicled his arrival thus:

Sad shukr ke zat deen panahi amad

Rounaq dah Mulk badshahi amad
Tarikh rasidnish bagosham Hatuf
Guft Ayat Rahmat Ilahi amad.
1150 H – 1737 AD

"Millions of thanks, that your Highness has come which brings glory to, the State and mysterious voice whispered in my ears, the year as date of his arrival, which is according to numerology equivalent to 1150 H 1737 A.D."

NADIR SHAH'S ATTACK

Nizam-ul-Mulk after reaching Delhi took charge of the post of Vakil Mutlaq (absolute viceregent). After restoration of the administration and the organisation of the army, he was busy crushing the power of the Marathas. In the environs of Bhopal, he discussed with Baji Rao the terms of a compromise. At that time, Nadir Shah attacked the North-West borders of India. Nizam-ul-Mulk marched on till he reached Delhi. He organised and arranged the royal army. He collected ammunition, and along with Burhan-ul-Mulk, he fought against Nadir Shah at Panipat in Febraury 1739. Burhanuddin was imprisoned by the army of Nadir Shah. After holding consultations with his military commanders. Mohd. Shah promised to pay penalty of four crores of rupees. When the preparations were being arranged for a royal banquet for Nadir Shah, word got round that Nadir Shah had been assassinated. On hearing the news, the people of Delhi massacred the followers of Nadir Shah. When Nadir Shah was informed about the situation, he rushed to the city on horseback to assure the people that he was alive but stones were hurled at him. That angered him and in the courtyard of Sunehri Masjid (golden mosque) he unsheathed his sword and sat down. It was the hint of an order for general massacre. Immediately the army of Nadir Shah plundered Delhi, burnt the shops and there was bloodshed in the lanes and the streets. In these horrible conditions, on the orders of Mohd. Shah, Nizam-ul-Mulk sought an audience with Nadir Shah. He stood quietly bareheaded with a sword hanging on his neck. On seeing him, Nadir shah asked him what he wanted. Nizam-ul-Mulk read a couplet of the poet Hafiz Shirazi:

Kase namand ke digar ba tegh naaz kashi
Magar ke zinda kani khalq ra o baz kashi

"None has survived, you may take pride in the art of wielding the sword only when you are able to revive the people you have killed".

Then and there the couplet touched the heart of Nadir Shah. He said " 'Ba resh safeed' bakshi dan". I declare a truce in respect for your white beard.

He placed his sword back in the sheath. Immediately, the massacre was stopped. Thereafter, on May 5, 1739, he collected the wealth of Delhi, cash and jewels and the Peacock Throne and koh-i-noor diamond, loaded it all on camels and turned towards Iran. When he was ready to depart from Delhi, he offered Nizam-ul-Mulk Asaf Jah the Empire of Delhi and observed: "You are the only man who deserves this". The magnanimous Nizam-ul-Mulk Asaf Jah as a loyal servant of the house of Taimur replied "Ma mardam naukar pesha yem mara uz Saltanat che kar dag namak harami ba farkh itaat rawa nami darim".

"We belong to the category of people who are servants by profession. What have we to do with kingdoms; we do not think the stain of unfaithfulness is permissible on the head of obedience." Nizam-ul-Mulk for all practical purposes was independent in the exercise of his sovereignity, but acknowledged that he administered his Government as a deputy or delegate of the Mughal Empire. All the coins of his State were stamped with the name of the Mughal Emperor, and in public prayers it was the Emperor's name that was used. He was designated 'Servant of the Emperor'. He could confer titles on his subjects, though he himself received his titles from the Emperor of Delhi. His designation "Subedar of Deccan" merely implied the Governorship of a province under an Emperor. Sometimes the Nizam was addressed as "Nawab" the literal meaning of Nawab being Deputy. "The Regulator Of The Country" was his title before he assumed the sovereignty of the Deccan. The same title was continued by his descendants who succeeded him. 'The Nizam' as a distinctive appellation was coined by the Europeans. (Captain Robert M. Gindlay, Scenery, Costumes and Architecture, 1826).

Mohammed Shah Rangeela again revived his flippant life-style. Nizam-ul-Mulk could not bear all this. On the other hand Nasir Jung at the instigation of some evil-minded nobles declared his subedari in the Deccan. After obtaining permission from the King, Asaf Jah turned towards the Deccan in 1741. In the beginning, he wrote to Nasir Jung in conciliatory terms advising him to abstain from childish actions but Nasir Jung was under the spell of power. His father's admonitions had no effect on him. Much against his will Asaf Jah proceeded to punish him. On July 23, 1741 a battle was fought between father and son near Daulatabad. When the battle between Nasir Jung and Nizam-ul-Mulk was concluded at the Idgah Maidan, Aurangabad, Nasir Jung was imprisoned by his father. (Chronology of Modern Hyderabad, Central Record Office, Hyderabad, 1954). The arrogant son had to face defeat. He looked downward with shame. When he was presented in front of his father he felt thoroughly ashamed with repentance. Nasir Jung then read the following couplet:

Kash ke madar na zade ba bude
Jaye shiram zahar dade ba bude

"I wish, my mother had not given birth to me. Instead of giving me milk, she should have given me poison."

Asaf Jah controlled his feelings, and moved by his

fatherly affection, pardoned him. Later, he presented to him his personal robes. After spending a few days in Aurangabad, he proceeded towards Hyderabad.

In 1743, Asaf Jah captured the fort of Trichnapalli from the Marathas and in 1744, the fort of Balkonda of Munawar Khan Deccani too fell into his hands.

In 1747, Ahmed Khan Abdali, the ruler of Kabul, attacked Shahjahanbad. Hearing this news, Asaf Jah went up to Burhanpur from Aurangabad, where he was informed of the victory of the royal army. Ahmed Shah Abdali after being defeated returned to Kabul. Meanwhile, Mohd. Shah passed away and Ahmed Shah became his successor. Asaf Jah himself felt sick and his condition deteriorated day by day. Nizam-ul-Mulk died in Burhanpur on 4th Jumadi ulsani 1161 H i.e. 1748 at the age of 79. He was a ruler for 29 years.

Nasir Jung on completion of all the formalities, saw to it that the body of Asaf Jah was bathed and covered with shroud; the final prayers were said and with pomp and final dignity the body was given in trust and buried at the same place where a tent was erected. This place become famous as his bathing place. Here a garden was laid. Auqaf (charitable endowments) were fixed and a treasurer and custodians were appointed. Later, his body was taken to Khuldabad where he was buried behind the tomb of Shah Burhan uddin Garib. He was called 'Maghfirat Maab', posthumously.

Maghfirat Maab got his 'Will' recorded in the presence of Nasir Jung, Ahmed Zia uddin Khan, the Chief Judge, Daroga Auli Khan, the superintendent and Munshi, and Peshkar Lala Mansaram which contained seventeen directives to Nasir Jung. This 'will' constituted the basic principles of the Hyderabad Dominion, which acted as the inspiration and guidance to the Asaf Jahi dynasty. Nizam-ul-Mulk not only laid the foundation of Hyderabad State but also was responsible for its consolidation and orgaisation. Nizam-ul-Mulk was a man endowed with lofty ideals, political sagacity and statesmanship of a high order. He brought peace ad security to the region. As rightly stated by the learned scholar, Nawab Ali Yawar Jang, he was a great scholar and a poet, no less an administrator in peace than a general in war. No chronicle of the 'Rulers of India' can be complete without reference to him. History has done scant justice to his achievements. He was not only in command of armies, but was indeed a leader of men. He not only founded a State, but also organised and established it. The basic divisions of Diwani, Sarf-e-khas, and Paigah owe their origin to him. He brought peace and security to a distracted land. He had the wisdom to seek the substance, not the shadow, of power. What is more, he had the stature and the sinew to maintain his position. And yet, when Nadir Shah rode with blood and thunder into Hindustan, he marched to the defence of Delhi, the scene of his ancient loyalty, against the invador of India.

Maghfirat Maab witnessed the rule of seven kings and fought 87 battles. During his last days, Asaf Jah's reign spread over a large area, 800 miles in length and 400 miles in breadth. There were six provinces under him. The early part of the life of Maghfirat Maab was spent under the training of Aurangzeb Alamgir. He was a great commander and a far seeing statesman. He tried to avoid battles as far as possible. Whenever the need arose, he would not hesitate to raise his sword, and adopt successful war strategies. He could in a short span and with less damage to the life of his soldiers, defeat the large army of his enemy. He was loyal, industrious, and a true lover of education. He preferred to spend his time in the company of scholars. He had an excellent command over the Turki and Persian languages and was also a poet. His Persian diwan has been published. He was the pupil of Mirza Abdul Qadir 'Bedil'. He had two published diwans to his credit (Ram Babu Saksena, History of Urdu Literature, Ram Narain Lal, Allahabad, 1927).

WILL IN THE NAME OF NASIR JUNG

1. "It is necessary for the Prince to be friendly and conciliatory with the Marathas, who control vast lands of the country. As far as possible, he by himself should not break peaceful relations with them, unless compelled to do so.
2. Avoid bloodshed, and destruction of human beings who are God's children. They are not foodgrains like wheat and jawar which can be cultivated every year. Criminals should be handed over to the Kazi, who should perform his duties with justice.
3. The greater part of life time should be spent in touring the country because one will then come into contact with new places and new events. He should make it a habit to stay in tents and organise administrative affairs from there itself. The soldiers of the army should be granted leave to visit their homes and families so that there is no break in family ties. As far as possible, the soldiers should be posted closer to their home town.
4. After discharging religious duties, you must thank God for having blessed you with the governance of a dominion and entrusted you with the affairs of human beings. In the pride of your royal authority, never forget the instability and non-permanence of Government. You should schedule your work according to a set time-table lest you waste time. Do not keep your work pending for the next day. When involved in one type of work, do not neglect the other. Keep a sharp eye on the principles and details of administration because details form part and parcel of the whole.
5. The foundation of our family was laid, when Bad Shah (Aurangzeb) appointed our grandfather, the late Nawab Abid Khan, (Killich Khan) to the post

of Premiership. Therefore, it is necessary for us to respect our benefactor. At the time of battle, seek blessings from saints and elderly people.

In accordance with Sunnat-e-Nabavi (Prophet's precepts) always strive for peace, for this will strengthen faith, and, in the world and in the hereafter, you will be suitably rewarded.

6. God has created the earth, sky and human beings. It is, therefore, essential for the King, who is the deputy of God, to meditate on nature and the world created by God. As the entire surface of the land is God's own, do not usurp the rights of others. The ruler as a human being should remain grateful and should not acquire property of others by force and terror, or else he will be answerable on the Day of Judgement.
7. The Deccan comprises six provinces from ancient times which were governed by selected ministers, nobles and officers. Each province had its separate army. Emperor Aurangzeb Alamgir brought these provinces under the control of one ruler. It is necessary, therefore, to honour and respect the members of ruling families and provide them jobs on a priority basis. None should be entrusted with more than one job, for it could affect the quality of work. Warn your advisers to always report to you the problems and affairs touching your subjects.
8. The Dominion of the Deccan is under the control of the Mughal Empire. The Mughal Emperors should be respected. During your reign you should not become a sinner by going against their wish. When Nadir Shah, the King of Iran, came to India, he wanted to favour me and offered to me the Indian Empire. When he asked me I replied: "It will not be of any use except that I will become notorious as a disloyal person and you will also get a bad

name for faithlessness". He appreciated my reply very much. Next day Nadir Shah entrusted me with absolute authority and left Delhi.

9. For high posts do not appoint person of lower status. Similarly, for menial jobs high-ranking persons should not be appointed. In either case, the administration of the Dominion will suffer. You will ask me why I have appointed a man of lower status, Puran Chand to the post of Dewan. The fact is that no nobleman was prepared to accept the post of Diwan, because the Diwan would have to face many problems. Hence, Puran Chand was appointed the Diwan to teach a lesson to the selfish and ungrateful nobles. Puran Chand proved himself a good administrator and collected more revenue from the Jagirdars than his predecessors. In my opinion, he should be given a chance to work for another three years.
10. As far as possible, there should not be any precedence in battle. Whether it is fought for acquiring wealth or for victory, wars should not be fought just to exhibit your rank and dignity or to express your belligerence. This will not be liked by God. As far as possible, try to settle disputes and conflicts so that administration can be run smoothly. While doing so if the results are not satisfactory and your motives are suspected then there would be no other alternative left but to fight as a last resort. In these circumstances, seek help from God and try to defeat the enemy. As far as possible you must try to ensure that there is minimum loss of life. Seek divine support and confront the enemy in the battle field with wisdom and courage.
11. Since I attained the age of maturity, it has been my experience that among the inhabitants of the Deccan,

the people of Burhanpur and Bijapur are less trustworthy. It is better to refrain from using their services, and one should not place trust in them.

12. The resources of the Government and the treasury should always be reviewed and one must have control over them. If the administration is run in this manner, the expenses of the Government will not increase. The resources will then be sufficient to last for the next seven generations. But in this connection, if you follow a different method without adopting economy measures, then in a year or two, the treasury will be totally empty.
13. It is necessary to keep the treasury under your personal care and control. In the event of unrest and disturbance when the soldiers ask for their salaries even though their salaries may not be pending for more than three months, there should always be provision of money for payment of their salaries without difficulty.
14. It is the duty of my children and successors to maintain the dignity of the family by following the time-honored custom of managing palace affairs.
15. Moru and Ramdas are the two Brahmin leaders of the Deccan who are determined to demolish the structure of the Government. I have therefore imprisoned them in the fort of Mohammed Nagar. It is necessary to keep them in prison for the maintenance of peace and for the conduct of good and efficient administration.
16. Treat your younger brothers as you treat your own sons. Take care of their education and training. Treat them as your wellwishers and raise their status. They will be a source of strength and glory to the empire. Mohiuddin Khan, among my children, will be a tower of strength for you. So make him your staunch loyalist and treat him with generosity and

kindness. Do not listen to those who speak ill of someone behind his back and do not give a chance to every person to become intimate with you. You must follow the dictates of religion and conscience.

17. Now go ahead and appoint your people to run the administration of the Government and trust them. I have entrusted you to the care of God who will guide you and be your guardian and protector."

Nizam-ul-Mulk had the vision and constructive genius to formulate sound principles of state administration in his 'Will' which is rated high as one of the most important political documents. It was an unfailing source of inspiration and guidance to all the Nizams after him.

The wisdom and experience of Nizam-ul-Mulk Asaf Jah-I is evident in this great testament which laid a strong foundation for his dynastic rule. The successors of Asaf Jah-I followed word by word the directives in the testament forging strong bonds between the royalty and the people.

Lala Mansa Ram wrote Risala Darbar Asafia 14 years after the death of Asaf Jah. He wrote that at the time of dictating his testament, Ziauddin, the Chief Judge, was also present. Mansa Ram wrote thus:

> "While the words of advice came out of the mouth of Asaf Jah his son Nasir Jung stood up with folded hands. Asaf Jah with fatherly affection, called Nasir Jung near to him and consoled him by wiping the tears rolling down his eyes with a handkerchief and said: "there is no use of crying like this. If this is your attitude then the work of the people will suffer. Perhaps the turmoil which has subsided will rise up again and the people may be destroyed by events. My heart wishes you good luck and let peace be with you".

Nasir Jung was not an erudite scholar nor a far seeing statesman like his father. As best, he tried to continue the good work done by his father but was soon caught up in the vortex of palace intrigues and power politics at Delhi. The situation was further worsened with the conflict between the British and the French who wanted to exploit him in order to serve their ends. Nasir Jung was gullible and believed in whatever the Nawabs of Cuddapah, Kurnool and Shahnoor said. In a battle against the French, Nasir Jung fell a martyr to the bullets of his treacherous ally, Himmat Bahadur Khan.

Nasir Jung was proficient in Persian, Arabic and Sanskrit. He was well versed in music, painting and calligraphy. He patronized poets and he himself was a poet in Persian and Urdu.

Among the other rulers Muzaffer Jung did not contribute much to the growth and development of the Dominion. Beset as he was by internal disorder and external pressure with the advent of British and French companies, he became the victim of their deceptive tactics. Muzaffer Jung shared the fate of Nasir Jung as he too was slain by Himmat Bahadur Khan.

Salabath Jung, the third son of Nizamul Mulk, had to fight wars with the aggressive Marathas and make peace with them by ceding a few districts. He found it expedient to make friends with the British in order to curb the French influence. He signed the Treaty with the British in 1759, in which he gave up Masulipatnam to the British and presented sanads to them. His eleven-year rule (1758-1761) witnessed the establishment of British influence in the Deccan in place of the French, and some degree of stabilization in the state administration.

NIZAM ALI KHAN – ASAF JAH-II

Nizam Ali Khan fourth son of Nizam-ul-Mulk, known as Asaf Jah Saani ascended the throne in 1761. He had to face secret intrigues of the French with Hyder Jung against him. He ruled for 42 years (1761-1803) which was mostly a period of violence and disorder. The British consolidated their political power and were able to use Nizam Ali Khan against their arch-enemy, Hyder Ali, and his son Tipu Sultan. It was the triumph of British diplomacy that they could break Nizam Ali Khan's ties of friendship with Hyder Ali. The British defeated the joint forces of Nizam and Hyder Ali. Nizam Ali Khan had to sign a treaty with the British in 1768 pledging mutual military assistance on the condition that the Nizam should bear the expenses of the troops and the artillery. This was, in fact, the beginning of the Subsidiary Alliance. In 1792 the combined forces of the Nizam and the British besieged Seringapatnam and inflicted defeat on Tipu. In this way the British with the assistance of the Nizam could destroy Tipu's political power. The valiant Tipu died a martyr in 1799 fighting the invaders on the battlefield. Nizam Ali Khan thus became increasingly dependent on the British East India Company. He entered into the Subsidiary Alliance with the British which virtually eroded the authority and sovereignty of the Nizam. Under the agreement the Nizam was compelled to keep British troops in Hyderabad at his own expense. The manipulations and machinations of the British Residents to tighten their stranglehold and defeat the designs of rivals began to increase day by day. The Residents began to interfere in the internal affairs of the Dominion and had a final say even in the appointment of the key post of the Prime Minister (Madarul Maham). In this way the British virtually became the 'king makers' and made their appointee Prime Minister a stooge in their hands. The Subsidiary Alliances signed in 1798 signalled the decline of the Nizam's sovereignty and the rise of British political power.

SIKANDER JAH—ASAF JAH -III

In 1803, Nizam Ali Khan passed away. He was succeeded by Sikander Jah, Asaf Jah Saalis, the second son of Nizamul Mulk. The British Resident had by this time become powerful enough to decide policy matters. Sikander Jah's choice for Prime Minstership was Raja Mahipatram, a great patriot known for his anti-British views and his resolve to liquidate the British power. At the instance of the British, Raja Mahipatram was dismissed and expelled. Mir Alam was strongly backed by the British Resident for the position of Prime Minister. The ambitious and crafty Mir Alam became the Prime Minister. Chandulal an ally of the British was made the Peshkar. The disricts of Northern Sircars were handed over to the British without any compensation.

CHAPTER III

GHUFRAN MAKAN MIR FARKHUNDA ALI KHAN NASIRUL DAULA ASAF JAH RABEY-IV

The signing of the Subsidiary Alliances in 1798 by the then Nizam was a watershed in Asafia history whereby the decline in the power and sovereignty of the Nizam began. The stationing of the British troops and the formation of the British Residency in Hyderabad was the beginning of the end. Having fallen a prey to the wily diplomacy of the British, the Nizams one after the other had to reconcile themselves to the inevitable. And yet the Nizams from Nasir ud Daula to Osman Ali Khan could not hide their resentment against this unfortunate development.

Nasir ud Daula was born in 1792 A.D. at Bidar when his father and grand father were busy with the arrangements for the Khadla battle. After the death of Sikander Jah Saalis he ascended the throne of the Asafia kingdom in 1828. Nasir ud Daula wanted to get rid of the incompetent Peshkar Chandulal, and disband the contingent, but the Resident was firm that he would maintain the contingent and Chandulal was to continue in his post as Peshkar. For him the two were the wheels of the chariot of British power. If the services of any one were to be terminated the entire British administration would be thrown out of gear.

In 1838, Gen. Frazer arrived in Hyderabad as Resident. He informed his Government about the extravagance of the contingent. He listed the shortcomings and acts of mismanagement by Chandulal.

DISMISSAL OF CHANDULAL

In 1843, Chandulal was dismissed. His nephew, Raja Ram Baksh, was given an opportunity to take his place. He could not keep the administration in good shape even after holding the reins of office for nearly three years.

LETTER TO DALHOUSIE

In 1853, Col. Frazer left Hyderabad. In March, 1853 Col. John Low reached Hyderabad as Resident. Lord Dalhousie sent word to Nasir ud Daula through him that in order to repay the loan of Rs.64,00,000 and payment of the monthly salary of the contingent on a regular basis, the Nizam should handover the districts of Berar, and the district of Painghat to the British Government. In reply to the suggestion of Dalhousie, Nasir ud Daula, wrote to Col. Low as follows: "For any ruler two actions are always considered a disgrace. One is to hand over a part of one's own ancestral and hereditary country to others and second to dismiss one's own brave loyal and tested army. People like you are sometimes in England and sometimes in India. Sometime you participate in the administration of the Dominion and sometimes you act as a soldier. Sometimes you act as a boatman and sometimes as a trader. (I heard that some of the members of your group are merchant princes). You will not understand my feelings and desires in these matters. I am a dignified hereditary ruler. I inherited an empire which has been ruled by my family for generations and will die in the same empire. Do you think that I will remain happy after giving up a part of my Dominion? I would consider it as the height of insult and disgrace. I understand, some of you are of the opinion that if you keep me in the same position as that of Mohd. Ghous Khan, the Nawab of Karnatak I would be happy and satisfied. It means you will give me a pension like an old servant and attender, and I should not attend to any matter except prayers, eating and sleeping. Well, you are unable to understand the feelings of a Prince and his perceptions. You say that if I gloss over this agreement, there would be a saving of Rs. 8,00,000 to me. That would be a matter of delight to me, but I tell you that if there is a four-fold saving by these Rs,8,00,000, even then I would not be satisfied because, I would lose my respect and reputation if I let down my country and kingdom," (Hyderabad Affairs, Vol II).

After replying to the representative of the British Government, Nasir ur Daula told Col. Low that the required loan would be paid within four months, and in future, the salary of the contingent would be paid monthly. The Resident however did not consider the royal promises worthy of attention Nasir ud Daula then wrote": Suppose I do not like the establishment of the contingent then what would you do?"

Col. Low replied that they would accept the disbandment of the contingent and that would take many years and that in any case, till that time the salaries would have to be paid and the districts would have to be handed over to the British Government. The designs of the Europeans were now revealed. It was clear that the contingent issue was only a pretext. In fact, the British wanted to seize more districts.

Nasir ud Daula did not agree with the proposal. A week later, Siraj ul Mulk received a letter signed by the assistant of the Resident mentioning that the talks between the Resident and the Nizam should be considered as closed. The Resident requested the Governor-General of India to move the army.

This was not a letter addressed to Madar ul Maham from the Resident but was a military threat of the British Government to his 'Faithful Ally' who had relieved the British from the clutches of the French, saved the British from the guerilla attacks by the Marathas and the Pindaries. It was the 'Faithful Ally' who saved the British from being slaughtered by the sword of Tipu Sultan.

The said letter from the Resident was received on May 19, 1853, Nasir ud Daula was quite aware of the result of deviation from an agreement which was a real disgrace to the people. On May 20, he was ultimately led to sign the Agreement of Berar. Siraj ul Mulk died after a few days after the Agreement was signed.

The succeeding years presented a gloomy picture because of the unfair policies of the British. By 1853, the Nizam owed a considerable amount to the British Government. According to the Articles of the Treaty of Subsidiary Alliance, the Nizam was paying handsomely, in fact, more than what was necessary for the up keep of the Subsidiary Force which was virtually the British Army. Gradually the British became more powerful and forced the Nizam for territorial cession against repayment. Therefore, in 1853, an agreement was entered into by which the Subsidiary Force was subsequently named the Hyderabad Contingent for the purpose of providing regular monthly payment to the said contingent troops and towards the payment of the debt amounting to Rs. 50,00,000. The Nizam agreed to "assign the districts of Berar (Dharaseo and the Raichur Doab) yielding an annual gross revenue of Rs. 50,00,000. According to Henry Russel, the troops in fact belonged to the Nizam's Army only in name, but for all practical purposes they were British Forces.

TURAB ALI KHAN, SIR SALAR JUNG-I (MADAR UL MAHAM)

Siraj ul Mulk, was replaced by his nephew, Mir Turab Ali Khan Salar Jung and appointed as Madar ul Maham. At that time, he was only twenty-four years of age. Economically, the State was bankrupt. Government was to pay a loan of two and half crore to the local money-lenders. Throughout the country, discontent, dissatisfaction and hatred prevailed. In such difficult and precarious circumstances, Salar Jung performed the duties of Madar ul Maham with great prudence and public spirit winning the confidence of the public and the ruler alike. The finances of the State steadily improved.

Sir Salar Jung laid the foundation of Hyderabad's future prosperity and ended the chaos and confusion left by his predecessor, Chandulal and continued to hold his authority as Prime Minister till his death in 1883. He declined to act as a puppet, unlike his predecessors, and soon began to extricate the State from its financial bankruptcy and maladministration with remarkable assiduity, efficient governance and competent management of resources.

ENCOURAGEMENT TO INDIGENOUS GOODS

The most important feature of the period of Nasir ud Daula was that, he passed a strict order that no British goods should be bought and that locally made articles should be used. In the Government offices the paper manufactured locally at 'Kaghazi guda' (name of a locality in Hyderabad) was used. The handmade paper industry has a long history in India. In 13th century, Allauddin Khilji brought the artisans from Delhi to Daulatabad. The paper makers, those days were called kaghazis. This industry was maintained by the kaghazis and Aurangzeb gave it further impetus. It was said that a cradle made out of handmade paper could bear the weight of a baby. This was presented to the Europeans.

Asaf Jah I and Mir Nizam Ali Khan took great interest in the handmade paper industry. Nizam Ali Khan-II accorded permission to kaghazis for manufacturing a special type of paper to be named after the Nizam himself.

There were more than six towns in Hyderabad State namely: Ellora, Gurud, Koratla, Warangal, Medak and Hyderabad city where this industry flourished. The encouragement and patronage of the Nizam's Government to the kaghazis is worth mentioning. The British obstructed the growth of this industry during the late 19th century, when they flooded the market with cheap imported machine made paper from England.

The 'nima' and 'jama' make of the cloth was manufactured at Nanded. One of the nobles purchased British-made cloth from a Bombay merchant. He stitched a jama of the cloth, wore it and attended the Darbar. Nasir ud Daula inquired about the place from where the noble had purchased that cloth. The unfortunate noble said he bought it in Secunderabad. The Nizam said: "You might have acquired it free. You must pay a large sum by way of penalty and retire till further orders".

After signing the Agreement, Nasir ud Daula survived for not more than four years. The Agreement on Berar proved fatal. After ruling for 29 years, he died at the age of 66 during the disturbances of 1857. He was buried in the courtyard of Mecca Masjid.

Nizam's crest

Gold-plated chair of Nizam VII at Jubilee Museum—1936

The Nizams VII, in Arab dress presented by king Saud of Saudi Arabia 1964 (AMI)

The Ruling Princes of India and Nizam VI in black Sherwani—1905

Osmania University

The Nizam VII with Queen Suraya of Iran. 1960's (SHER)

A meeting of the Council of Ministers of Nizam VII, In the picture: Maharaja Sir Kishen Pershad (Prime Minister), Nawab Zulqadar Jung, Nawab Mahdi Yar Jung, Sir Akbar Hydri, Mr. Taskar & Raja Shyam Raj Bahadur, Nawab Mehdi Nawaz Jung in the rear seat.

The Nizam, in conversation with Moulana Azad

The Nizam, Mir Osman Ali Khan, with Pandit Jawaharlal Nehru and Moulana Abul Azad - 1951

Lord Curzon, Viceroy of India, with Nizam VI, in Haveli Manjhli Begum. Prince Mir Osman Ali Khan is also seen (third from right) March 28. 1903

An historical group photo of Nizam's Family taken in Afzal Mahal in 1905. Seated (from left) : Nizam VI, Prince Osman Ali Khan and Maharaja Kishan Pershad

CHAPTER IV

GHUFRAN MAKAN MIR TAHNIYAT ALI KHAN AFZAL UD DAULA ASAF JAH (KHAMAS)-V

Afzal ud Daula was born in 1827 A.D. He ascended the throne in 1857 A.D. Four days after his accession, the flames of the independence movement started blazing in many parts of India. The sparks of the freedom struggle turned into a wild fire touching Delhi, Meerut, Lucknow, Jhansi, Gwalior, Ghazipur and Punjab. When Col. Davidson, Resident of Hyderabad received a telegram mentioning that the rebels had taken Delhi under their control, he consulted Salar Jung. Salar Jung said, that the news was making the rounds in the city for the last four days and assured him that Hyderabad would remain peaceful during the disturbances. When the news of the mutiny reached Hyderabad, the people of Hyderabad city woke up from their sleep and came out of their houses to find anti British feelings all over the place.

ATTACK ON RESIDENCY

The masses in their excitement and fervour raised a green

flag and their fury was about to take a serious turn in the streets, when Salar Jung with his Arab army, used force to disperse the unruly mobs. On July 17, 1857 a large group of Rohillas suddenly attacked the Residency. The leaders of the group, Turrahbaz Khan, and Allauddin, were arrested. The former was shot dead by a bullet and the later, Allauddin Khan, was sent to the Andamans. It would not be entirely wrong to say that had the Nizam joined the Revolt of 1857, the consequences might have been very serious for the British, and perhaps they might have been completely rooted out of the country.

The Raja of Shorapur joined the rebels at that time. He was also overpowered, arrested and handed over to the Resident by Salar Jung. When the rebellion was over, Shorapur was included in Hyderabad. A loan of Rs. 50,00,000 which Hyderabad was to pay was waived. Thirteen other regions on the western boundary of Hyderabad adjacent to Ahmednagar and Shorapur were also handed over to the Nizam. During the period of Nizam-ul-Mulk Asaf Jah—I, the position of the East India Company was not more than a group of traders from England who did not enjoy any importance. On the contrary, it was the tradition of European nationals to associate themselves with a native ruler and to acquire jagirs from the rulers who won the battle. They always changed their sides and joined those who were powerful. The entire period of Nizam Ali Khan (1761-1803) witnessed the non-operation from the Company. Their policy was to stop Nizam Ali Khan from joining hands with Tipu Sultan. Had the Nizam joined Tipu Sultan the situation would have completely changed and it would not have been possible for the British to establish their rule in the Deccan. Nizam Ali Khan always observed their policy of changing sides. Whenever the Company did not assist him during the Maratha and Mysore wars, he was sore with the British army every time for breach of faith.

Subsequently, when the British succeeded in establishing their rule, they concluded a number of agreements with the Asaf Jahi rulers but they never honoured it and were accused of breach of faith when they interfered in the affairs of the State. On the one side, they tried to impress upon the minds of the Asaf Jahi rulers that they were weak and not capable of ruling over a State. On the other hand, after the mutiny of 1857, there was a general feeling among the British, that if the Nizam had not associated with them and if Hyderabad too had joined the freedom struggle, the British rule would have come to an end.

CHANGE IN COINAGE AND SERMON

On January 27, 1858, under the orders of Sir John Lawrence, Chief Commissioner of Punjab, a case was filed against Bahadur Shar Zafar in the Red Fort. After hearing false witnesses, he was accused of rebellion, and was banished and sent to Rangoon. As Bahadur Shah Zafar's coin was still in circulation in Hyderabad the British did not like this. Lord Canning, through Salar Jung, appealed to Afzal ud Daula to change the currency, but Afzal ud Daula turned a deaf ear. The Resident of Hyderabad, Col. Davidson, through Amir Kabir Shams ul Umara an uncle of the King again sent a message to force the change. Afzal ud Daula continued to circulate the coin as long as Bahadur Shah was alive. Afzal ud Daula under compulsion agreed to change the coin. Hence, the new coin which was introduced was engraved "Nizam ul Mulk Asaf Jah Bahadur" on one side and on the other "Jaloos mamniyat Manoos Zarb Farkhunda Buniyad Hyderabad". This coin was called 'Sikka Hali'. Coins of this period had the initial letter 'Alif' from the name of Afzal ud Daula inscribed on it. Later, the initial letter'M' of Mir Mahbub Ali Khan's name and finally the initial letter of the name of Osman Ali Khan was inscribed on the coins. Thus from 1858, Afzal ud Daula possessed his own coins and the name of Bahadur Shah Zafar was deleted from the sermon in Friday prayers.

THE HISTORIC LETTER: ANTI-COLONIAL BIAS

The fact that Hyderabad was a sovereign State is confirmed by a historic letter which Sir Salar Jung wrote to Sir John Lawrence at the insistence of Nawab Afzal ud Daula, Nizam V. when the province of Orissa was ravaged by famines and floods. The Prime Minister wrote:

> "The Government of Hyderabad is grieved over the unmindful attitude of the Government of British India towards the welfare of their subjects. The callous indifference of the authorities is responsible for the deaths of lakhs of people during the recent floods. The authorities should not forget that it is because of the Hyderabad Government that the British could establish and maintain their rule in India. Hence, they are responsible for the welfare of the British India. If the authorities at Orissa are unable to cope with the situation, the Government of British India would be well advised to hand over the province of Orissa to the management of Hyderabad, to administer the province in the interests of the people and remit to the British Exchequer the balance of the revenue receipts. Hyderabad cannot sit silent while lakhs are dying in Orissa, despite the fact that the treasury of the said province is replete with cash". (Abid Hussain, Whither Hyderabad, 1935, PP. 136 – 137).

The letter brings out the Nizam's anguish and anger at the 'paramount power' turning a blind eye to the countless deaths in Orissa and doing nothing to mitigate the sufferings of its subjects in the British India. Such a callous behaviour on the part of rulers was the worst example of the colonial mentality that wielded power without responsibility. While there is an under-current of sorrow in having helped the British to rule over India, the Nizam in this letter, virtually admonishes them for their total indifference and offers to take over the responsibility of administering relief and rehabilitation measures to the afflicted in the hour of national calamity.

REFUSAL TO ACCEPT BRITISH TITLE

When Queen Victoria conferred the title of G.C.S.I. on Afzal ud Daula for his friendship and support to the British, he hesitated to accept the title. Earlier, the rulers of the Deccan had not accepted titles from the British. When the Resident assured him that it was not meant for any political purpose, Afzal ud Daula agreed to accept it. Besides, the Nizam and Salar Jung, Sham ul Umara Amir-I-Kabir, Narender Pershad Peshkar and other nobles were presented valuable gifts by the British Government. In 1861, a new order of the Star of India was created. The British Government desired to recognise the services of those deserving persons who rendered them assistance during the Mutiny of 1857, by conferring honours and distinctions upon them. This award was similar to those which the Mughal Emperors conferred upon their subjects. These distinctions emanating from the Crown formed a connecting link with the Indian Princes. It was a political ploy to wean the Princes away from the freedom movement.

The Nizam, Afzal ud Daula, raised objection to his acceptance of the Star of India on religious grounds.

In 1866, there was some misunderstanding between Salar Jung and a few companions of Afzal ud Daula. As a result, Salar Jung resigned from the post of Prime Minister. During this period, Sir Charge Pole was the Resident. He met Afzal ud Daula and told him that the developmental work of the State would be hindered without the guidance of Salar Jung. Accordingly Afzal ud Daula re-appointed Salar Jung to the post of Prime Minister.

FORMATION OF SUBAS AND DISTRICTS

In 1866, the Dominion of Hyderabad was divided into five subas (Provinces) and seventeen districts. Each suba was under one Subedar (commissioner) and for each district Awwal Tauqdar (Collector) was appointed. In each of the Taluqa Tehsildar (Revenue Officer) was also appointed. Departments of Buildings, Medicine, Sanitation and Education were established. All these organisations were the outcome of Salar Jung's devotion to duty, who left no stone unturned to achieve the welfare and well-being of the State and the public.

The period of Afzal ud Daula is very significant in the history of Asaf Jahi rule. On the one hand, the Deccan remained aloof during the mutiny and, on the other, many regions were returned to Hyderabad State. During the Prime Ministership of Salar Jang regulatory-codes and conducts were formulated to streamline the functioning of Government.

Afzal ud Daula was very frugal in his ways, a man of piety, and an excellent scholar. He hated amusements. He honoured learned and virtuous people. All the liquor shops were shifted outside the city by his orders. The locality called Afzal Ganj, Masjid Afzal Ganj and Afzal Ganj Bridge constructed during his time are reminiscent of his benign rule.

HIS LIBERALITY

His generosity crossed the borders of Hyderabad and became the talk of the entire Indian subcontinent. He extended his patronage to literary men, scholars and artists. Nawab Afzal ud Daula was very generous and cared for the poor. He was known for his liberal outlook. His generous donation to the needy was never less than a lakh of rupees. The prevalent coin during his time was made of silver. These were not in circulation. His companions and servants of the court were astonished to see the heap of one lakh rupees which he gave to the needy. They assumed that the Nizam was not aware of how much one lakh rupees really amounted to and that if the Nizam saw the heap of one lakh rupees then he would not have given to anyone. They decided among themselves that the Nizam should be shown a heap of one lakh rupees. They therefore, decided to keep a heap of one lakh rupees on the way from where he came. When the Nizam passed by the heap he inquired about the money. One servant submitted respectfully that His Highness had ordered to pay rupees one lakh to a certain person. Nawab Afzal ud Daula stopped, and with astonishment he said one lakh rupees was too little and instead gave him two lakhs of rupees.

He was well built and was handsome. In 1869 A.D. after ruling for twelve years, one month and twenty days Afzal ud Daula passed away at the early age of 42. He was buried at Mecca Masjid and after his death he was posthumously awarded the title of Maghfirat Makan. At the time of his death, his son and successor, Mahbub Ali Khan, was only two years and seven months old.

CHAPTER – V

GHUFRAN MAKAN MIR MAHBUB ALI KHAN ASAF JAH (SADAS) -VI

(1869-1911)

Mir Mahbub Ali Khan was in every sense a darling of the people. He loved his people and was profusely loved by them irrespective of class, caste, religion and community. Hindus named their children after him. Totally unbiased in his outlook, he had profound respect for all religions. This was reflected in his day-to-day administration. In his reign, communal amity and harmony became an essential component of Hyderabad culture. Mir Mahbub Ali Khan was one of the finest representatives of the secular tradition set by the Qutub Shahi and Asaf Jahi Kings.

Mir Mahbub Ali Khan was born in 1869 A.D. When Afzal ud Daula died, the lone successor of the Asaf Jahi family was only two years and seven months. Being a minor, the British wanted to appoint Roshan ud Daula, brother of Afzal ud Daula, as his successor. Khursheed Jah desired that his son, Mohd. Hafizuddin become his successor, he being older than Mir Mahboob Ali Khan. Salar Jung soon after the death of the Nizam in tune with the prevailing custom ordered the closure of all entry points to the old city ramparts. In 1869 A.D. in the Royal Palace a Darbar was arranged to mark Mahbub Ali Khan's accession to the throne. A maid servant came out from the harem with the infant successor to the Asaf Jahi throne in her arms. Shams-ul-Umara, Amir-I-Kabir Mohd. Rafi uddin Khan took Mir Mahbub Ali Khan from the arms of the maid servant and made him sit on the royal throne with the help of Salar Jung. First of all, Shams ul Umara and Salar Jung presented the nazr, and were followed by the nobles and court officials. Their greetings were conveyed with great respect, honour and royal etiquette. They took their turns to present their nazr which was received by Shams ul Umara on behalf of the King. There was a rejoicing with the sounding of the kettle drums, musical pipes and loud trumpets and the entire city echoed to the sound of ceremonial music.

RESIDENT'S OBJECTION ON THE OCCASION OF ACCESSION

On this occasion, the Resident held out a threat that he would not attend the accession Darbar since he was kept in the dark and not consulted regarding the accession. The experienced Salar Jung and the seasoned Shams ul Umara observed that in keeping with the Asaf Jahi custom, it was the voice of the people that mattered in the selection of the King. There was no question of seeking an opinion or to make a reference to the British Government. Finally, the Resident and his companions agreed to attend the accession Darbar. A decision was taken to provide chairs to the Resident and his staff and military officers. Hitherto, the Darbar used to be organised in the Mughal tradition and the British sat on the carpet.

It is well known to every student of history that up to the times of Afzal ud Daula, the Governor–General used to sign himself as 'Niaz Mund' while the Nizams on their part referred to themselves as Mabadaulat wa Iqbal' 'Mir

Alam was the Nizam's envoy at the British court.

The Resident of Hyderabad was never allowed a chair in the presence of the Nizam. There is a documentary evidence to prove that on certain Darbar occasions the Resident petitioned the Nizam that the practice of squatting on the floor was highly inconvenient to a man who wore breeches and so he should be allowed to use a chair at the Darbar. The Nizam ordered that a pit should be dug to enable the Resident to place his feet down and thus the question was settled. The claim of equality with the Nizam was thus denied". (Abid Hussain, Whither Hyderabad), 1935, P. 138.

FORMATION OF REGENCY

Soon after the declaration of succession, a Regency was formed comprising Salar Jung and Shams ul Umara. The position of Salar Jung was Regent and Shams ul Umara was, co-Regent, and the Resident was to be consulted on some issues.

PARTICIPATION IN IMPERIAL ASSEMBLAGE AND HISTORICAL ADDRESS

Perhaps it will be a rare example in the world, when nobles, distinguished personalities and elderly persons of any nation presented a welcome address to a person who had completed ten years of his age. The address was presented by Darul Uloom which was supported with royal grants. Similarly the Committee of Khazinat ul Bzai, Aligarh decided that some selected members of the Committee should go to Delhi and present a welcome address to His Highness Mir Mahbub Ali Khan Asaf Jah Sadas on his arrival there to attend the Imperial Darbar.

When this application was approved by the Royal court, a deputation of fifteen persons went to Delhi under the leadership of Maulvi Samiullah Khan. On January 3, 1877, this deputation was allowed at the Darbar. When all the members assembled there, His Highness arrived. All the members, after their respectful salutations, presented their nazr. Maulvi Samiullah Khan read the welcome address written in Persian and presented it in a silver box. Thereafter, His Highness stood up and Nawab Rasheed ud Daula read a written reply on behalf of His Highness. Then His Highness the Nizam presented the reply with his own hands to Maulvi SamiUllah Khan, and with great affability and respect bade farewell to all the members.

In the address besides thanking the Government of His Highness for the grants and expressing their faith, the Committee requested that the museum building of the university be named after him. The address, though very brief, was well worded conveying a sense of deep loyalty, sincerity and wholehearted support.

When Mir Mahbub Ali Khan grew up he received the best education and training from expert tutors and teachers and acquired skills in every field of art and science. By way of companionship of His Highness, highly qualified and experienced persons were appointed. Maulvi Mohd. Zaman Khan, Maulvi Anwar Ullah Khan, Hafiz Mohd. Anwar, Mohd. Ashraf and others were entrusted with the teaching of Arabic, Persian and Urdu. Captain Clark was appointed to teach him English. Mir Mahbub Ali Khan attained quick proficiency in many fields. In the art of soldiering, he was second to none. In shooting, nobody could equal him. He displayed deep knowledge of Persian and Urdu, and could write poetry in Urdu. His penname was "Asif'. Till 1883, Salar Jung performed the duties of Prime Minister and Vicereagency with loyalty and extreme diligence. He had become Prime Minister only a week after the signing of Agreement for cession of Berar. Salar Jung continued his best efforts to regain Berar till his last breath. He died in 1883 A.D.

Regarding the restoration of Berar, Salar Jung during his life time challenged the authority of the British Empire. This issue arose when certain territories were transferred to the British Government under duress by the Nizam. All his subsequent efforts to regain the lost territories proved fruitless as the British refused to consider the claim on legal, financial or moral grounds. The reopening of the issue was displeasing to the British, but Oliphant, the Secretary of State Affairs of the Nizam's Government wrote strongly and fearlessly about Berar, with the result that he incurred the displeasure of the British Government and had to quit Hyderabad.

In consultation with the Resident, a Council was entrusted with the administration of the Dominion. The Council comprised of Mir Laik Ali Khan as the Secretary and Narender Bahadur as a senior member.

CELEBRATIONS OF CORONATION

In 1884, Mir Mahbub Ali Khan met the Viceroy of India, Lord Rippon, and invited him to visit Hyderabad. After a few months, Lord Rippon visited Hyderabad. He was the first Viceroy to visit Hyderabad. On 6th Rabul ul Sani 1301 H i.e.1884 A.D a grand Darbar was organised in which Lord Rippon performed the coronation ceremony and the entire powers wielded by the Regent were entrusted to Mir Mahbub Ali Khan on his attaining majority.

After taking over the reins of his Dominion in his hands, Mir Mahbub Ali Khan ran the administration on the guidelines laid down by Salar Jung. He followed old customs and traditions of the Asafia dynasty and maintained royal etiquette and dignity. Even though he ascended the throne when he was just a minor, he followed the old traditions and was able to hold the Darbar as in the past. It seemed as if the grandeur of mediaeval period had returned. People from far off places came to watch the royal Darbar and royal procession.

Mir Mahbub Ali Khan appointed Mir Laik Ali Khan Salar Jung [Mukhtar ul Mulk Imadus Saltasnat] to the post of Prime Minister, on the day of his accession. He set up a Council of State [Majlis Saltanat). He himself was the Chairman and Bashir ud Daula, Khursheed Jah, Viqar ul Umara and Narender Bhadur were the other members.

In 1886, Imad us sultanat resigned due to some differences with Mir Mahbub Ali Khan. Mir Mahbub Ali Khan ran the administration without a Prime Minister for one year.

In 1889, Sir Asman Jah Bashir ud Daula was appointed Prime Minister of the Dominion. Lord Dufferin came to Hyderabad in the same year.

In 1888 an order was passed by the High Court that no lawyer of the Government Court could speak in English as a matter of right.

In 1888, the Duke of Connaught son of Queen Victoria visited Hyderabad. There was great rejoicing and he was given a warm welcome.

In 1890, the Unani Hospital was opened in the city and a post card was issued to mark the event.

PROMULGATION OF KHANOONCHA MUBARAK

In 1892, Sir Asman Jah took six months' sick leave. The Nizam was unhappy with his Prime Minister Sir Asman Jah. During his Prime Ministership the administration of the Government was run by subordinates, and the real power was in the hands of Assistant Ministers. As a result, there was grave financial mismanagement involving public scandals. It was also alleged that Asman Jah tried to sabotage the new schemes of the Nizam.

In his place, his cousin, Viqar ul Umara was appointed. During the first year of Viqar ul Umara as Prime Minister Mir Mahbub Ali Khan promulgated Khanooncha Mubarak in which he spelt out a scheme for the delegation of powers and the allotment of duties to the Prime Minister and Asst Prime Minister in order to run the administration of the State smoothly. A remarkable feature of the changed administration after Mir Mahbub Ali Khan took over the reins was the onset of an important constitutional change. During the 1890's, a body of advisors known as Council of State or Cabinet Council was formed for the first time. The Council recognised the right of the people's representatives to participate in framing the laws and laid the foundation of a democratic polity under the Nizam's Government.

ESTABLISHMENT OF LEGISLATIVE COUNCIL

In 1893, a Legislative Council was established to enable the Government officers and non-Government members to draw up suitable regulations after mutual consultations and discussion which would be issued after approval by the Nizam. The Prime Minister was the President of the Council. The Legislative Council was constituted with nineteen Ministers i.e. President, Vice-President, eleven officials and six non-official members. The eleven officials included the Chief Justice, the Judicial Secretary and the Legal Advisor as ex-officio members, the remaining eight official members were nominated by the Minister for two years. Of the six non-official members, two were elected by the Jagirdars and land owners, two seats were reserved for First Grade Pleaders of the High Court of Hyderabad, and the remaining two members were nominated by the

Prime Minister including one from the Paigah area. The non-official members were appointed for two years but retiring members were eligible for re-election (Hyderabad Residency Records, NAI, Microfilm, No. 2 1900, pp.2-7).

In 1899, Mir Mahbub Ali Khan accepted the invitation from the Viceroy of India Lord Curzon, and went to Calcutta accompanied by the heir apparent Mir Osman Ali Khan. In 1899, a quarter anna stamp was issued for the despatch of newspapers. Also law classes were inaugurated for the first time.

There was a famine in 1900. Thousands of poor were employed on relief works. Seven lakh rupees were spent from the royal treasury to solve the problems of scarcity. The Indian Famine Fund Committee offered a grant for relief works to the Nizam's Government. The offer was declined with thanks because it was felt that the Government itself had sufficient funds and could bear the necessary expenditure for famine relief. It has always been observed during the time of famines, that the economic conditions of the people of Hyderabad were far better than the subjects of the Company. However the military burden imposed by the East India Company and its successors on the Hyderabad exchequer, and the manner in which the commercial and industrial interests of Hyderabad were given a low priority had, in fact, impoverished Hyderabad to such an extent that the State was in no position to compare itself with the other parts of India. Once a rich and prosperous State, Hyderabad was persistenly victimized and exploited by the British for their own ends.

In 1900 the opening of the Secunderabad-Manmad railway line was a landmark in the history of Hyderabad because the doors were opened for the Bombay market to get access to the rich resources of Hyderabad State.

In 1901, Viqar ul Umara was relieved of the post of Prime Minister and Maharaja Kishen Pershad the then Peshkar was appointed officiating Prime Minister.

In 1902, a decision was taken to hand over the Berar region to the British Government in perpetuity and it was decided to give rupees 25 lakh annually to the Nizam in reciprocation. Most of the contingents were disbanded and after retrenchment of the soldiers, the army was merged with the Madras Regiment. On November 5, 1902, a new Agreement was concluded between the Nizam's Government and the British for the administration of Berar. Under this Agreement, the Nizam's sovereignty over Berar was re-affirmed, and Berar province was leased to the Government of India in perpetuity in return for an annual rent of Rs.25,00,000. The Government of India was empowered to make proper arrangements for the administration of the Province which had been earlier placed under the administration of the Central Provinces. At the same time, it was agreed to reduce the costly and ineffective establishment of over 18,000 irregular troops to 12,000. In the same year, Maharaja Kishen Pershad was appointed Prime Minister and awarded the title of Yamin ul Saltanat, with Zat mansab of 2000, five jewels sarpatti with turrah, har, bhujband, navratan and dastband. Later, he was honoured with G.C.I.E. by His Majesty the King Emperor. Such a distinction had not been conferred on any Prime Minister of Hyderabad since Salar Jung I who was awarded G.C.S.I.

WHERE ARE YOUR JEWELS ?

On Thursday January 1, 1903, a Darbar was arranged to celebrate the coronation ceremony of Emperor Edward VII, at Delhi. Lord Curzon, Governor-General and Viceroy of India, invited all the Princes and Rulers of the Indian States and Burma. There was a procession of elephants. The elephants were decorated, and studded with gold and silver, with brocade covers. All the Rajas and Maharajas wore glittering jewellery. Compared to the other rulers of State. Mir Mahbub Ali Khan was in simple dress. On seeing his simple dress Lord Curzon asked him "Where are your jewels?" Mir Mahbub Ali Khan smiled and pointed to the nobles and ministers of his Kingdom and said "These are my jewels".

FLOOD IN RIVER MUSI

In September 1908, there were floods, in the Musi river. The floods caused great havoc and distress. Thousands of lives were lost, 19,000 houses were washed away. Many people were drowned and houses close to the bank of the river collapsed. Thousands of children became orphans and many women became widows. Members of the entire army and the police of the Government were drafted for relief work. Mir Mahbub Ali Khan was deeply moved by the sudden disaster which had overtaken his people. Shedding tears at the calamity he consoled the affected persons and inspired them to undertake rescue works. His love for his subjects was clearly evident when on the advice of pundits he performed puja to propitiate the angry river goddess and stepped boldly into the swirling waters with the arti.

While he was busy with the assessment of the fury of the flood, affected people cried out and said that they were ruined, and had been rendered homeless. When the Nizam heard their cries of anguish, he was in tears and said: "The house of this slave is there." The doors of the royal palaces were opened for the flood-stricken people. Five public kitchens for Muslims and five for Hindus were established in the city. Maharaja Kishen Pershad, the then Prime Minister was very active and readily participated in all the arrangements. The Nizam went round the affected areas in vehicles or on foot and supervised the relief operations personally. He set up a kitchen at his palace for several days where thousands of people were fed day and night. A Commission was set up to assess the losses suffered by the flood-affected people. Efforts were made to compensate the loss of each and every family. When the car of His Highness reached the new bridge, it was suddenly entangled in the flood waters but he remained calm. Members of the public, army and police pushed the car and brought it out of the floods.

During Mir Mahbub Ali Khan's, reign reforms were introduced on a large scale. Many new departments were set up and many administrative changes were introduced. Mir Mahbub Ali Khan was a remarkable man and the ablest Indian of his times who possessed a great talent for administration combined with a capacity for hard work. His rule was an example of royal munificence, grandeur, hospitality and patronage. Mir Mahbub Ali Khan was tolerant, humble and also a man of integrity. Lord Curzon, the then Governor General had rightly said that he was not one who would go back on his word. On an average four Darbars were usually held in an year at the time of his birthday, Id ul fitr, Id-uz-zuha and Nouroz, which were conducted in the Mughal style and were arranged usually late in the night. In the olden days, the Darbars were usually held to discuss issues of political importance. However Darbars were not only held on the occasion of Muslim festivals but were also held during Hindu festivals such as Holi, Basanth, and Dassera. The Royal Palace dazzled with lights. The king appeared in public with his companions late in the nights. No sooner did he appear on the royal masnad than the proclaimer would raise his voice informing the courtiers of the arrival of the Nizam. All those present would salute him respectfully making a dignified low bow. The royal kawwal would sing a welcome song. The nobles, ministers and mansabdars used to present nazr according to their ranks and status. The highest nazr presented to the Nizam was eleven gold coins from the members of the Paigah family, and the lowest was rupees two. Titles were conferred during these Darbars. At the time of conferring the titles, robes and jewels were awarded. The Nizam himself would tie the sehra of the bridegroom and would present the title holder with studded serpech and har. Finally, the Darbar used to conclude at dawn.

The ceremony in which sehra is fastened on the Dastar of the groom is known as sehrabandi. This is a Hindu custom adopted by the Muslims. Sehra is usually tied by an elderly person of the family. In case of Paigah and other nobles, it was tied by the ruler. For instance, when Iman Jung, son of Khursheed Jah, was married to the sister of NizamVI, the Nizam tied the Sehra and presented the bridegroom, a sarpatti studded with precious stones and a pair of dastband.

SHOOTING, HUNTING AND RIDING

Mir Mahbub Ali Khan was very fond of hunting and his favourite pastime was hunting of tiger. The sixth Nizam, was a crack shot and a keen 'shikari' and it is said that a special train was kept ready to take him out on 'shikar' at the drop of a hat. He used to throw coins in the air and aimed at them successfully with his gun. He was a perfectionist in spear-throwing. Usually he used to carry three pegs one spear, and all the three pegs were attached to the spear. In 1890, on the visit of Prince Albert there was a demonstration of spear-throwing and tent-pegging at Purani Haweli in Hyderabad. In this demonstration, Mir Mahbub Ali Khan displayed his talents. Prince Albert was astonished on seeing his amazing feats with the spear.

It is interesting to note an incident in connection with hunting. Once he was busy hunting a deer, when he saw a small baby deer running near Saroornagar. Mir Mahbub

Ali Khan ordered his companion to catch the deer and bring it alive. People chased the deer up to one and half to two miles. Afsar ul Mulk was also watching the scene. Finally, he spurred his horse and in a short time caught it alive and presented it to the King.

In horse riding there was none to compete with Mir Mahbub Ali Khan. In the royal stable once a very beautiful, well-built horse was purchased. The horse had the ferocity of a tiger and would not allow anyone to put the saddle on its back. Even if somebody, with great difficulty tightened the saddle, it was not easy to sit on its back. Even renowed horse-riders accepted defeat. No sooner did the rider reach near the horse than it used to kick him with the hind legs. Mir Mahabub Ali Khan who was proud of his manhood and good horsemanship one day ordered that the same ill-tempered horse be brought to him for riding. His companions, Ministers of the Government, famous horse riders requested His Highness to abstain from riding the horse. He brushed aside everyone's request. When the horse was brought closer to him, as usual conversing with the people, he suddenly leapt and mounted the horse. He took the bridle in his hand and went forward riding, covering a distance of five to six miles. When he returned, the horse was tired and weak. It is said that from that day onwards the horse ceased to be unruly.

GREAT FAITH IN RELIGIOUS SAINTS

There are innumerable instances concerning the firm faith of Asaf Jahi rulers in religious saints. Most of the rulers of the Dominion participated in the funeral prayers whenever a religious saint or eminent scholar expired. But Hazrat Ghufran Makan, Mir Mahbub Ali Khan, on such occasions not only attended the funeral prayers but helped to carry the body on the pyre.

Mir Mahbub Ali Khan offered his shoulder to carry the funeral pyre when Ismail Shah Majub, a saint, died.

HE WAS A CONJURE FOR SNAKE BITE

Mir Mahbub Aki Khan was known to possess healing power for snake bite. With his spell it is said that the venom of the snake would abate. It was his order that if anyone from the public had a snake bite, he could approach him any time. It happened a number of times when he was awakened from his sleep.

It is said that Nawab Muneer uddin Khan Taluqdar who knew this spell taught the mantra to Mir Mahbub Ali Khan. When a man suffered from snake bite the name of the Mahbub Ali had to be mentioned in these terms: "Mahbub Ali Pasha Ki Dohaee". Then the venom would not spread further or in other words the venom of the snake would abate. Hence the name of Mahbub Ali Pasha and the practice of spell of snake bite became famous throughout Hyderabad State. (Hidayat Ali Khan Mandozai, Mahbub ki Dohai, Siasat Daily, November 16, 1987).

DEATH

In the month of Ramzan 1911 A.D. Mir Mahbub Ali Khan suddenly fell ill. On the 4th of Ramzan the King who was a protector of his subjects bade goodbye to them and went away in peace. He was buried beside his father Afzal ud Daula, in the courtyard of the Mecca Masjid. He ruled for 42 years. It is said that Mir Mahbub Ali Khan died at Falaknuma Palace. In the article, 'Unravelling the Falaknuma legend' Ratna Rao Shekar wrote: "Indeed it has been an irony of history, that Falaknuma, one of the finest examples of Georgian architecture, in style and design rated higher than palaces built in similar style, such as, Churchill's Blenheim Castle in England, was never really fully occupied. It is believed that the scorpion like shape of the palace proved unlucky for all those connected with the palace. The Italian architect, who built the palace, died while boarding a ship in Bombay on his way to Italy. Nawab Viqar ul Umara who built the palace lived in it for less than a decade before handing it over to the Nizam. He was poisoned to death at a shikar camp in his private forests. He died at the age of 48. The Nizam to whom the palace was handed over in 1895 died in the palace in 1911."

CHAPTER – VI

JANNAT MAKAN MIR OSMAN ALI KHAN–ASAF JAH-VII NIZAM UL MULK ASAF JAH SABAY (1911-1948, 1948-1967)

Seventh in the line of succession to the great Nizamul Mulk-I, the founder of the Asafia dynasty, Mir Osman Ali Khan was the last King whose attainments in diverse cultural, administrative, educational and philanthrophic fields made his 37 year rule (1911 to 1948) unique and memorable in the history of the Deccan. During his time pioneering and innovative measures were taken to democratise the polity by initiating functional representation and separation of executive from the judiciary. His concern for the Harijans by opening special schools for them earned the gratitude of Dr. Ambedkar. The success in enforcing universal primary education in the State was an achievement. The establishment of the Osmania University stands out as a lasting monument to his wisdom and foresight. Endowed with excellent qualities of head and heart, the Nizam as a person was simple, pious, and God fearing, compassionate and charitable, frugal in personal life yet munificent in serving public causes.

Mir Osman Ali Khan was born on April 6, 1886 A.D. His father evinced keen interest in his education and training. Replying to a query from then Viceroy whether the heir-apparent was making progress in his education, the Nizam, Mir Mahbub Ali Khan, replied that the heir-apparent was being carefully tutored. From early childhood, the best intellectuals were appointed as teacher and tutor to coach him in different subjects and for his general education. Since his succession had already been declared, he was being groomed for his future status by being trained to acquire knowledge, wisdom and sagacity. He was also being trained in the methods and skills of governance and organising the Government administration. The Secretaries of different Departments, and their assistants were asked to present official papers to him so that he could study them and thus get acquainted with all the complicated official matters and legal issues.

Mir Osman Ali Khan was a linguist and had command over six languages. Besides Urdu, he was well conversant with English, Turkish, Arabic, Persian and Telugu. He was good at shooting and horse-riding and was an expert in swordmanship. It is said that while riding on a horse, he could cut a goat hanging from the tree into two pieces with a single stroke.

In 1903, he visited Delhi along with his father to attend the coronation ceremony of King Edward.

In 1907 A.D. he was married to the daughter of Jahangir Jang at Adenbagh. In a report to the Viceroy, the Resident of Hyderabad wrote that the marriage of Mir Osman Ali Khan, took place with Azim Unnisa Begam, daughter of Jahangir Jang, on April 19, 1906. When he suggested to the Nizam that there should be some public rejoicing for the benefit of his subjects, the Nizam told him that this was not customary in his family. The marriage was a simple ceremony as the Nizam disliked ceremonial pomp (NAI, FD. Internal – B. Procs. June 1906 Nos.483-485, P.2).

On August 29, 1911, Mir Mahbub Ali Khan died and

Mir Osman Ali Khan was proclaimed as the Nizam.

The credit for the smooth transition was due entirely to a compact group of officials headed by Maharaja Sir Kishen Pershad. The Residency was nowhere involved in the proceedings for the installation.

In 1911, Friday at 4 pm in the evening, the royal procession started and a Mughal Darbar was arranged at Chow Mahalla Mubarak in the night.

At that time Maharaja Kishen Pershad was the Prime Minister. Maharaja Kishen Pershad, one of the closest and most loyal ministers of Mir Mahbub Ali Khan, had played significant role in ensuring the succession of Osman Ali Khan after the death of his father. Loyalty to his master was in the Maharaja's very blood and he transferred the same unquestioning loyalty to the new ruler. For some time everything appeared to proceed smoothly. It was known demonstrably that Maharaja Kishen Pershad was indeed close to him. Then suddenly matters changed and Kishen Pershad lost ground rapidly and unaccountably. His relations with the master deteriorated so fast that within a year of his accession, Kishen Pershad was obliged to go on long leave which as everyone understood, meant tha the had lost favour with the ruler. What actually caused his downfall was a sinister plot master-minded by Abdul Karim Khan who later became the Commissioner of Police.

Two weeks prior to the date of accession, the city was bustling with activity. In lanes and bylanes, the procession was the common talk. The general public eagerly awaited the happy occasion. When the day of accession arrived, people thronged the roads and even the public from the districts and villages reached the city as eager spectators and gathered after the early morning prayers. The procession began at 10 o'clock from Purani Haveli with great ceremonial pomp. The elephant of His Highness had a red golden cloth on its back which was adorned with old and silver-studded jewellery. The Nizam was seated alone in the amari and wore the royal costume. He had put on a dastar decorated with diamonds and jewels, on which a very glittering and bright turrah was shining. The glitter of diamonds, jewels and rubies was simply dazzling. The oscillating movement of the elephant presented a different scene. It gave the impression that the elephant was overjoyed. The elephant raised its trunk in salutation for which it was trained. The mahawat wore a red uniform laced with gold work. The goad which the mahawat was holding had unique splendour. The poor and needy persons with bags hanging on bamboos were seen all around the elephant. His Highness with his own hand distributed money from the trays to the needy. It contained silver coins, two anna coins, four anna coins, eight anna coins and rupee coins, besides two anna gold coins. The money bags were raised high enough and hardly any coin fell on the ground. The entire place resounded with joyous voices and clapping of hands. Behind the elephant of His Highness, Maharaja Kishen Pershad wearing his Darbar costume was seated on another elephant. The procession with all its splendour entered Khilawat Mubarak at one o'clock. Maharaja Kishen Pershad was present with morchal. Col. Afsar ul Mulk's elephant was behind the elephant of His Highness. There were 35 decorated elephants participating in the procession.

IMPORTANT EVENTS

In 1911 A.D. Lord Harding, Viceroy of India, arrived in Hyderabad and condoled the death of the Nizam's father, and congratulated the new ruler on his accession to the throne. He also invited His Highness to participate in the Delhi Darbar for the coronation ceremony of the Emperor of India. In 1911 A.D. His Highness with Ministers and staff proceeded to Delhi to attend the Imperial Darbar and met the Emperor of India who conferred the title of G.C.S.I.

on His Highness.

In July, 1912, Maharaja Kishen Pershad was relieved of the post of Prime Minister and Mir Yousuf Ali Khan Salar Jung was appointed in his place. Salar Jung was also relieved from his post in August 1914. When Maharaja Kishen Pershad was appointed to the post of Madur ul Madam the total income of the Asafia Dominion was four crores of rupees. It rose to five crores of rupees in 1908. It gradually increased and touched seven crores of rupees in 1912 at the time of Maharaja's resignation.

The Department of Archaeology was established in 1914 during the short tenure of the Prime Ministership of Nawab Yousuf Ali Khan Salar Jung-III. An amendement was made in the Forest Act and a Forest School was opened at Nizamabad.

Soon after the Nizam's accession the State was caught up in the whirlpool of war. The World War broke out in 1914 and became a life and death struggle for the British people and the British Government. At this critical juncture His Highness himself assumed the charge of the duties of Prime Minister. Four years later, under the pressure of the British Government an Executive Council was constituted to assist him in the administration but the Nizam continued to exercie his powers concerning all aspects of the administration. From time to time the British Residents had to support the authority of the Ministers against him. The Nizam naturally resented this and when the British declared their intention to withdraw the paramountcy he felt that a new era had dawned.

During the War, the Nizam rendered great help to the British Government. All the resources of the State were dedicated to the British Empire. Thousands of soldiers were sent to the battlefield. Financial assistance amounting to several lakhs of pounds and Rs.50 lakhs worth of silver bricks were given. The Nizams of Hyderabad were always loyal to the British. The British however, had a vested interest in befriending the Nizams. History bears witness to the fact that the British took undue advantage of the friendship. The British imposed the Hyderabad Contingent in Hyderabad and weakened the position of the Nizam and the State.

After the end of the war the British Government in recognition of the friendship of Mir Osman Ali Khan, honoured him with the title of 'His Exalted Highness' and 'Faithful Ally'.

SETTING UP OF THE OSMANIA UNIVERSITY

In 1917 A.D., Sir Akbar Hydari, who was Secretary of the Education Department, presented a petition to His Highness outlining the defects of the then prevalent education system and recommended the setting up of a University in Hyderabad.

The historic impact of the Farman issued by His Highness will remain as long as Urdu language subsists. His Highness not only agreed to the setting up of a university but also announced that the medium of instruction of the university would be Urdu. By taking this decision his Farman-I-Mubarak revealed his wisdom and farsightedness. The Farman was as follows :

'I agree with the petition and memorandum to set up such a university in the Dominion so that it will have a union of the old and new, arts and sciences of the East and West, - which will remove the defects from the existing system of education. This will combine what is good in the physical, mental, spiritual education of the old system with the new skills and methodology and will be conducive to the reformation of the students; and encouragement of innovation and research.

The main principle of this University would be that Urdu language should be made the medium of instruction for higher education. English would however continue as a language and would be a compulsory subject for the students. Hence I am very happy to permit, on this memorable occasion of my accession, the procedure for the setting up of a university in the State of Hyderabad on the principles mentioned in the memorandum." The University played a major role in the political awakening of the State since its inception in 1919. Urdu became the language of instruction. The political awakening created a demand for the introduction of regional languages in the educational curricula.

In 1918, a Royal Mandate was issued to constitute the University. The constituents of the Royal Mandate read as follows:

"As the prosperity and welfare of his beloved and loyal subjects is very important and dear in the eyes of His Highness this objective could only be best achieved when the current educational methodology of the Government of the Nizam would be liberated the from the outmoded system of the older Universities. In accordance with the special requirements, excellent arrangements could be made within the State itself. Accordingly, His Highness issued the following orders:

1. In Hyderabad Deccan one University namely Osmania University should be set up.

2. The main aim of the Osmania University would be to impart knowledge and skills in the various disciplines including religion, morals, literature, arts, science, medicine, philosophy, history, law, agriculture and other subjects beneficial for the development of professional expertise.

3. The main feature of Osmania University would to impart education in all subjects through the medium of Urdu and to have the study of English language and literature as compulsory subject.

The Osmania University became a living symbol of commitment to education and an enduring investment in excellence. It was the first university in India to have an Indian language, Urdu, as the medium of instruction. Expressing his approbation, Rabindranath Tagore wrote "I have long been waiting for the day when freed from the shackles of the foreign language, our education becomes naturally accessible to all our people". C. RajaGopalachari termed the University the "Ture Vidyapeeth, the swadeshi University of all India".

It is evident from the above mentioned Royal Mandate that His Highness himself had suggested the name of the University and decided that the medium of instruction should be the Urdu language, and the monogram of the University was subject to royal approval.

Prior to the establishment of the Osmania University a question arose about the availability of books which could be helpful in making the Urdu language the medium of instruction.

To overcome this difficulty a Translation Bureau was formed in order to translate books from other languages. In the Publication Bureau, books translated by the Bureau were published in a given time-frame.

The stupendous task of translating books from English to Urdu was entrusted to teams of experts subject-wise in each faculty. Basic lecture in each discipline was published in Urdu. These publications testify to the knowledge and expertise of the translators who besides having a mastery in both Urdu and English were conversant with the latest developments in their respective subjects and possessed the expertise necessary for a good translator. Osmania soon established itself as the first premier Urdu university in India to produce scholars and specialists who proved their mettle in every field, some of whom were outstanding, comparable in academic excellence to the best products of any other university in India and elsewhere.

In the beginning of 1918, the British Government dispatched the following letters to the Nizam:

"It has given me great satisfaction to express my sincere appreciation of the eminent services which you have rendered to my Empire during the War by conferring upon you the special title of 'His Exalted Highness' and by conferring on you formally the honorary title of 'Faithful Ally' of the British Government. Your Exalted Highness and your predecessors have shown loyalty to my ancestors and myself. Following the lofty example of your illustrious predecessors at the time of the signing of the early treaties between the British Government and the Hyderabad State. Your Exalted Highness has given in your own person a clear proof of your right to bear that historic title. In the prominent position enjoyed by Your Exalted Highness as the leading ruler of India, your loyalty was displayed in the early months of the present War by the proclamation calling on your subjects and impressing on your co-religionists throughout India the duty of firm and steadfast devotion to my throne and empire. The munificent contribution made by your Exalted Highness from time to time for objects connected with the war have borne striking and public testimony to the strength of enduring bond which unites the destinies of Great Britian and Hyderabad.

Trusting that Your Exalted Highness may long continue to enjoy good health and prosperity, I sign myself.

Your sincere friend and Emperor, (George R.A.).

In 1919, Sir Ali Imam was appointed to the post of Prime Minister as a result of which the administration improved and the income of the Government increased. In 1919, Mir Osman Ali Khan thought of a scheme for the constitution of an Executive Council in order to have better and more efficient administration in Hyderabad. The post of the President of the Executive Council was offered to Sir Ali Imam, who was then a Member of the Executive Council of Bihar and Orissa. He was considered the most qualified person to shoulder the onerous responsibilities by virtue of his experience and educational attainments.

ESTABLISHMENT OF BAB-I-HUKUMAT

November 17, 1919, is reckoned as the golden day in history of the state the Osmania period, when on this date, the Nizam issued the fundamental principles of the consititution, and Constituted Bab-I-Hukumat (Executive Council). A Darbar was convened for the inauguration of the Executive Council.

Two troops of the Deccan Horses and Imperial Service Lancers which were well trained and fully provided with the best equipment were sent to the battlefield by the Government of Hyderabad. This was done at at the request of the Government of India in 1914, soon after World War I broke out.. In 1920, these troops returned to Hyderabad after being at the battlefront for six years. During the War, the armies of His Majesty and his Government recognised the spirit and bravery of these troops in impressive words. Since the accession of His Highness, the renowned Gen. Nawab Sir Afsar ul Mulk remained the Commander-in-Chief of the Asaf Jahi troops for a long period.

A Department of Sports was set up in 1920. In the beginning, the Department was semi-official. Nawab Masood Jang Bahadur was the President. In the beginning, mass drill and football tournaments were conducted, in which only the local schools of the city participated. Later, Secunderabad and other district school teams participated in these tournaments. Gradually, besides football, annual tournaments in hockey, cricket, tennis, badminton and mass drill were held. Then there was a time when the sportsmen of Hyderabad participated in the Olympic Games. In the swimming contests across the English Channel, a student of Hyderabad gained prominent success.

The Singareni Collieries Co. was set up in 1920 to mine mineral coal.

In 1921 through a Farman a rural development programme was commenced.

In 1922, Sir Ali Imam was relieved of his post and Faridoon Mulk was appointed as the President of the Council.

SULTAN UL ULOOM

Keeping in view, the extraordinary interest taken by the Nizam in education and particularly as the Chief Patron of the Osmania University, the members of the Council after its establishment presented in 1933, to H.E.H. the Nizam the title of 'Sultan ul uloom' (King of Sciences). The address presented on this occasion reads as follows:

> "By the grace of God, today is an auspicious day not only in the history of the Osmania University but a memorable day in the history of the academic institutions when the Founder and Chief Patron of this university has honoured the members of the Council by accepting the honorary degree."

'It is evident from the history of the world that enlightened rulers always participated actively in patronizing arts and literature. The devotion and interest shown by H.E.H. the Nizam in the promotion of education and his patronge of learning constitute a shining example for the rest of the country.

There is no greater occasion of joy and pride, for the people of the State and the University itself, than this to present H.E.H. Highness its first and foremost honorary degree to such an eminent patron and the supporter of the cause of education. The Members of the Council of the Osmania University have the honour of presenting the honorary degree of "Sultan ul uloom'to His Exalted Highness".

ROYAL SPEECH ON THE OCCASION OF THE CELEBRATIONS OF THE TWO HUNDRED YEARS OF INDEPENDENCE OF ASAFIA KINGDOM

Celebrating 200 years of Asafia rule the Nizam paid tributes to Nizamul Mulk-I for his valued vision and humility while praying for the happiness and prosperity of his subjects. An excerpt from his address in 1923 is reproduced below:

> "God had endowed Nizam ul Mulk with the rare qualities of courage & prudence. Moreover, he had attained the highest position because of his military prowess. He strode the 18th century because of his commanding personality and outstanding abilities. The Mughal Empire at Delhi was almost on the verge of collapse. It was generally believed that if there was any person who could avert the downfall and revive the Empire's strength and glory, it was Nizam ul Mulk. There was not a single part of the kingdom which had not seen the feat of his arms. Deccan had won over his heart, because he loved this State like his own child. His Government was free and independent, in all respects. Renouncing personal ambition, he remained loyal to the Mughal Emperor hoping to regain the lost grandeur of the house of Taimur. In a short time, however, he realised that the foundation of the Empire had become very weak. His self-respect did not permit him to continue his relations with the Delhi Mughal rule which had fallen in total disgrace. He felt compelled to declare his independence to save the Deccan from chaos confusion and war for the welfare and betterment of the people.
>
> Since then two centuries have passed and the establishment of the rule of my family now entering the third century, is a matter of glory, pride and honour for me. The rulers of the Asaf Jahi dynasty have ruled

over this State to ensure that the people of the State should be prosperous and peaceful. The declaration of independence by Asaf Jah added more links to the chain of loyalty, which joined the Ruler and the subjects both in a common endeavour. I know my subjects will feel the same pride over this declaration as I do. The memory of this magnifient event is dear to all of us, because it is the symbol and sign of patriotism.

Finally I pray to God that he should save my kingdom from evil and violence and grant prosperity and progress to the State. The friends should be happy and successful & the foes be unhappy and disgraced Amen (So be it)".

Fakht
Sd/- Ala Hazrat
From Jarida Extraordinary
Dated 1st Shahban 1342 H – 1923.

BERAR ISSUE

The Nizam wanted to take an independent line with the British on equal terms on the issue of Berar. The English, however, invoked the doctrine of Paramountcy and invoked their prerogatives as a colonial power and the subordinate status of the ruler. Lord Reading the Viceroy rejected the claim of equality and made it quite clear that the Agreement on Berar could not be reversed.

Lord Reading in a letter affirmed as follows:

"You have stated that in internal affairs of Hyderabad, you enjoy a position similar to that of the British Government concerning the internal affairs of Britain. It is clear from these words that your Exalted Highness has formed a wrong impression regarding the relationship between the ruler and Paramount

Power. As a representative of His Imperial Majesty, I am bound to state the position in clear terms as at this stage my silence on such a issue would possibly be considered later on as acceptance of the claim which you had made.

The sovereignty of the British Crown is supreme in India. On this basis, no ruler of the State is justified in claiming to discuss with the British Government on equal terms.

I want only to tell that your Exalted Highness, who bears the title of 'Faithful Ally' that despite this your State has no special status compared to other States which are governed by the British Crown".

The Nizam was sorely disappointed and had to bide his time until 1936. The issue was raised at the Round Table Conference held in London between 1931-33. Ultimately after protracted negotiations, on October 24, 1936, an Agreement was concluded between His Exalted Highness and His Majesty King Emperor regarding the issue of Berar. According to the Agreement, the British Government accepted His Exalted Higness's proprietary rights on the Berar region. Sir Akbar Hydari had represented the Berar case at the Round Table Conference. An announcement was made in 1933 by Lord Wellington to resolve the issue. According to the Agreement, the sovereignty of the Nizam over Berar was accepted and acknowledged by the British on October 24, 1936 A.D. How ever the administration of Berar rested with the British. It was also agreed that the British would pay the surplus revenue to the Nizam. The titles of the Nizam and his heir-apparent were revised by the Viceroy and notified as 'His Exalted Highness, the Nizam of Hyderabad and Berar' and his heir-apparent was entitled 'His Highness the Prince of Berar.

The other important developments that occurred between 1930 and 1936 are highlighted below:

1. At the Round Table Conference (1931-33) it was decided that if Hyderabad joined the Federal Govt., it would have its own post and currency.

2. Weightage to Harijans in education : Dr. Ambedkar in a resolution on October 1931 expressed his gratitude to the Nizam for opening schools particularly for the Harijans and said that this gesture had no parallel in India and wanted the rest of India to emulate it.

3. It was a red letter day for Hyderabad when the British returned the Residency area to the Nizam in 1933.

FUNCTIONAL REPRESENTATION

The Reforms Committee submitted its report on August 31, 1938 to the Department of Legislative Affairs and acting on the recommendations of the Committee, the Government approved constitutional amendements of a far-reaching nature. In these constitutional amendments, the principle of representation adopted for the participation of Government and the public was totally a new concept for India. This principle meant that instead of electing representatives on a regional basis as was the practice in British India, the people were entrusted with the right to elect representatives to the legislative assembly on the basis of their occupations, such as representatives of cultivators, workers, lawyers and doctors.

The Farman of His Exalted Highness which was issued in connection with the consitutional amendments, which are briefly described in the following terms:

> "Since the time when Asaf Jah–I laid the foundation of the State which is the largest State of India, all the people had equal civic rights without any discrimination of caste, religion or nationality. I hope, that in the implementation of their rights, every one will maintain the traditions of mutual respect for

the feelings of others and their aspirations. I am sure that in framing this constitution, the underlying purpose is to equip the administrative machinery to implement the new reforms in order to stimulate the progress of the maintain its present state on all fronts and open new vistas of experience and diverse opportunities for the welfare of the people. I hope both the Government and the people will join hands in a common effort for the purposeful advancement of the State to achieve the greatest good of the greatest number. This is my ardent desire".

"With the blessings of God, in exercising my authority, I am conscious of the great sense of responsibility that rests on my shoulders to rule according to the dictates of my conscience. I am confident that in the proper discharge of my duties and responsibilities my sincere efforts will be supported by the people. Both I and my family have always cherished the loyalty and faith of my people".

HYDERABAD'S ACCESSION TO THE INDIAN UNION

Indo-Hyderabad talks for an amicable solution of the issue after a 'Standstill Agreement' in 1947 failed in June, 1948. A White Paper on Hyderabad was presented by the Government of India stating its policy. The Government of India declared that "it cannot afford to be a helpless spectator of orgies of misrule in Hyderabad. It said further that the only way to resolve the Indo-Hyderabad political deadlock was to accede to India and democratise the administration." The Nizam, however, did not comply with the requests of the Government of India on the advice of his Ministers. The Indian Government at last was forced to send its troops to Hyderabad on September 13, 1948.

The Nizam surrendered on September 17, 1948. This was the well-known 'Police Action.' Maj-General J.N. Choudary was appointed the Military Governor of Hyderabad by the Government of India. Mohd. Syed Qasim Razvi was arrested on September 19, from his room at the headquarters of the Ittehad-ul-Muslemeen. Mir Laik Ali and his other Ministers were kept under house arrest.

All the former Ministers were not allowed to leave their houses without the permission of the Military Government and they were not allowed to have contacts with anyone. There were no restrictions, however, on the members of their families. Syed Qasim Razvi was charged with murder and dacoity and a case was registered against him. He was sentenced to rigorous imprisonment for seven years in the dacoity case. After the completion of his jail term he proceeded to Pakistan.

On January 26, 1950, His Exalted Highness the Nizam Asaf Sabay, relinquished his throne and Hyderabad came completely under the control of the Government of India. The Nizam was made the Rajparmukh on January 26, 1950.

In March, 1953, under the leadership of B. Ram Krishna Rao an elected Government was formed. Huzur Nizam was appointed as the constitutional Rajparmukh of the Hyderabad State. Prince Mukarram Jah Bahadur the grandson of the Nizam, was accepted as his successor by the Government of India.

In 1956, the State of Hyderabad was reorganised on linguistic basis. On October 31, 1956 the status of the Nizam as Rajparmukh of the erstwhile Hyderabad State ended.

THE NIZAM'S SENSE OF PIETY

In 1935, after visiting the tomb of the saint Hazarat Nizam uddin Mahbub Ilahi, His Exalted Highness visited Jama Masjid to perform the Friday prayers. At that time, one poet desired to read a 'quasida' but the Nizam told the poet that, "the greatness of a servant should not be recounted in a mosque. In the abode of God, a king and a beggar are both equal, for in the eyes of God there is none superior or inferior."

In 1935 H.E.H. the Nizam considered it his duty to participate in the urs at Gulbarga. He joined the procession Sandal 'sharif' and walked up to the Astana Hazrat Khwaja Banda Nawaz. At that time a salutation and guard of honour was arranged near the stairs but Hazur Nizam said: "I have myself come here to salute God, and hence there is no need for salutation." Accordingly salutations were forbidden.

It is said that once Hazur Nizam attended a sermon. One of those persons present at the sermon tied an ornamental belt around his waist. When the Nizam saw him he pointedly asked him: "Is this my Darbar or a divine assembly"? This was enough for the man to remove his belt immediately from the waist.

Once the Nizam attended a meeting, when the preacher saluted him. On this act of the preacher, the Nizam told him: "Maulvi Sahib, I have entered here, salutation is binding on me. Sitting on the pulpit of the Prophet it is not necessary for you to respect a worldly person like me".

ELECTRIFICATION AT HOLY MADINA

Nawab Sir Nizamat Jang, while proposing a scheme for the electrification at Madina Tayabah appealed to the people for Rs. 30,000. When the news of this appeal reached Mir Osman Ali Khan he sanctioned the entire expenditure for electrification. Then he issued a Farman Mubarak which read thus:

FARMAN MUBARAK

"I have ordered to set aside a reasonable fund particularly for the electrification at Madina Tayabah and for the management of other connected affairs from the donations of the Silver Jubilee Celebrations, and hope that shortly, this auspicious and religious work will be performed so that it should herald good fortune for the State".

Barely within eight days, another Farman in this connection was issued, which was published as Khand Mukarar as follows:

"On the occasion of my Silver Jubilee Celebrations, out of the donations collected by Sarf-I-khas a minimum sum of Rs.20000 has been kept aside. An order to this effect has already been issued to Sarf-I-khas so that certain projects are executed with this money at Mecca and Madina. The execution of this work in holy places will be done through a committee, which will be appointed by the Government. The President of the committee will be Sir Nizamat Jang and members Khwaja Moin Uddin and Yaseen Khan (Secretary Sarf-I-khas). I hope the work will be satisfactorily completed in time".

LOVER OF PROPHET MOHAMMED

A responsible official of the Hyderabad High Court stated "When I reached Hyderabad after having the honour of performing the pilgrimage to Kaba & Madina Munawara, it was Friday. I thought of presenting myself on Monday for salutation to His Exalted Highness. The next day when I was getting ready to go to the court the chobdar came and told me 'His Exalted Highness has asked you to meet him before going to the Court.' I immediately went to the royal palace and against the normal practice, was called in immediately. Compared to my other visits, I was most warmly received and extraordinary affection was shown to me. His Exalted Higness inquired for a long time about the details of the travel in general and my spiritual experience at Madina Munawara in particular. As it was getting late, he permitted me to leave but told me to meet him again. I went on the third day, I carried with me nazr and tabarrukat from the holy pilgrimage and a piece of sheet or cover used at Madina Munawara which I got it fixed in a golden frame. After presenting myself, I submitted that I had brought some tabarrukat from Madina which were in my car. His Exalted Highness ordered chobdar to bring those things. At that time he was smoking. He discarded the cigarette after the chobdar left and ordered another chobdar to bring water for washing his hands. When the chobdar brought water, he cleaned his mouth properly and washed his hands. Meanwhile, the other chobdar brought the tabarrukat. His Highness rose and stood up, stepped forward, took the tabarrukat in his hand, kept on his head and then kissed it. He ordered the chobdar to keep them in his bedroom safely. He then listened to the interesting facts about the Gumbad khizra and the land of Madina. He expressed great love for Madina and with rapt attention listened to the accounts of conditions in Madina while none of my friends or relatives made such enquires".

In 1933 the Nizam had written in a Farman:

> "As a nobleman, I have another religion which is known as Sulehkul or peace-loving. Under my regime, people belonging to different castes and creeds are settled and it is the custom of my kingdom for long to ensure protection of the places of their worship."

In the above mentioned document, the Nizam has thrown light on the 'Asaf Jahi Customs'. At another place, he had written thus :

> "My biggest wealth is my ancestral religion. In

reality if there is anything which could be utilized by me as a provision for the life hereafter, anything which will go along with me, it would be only the light of faith and the longing of my heart and nothing else."

In spite of being the richest man in the world, the Nizam led a very simple life. He wore simple dress and ate simple food. He hated extravagance. His frugality was limited to himself only. In giving charity, he was very generous. His traditional dress was a Turkish cap without tassel and shervani, half sleeves jacket, coarse cotton cloth pajama and salim shahi slipper. In spite of his simplicity he appeared so dignified that very few people could look into his eyes and stare him in his face. His lifestyle was in the manner of the style of the early Caliphs of Islam. He was one of those kings who considered himself a trustee of the State funds which belonged to his subjects.

FRUGAL YET MUNIFICENT

The Nizam believed that God had placed on him the responsibility of administering his kingdom to keep his subjects, secure, happy and prosperous. He had great compassion for the poor and the deprived and his heart went out to relieve their sufferings. God blessed the Nizam with qualities of self-denial. He opted voluntarily for poverty and like a dervish led a life of "plain living and high thinking". It should be noted, however, that he was generous and munificent in his charity for the downtrodden and for noble causes and public welfare institutions which needed money. As a benevolent guardian of the lowly and oppressed, he did not brook injustice and worked ceaselessly to rule the State with justice and generosity.

Maulana Khwaja Hasan Nizami a noted intellectual described the personal life of Nizam in these words:

"When the King used to sit in the Royal Palace there was a small chamber with a simple carpet and ordinary chairs placed on it. Everybody, whether big or small, relatives or strangers, all were received at the same place. The king used to wear very simple dress, but God gifted him with dignity and grandeur. Even important dignitaries were impressed by his royal bearing".

The Nizam never liked to see anybody standing in the sun or to get wet in the rain. If anyone among the servants got sick, he was immediately permitted to take rest. The King of the Deccan used to lookafter his ordinary day-to-day needs himself. He himself used to acknowledge in his own hand-writing the receipt of papers and would himself close the envelopes with gum.

If any member of the family fell sick he would arrange treatment and offer his personal advice.

Once the Nizam visited the Osmania General Hospital to inquire about the health of a Khanazed. While passing through a ward he saw a man who had lost both his legs and was dragging himself around with leather tied to his amputated legs. The Nizam inquired from one of the doctors accompanying him whether that man could be given artificial legs. The doctors said that there is no such factory in Hyderabad which manufactured artificial limbs and that it was very costly and that it was expensive to import artifical limbs from abroad. The Nizam was very much moved and upset. He consulted his advisors and expressed his desire to undertake construction of a hospital. Land was soon purchased for thirty lakhs of rupees at Panjagutta. A grand building was constructed for the provision of artificial limbs and free treatment for the poor was made available. The hospital was particularly meant for the treatment of polio cases, and the treatment of bone diseases. Free limbs were supplied to the poor. This hospital has now expanded in other directions.

The Nizam was kind to the animals also. Once his cavalcade was passing by and a goat was run over by his car. The King ordered treatment and made arrangements for treatment of the injured animal in the Royal Palace.

The Nizam's mind was so sharp that while he dictated a letter to the Viceroy of India, he would at the same time recommend medicine for the ailment of a child of his servant and prescribe a fixed diet for the sick.

The frugality, generosity and charity of the Nizam provided many lessons for all to learn, Nawab Samad Yar Jang Bahadur was Peshi Secretary. The Nizam once called him during the winter season and ordered him to buy a blanket saying :

"My blanket is very old. Please buy a blanket from the market but please ensure that it does not cost more than Rs. 15".

The cost of the blanket available in the market was Rs.18. Samad Yar Jang however told the Nizam that the cost of the blanket in the market was not less than Rs.18 and that if ordered, he would purchase one. After hearing him the Nizam said:

"No, I will manage with this blanket this winter. I will consider it next year."

Later, Maulvi Syed Ahmed: Pesh Imam from Delhi was allowed to see the Nizam. He made a request for his help in laying one-fourth of the flooring of the courtyard of Jama Masjid in Delhi, which was estimated to cost about four lakh rupees. Huzur Nizam said that "laying of one fourth courtyard was just like a patching of coarse cotton cloth on velvet and that he would like the entire flooring of the courtyard of the mosque be done up for which Rs.16,00,000 will be paid from the Royal Treasury". One cannot but note that he did not spare money for a noble cause.

DEATH OF ASAF SABE KING OF DECCAN

Asaf Sabay Mir Osman Ali Khan died on February 24, 1967 exactly at the time of Friday prayers.

His body was carried in an ambulance car from his residence to Mecca Masjid. The famous saint of the city, Hazrat Habib Idroos, headed the divine service at the funeral. Asaf Jahi flag was laid on the body, and the funeral procession proceeded on a gun-carriage with full military honours. Nearly ten lakh people accompanied the funeral consisting of Hindus, Muslims, Sikhs, Parsis and Christians.

TRIBUTE BY NEWSPAPERS AND JOURNALS TO LATE HUZUR NIZAM MIR OSMAN ALI KHAN

Every one will bear testimony to the fact that from 1911: when Mir Osman Ali Khan ascended the throne till 1948, a long period of 37 years, Hyderabad Deccan enjoyed the unique distinction of being a vibrant cultural center of India. The main reason for this was the personality of Mir Osman Ali Khan. At the cultural level, there is hardly any movement in which Mir Osman Ali Khan had not taken interest. The formation of the Osmania University and the Translation Bureau are the enduring symbols of his love for learning. Likewise, he patronised poets and men of letters. In fact, the death of the Nizam of the Deccan brought to an end an era rich in history and his death marked the end of a golden age

NIZAM ESTABLISHED THE FIRST CONSTIUTIONAL GOVERNMENT IN THE SUB CONTINENT

While the Nizam as a ruler always maintained the dignity of the high office, he himself led the life of a carefree fakir.

The Nizam was totally different from his ancestors and other rulers of the State. He was not interested in leading a luxurious life given to amusement. He was never seen in clubs, the beaches of Europe or on the race course. There is hardly any renowned poet, writer or any educational institution in the sub-continent that has not benefited from his generosity. When he assumed reins of power in his hands the treasury was empty. When he was deprived of his power, Hyderabad was the most prosperous and progressive State in the sub-continent. His predecessors on the throne never wore their clothes for the second time. The late Nizam not only wore clothes after washing but he never hesitated to wear clothes which were patched. Hyderabad symbolized a rare culture which is fast disappearing. Few are aware of the fact that Mir Osman Ali Khan established the first contitutional government in the sub-continent. ('Anjam' Daily Karachi, February 26, 1967).

Hakim Ahmed Shujah in his speech said:

> "The life of His Exalted Highness was very simple but dignified and attracted attention. He kept away from the artificiality of the world. He was not a hypocrite but was a portrait of culture and refinement. He was a shining example of Islamic toleration. He adhered strictly to religious fasts and prayers. He dedicated his life for the good of the people and enriched the quality of their lives.
>
> The establishment of Osmania University was indeed a great educational and cultural achievement. By making Urdu the medium of instruction in the Osmania University, the Nizam wanted to free his people from the shackles of a foreign language. His Exalted Highness's generosity was endless and there were no limitations to his large hearted generosity. His generosity crossed the limits of land of the Deccan and benefited people in the rest of India, and in Islamic countries.

The death of Mir Osman Ali Khan was not the mere death of a single person; he was an institution by himself and represented the best in Indian culture.

A man of ability and learning he was Sultan-ul-uloom 'Absolute Monarch of Sciences' in the real sense of the term. The obligation of a benefactor can only be paid back in exchange for his services. His rich traditions should be maintained. His qualities of head and heart and his noble principles must be fostered and adopted. Institutions should be established in his name. Efforts should be made to establish universities like Osmania, so that the memory of the great Patron should always be kept alive in the hearts of the people. At least our heartbeat should feel that the name of our patron is alive and will continue to be alive."

UNIVERSAL RESPECT

Soon after the Police Action, Pandit Jawaharlal Nehru as the Prime Minister of India arrived in Hyderabad for the first time. He sent word that His Exalted Highness Nizam should not be bothered to receive him at the airport, but only the presence of the heir–apparent of the Dominion would be enough.

When Dr. Zakir Hussain visited Hyderabad as the President of Republic of India, he also issued special orders that he himself would visit the palace and meet His Exalted Highness the Nizam. The first sentence the President uttered at the meeting was "My position is of another nature. Beside the position of the President of India, my father was a servant of Darbar Asafi. My conscience does not permit me to trouble His Exalted Highness to attend the reception, when, by birth, I enjoy the position of being your subject".

CHAPTER – VII

SYMBOLS OF SOVEREIGNTY

It is noteworthy that the Nizam was the only ruler among the Princely States who–in the historical circumstances obtaining in the colonial India–had developed fully the infrastructure of an independent prosperous and self reliant State. There were many symbols of his sovereignty.

The imperatives of an independent State and the symbols of the Nizam's sovereignty were a separate State anthem, flag, army, currency, post and telegraph and the Nizam's State Railway.

STATE ANTHEM

Ta abad khaliq-I-alam ye riyasat rakhe
Tujh ko Osman basad ijlal salamat rakhay
Jaise to fakhr-I-salateen hai bafazal yazdan
Yun hi mumtaz tera daur-I-hukumat rakhay
Al o aulad ko allah de umr-e-khizri
Unse abad tera khana-e-daulat rakhay
Jod-e-Hatim rahe sharminda-e-ahsan tera
Adl-I-khusrau ko khijal teri adalat rakhey
Khandazan surat-I-gul tere hawa kha rahen
Ake qadmo pe adu farkh ita'at rakhey

Ban ke saqi tere Iqbal Nizam-e-sabay
Tujh ko sahba kash khumkhana ishrat rakhay.

"May the creator of the world bless this kingdom till eternity and O! Osman, keep you sound and healthy, and live with dignity for a hundred years. By the grace of God you are the pride of rulers. May the Almighty keep your rule illustrious. May God grant long life like khizr to your children and maintain the continuity of your noble descent. May the proverbial Hatim's charity pale before your glorious munificence. May your sense of justice surpass even the legendary justice of Khusro. May your well-wishers glow in happiness like the full blown flowers and your enemies acknowledge your superior prowess. O! Osman may your glory as Saqi (giver of wine) make your tavern an abode of joy and ecstasy".

ASAF JAHI FLAG

A story quite current about the Asaf Jahi flag states that once a saint while presenting seven loaves of bread and a yellow shawl to Nizam ul Mulk conveyed the good news that not only he but his dynasty would rule the Dominion for seven generations. According to some historians, the name of the saint was Nizamuddin Aurangabadi while others are of the view that his name was Shah Inayat. According to some chroniclers, Nizam ul Mulk once sought the audience of Shah Inayat at a time when he was having his meal. Shah Sahib presented Nizam ul Mulk seven Kulchas (a kind of bread) one after the other. When the eighth kulcha was offered, Nizam ul Mulk pleaded to be excused. Immediately Shah Sahib revealed to Nizam-ul-Mulk that he would be the ruler and that his kingdom would last for seven generations in the Deccan region.

According to some historians the story runs that when Nizam ul Mulk was unhappy with Mohd. Shah Rangeela, the ruler of Delhi, and resigned from the Subedari of Malwa, he proceeded towards the Deccan. At Balapur (Berar province) he presented himself before Shah Inayat and sought his blessings for his well-being. On this occasion, Shah Sahib while giving him seven kulchas and a yellow shawl, conveyed the good news that he would be a ruler. After this incident Nizam ul Mulk attacked the Deccan and emerged victorious in 1724.

Mohd. Ashraf Engineer a historian gives another version of the story. He says:

"Nizam ul Mulk reposed great trust in the saints of the Chistiya family. When he went into seclusion in Delhi, he frequently prayed at the tomb of Hazrat Nizamuddin Auliya Mahbub Ilahi. As was the prevailing custom, the spiritual supervisor of the dargah tied a yellow pagdi on the head of Nizam ul Mulk which was the saint's favourite colour. With the announcement of his independence Asaf Jah considered the yellow colour as a good omen and chose the yellow color for his headgear, his flag and amari and the same yellow colour was later adopted as Asaf Jahi colour. While opting for the yellow colour for his flag, he had the sign of kulcha impressed on the flag as an expression of his faith.

Earlier the Asafi flag was yellow in colour with a white circle in the center which was the impression of the kulcha of Shah Inayat. Later, green and white lines were added. The green colour stood for the Syed lineage because the mother of Asaf Jah-I was a Syedani. The white colour was attributed to Hazrat Abu Bakr Siddique. On the circle of the flag, there was a dastar of Asafi and on the Dastar 'Al-azmatu- Lillah' was written meaning 'God is great'.

The significance of the constituents of the flag are as follows:

The yellow colour originated from the yellow cloth wrapped round the head of the Nizam-ul-Mulk by the guardian of the tomb of the famous saint,

Hazrat Nizam uddin Auliya at Delhi, and from that time yellow became the official Asafia symbol.

The green colour is Islamic. On the maternal side, Nizam ul Mulk traced his genealogy to Prophet Mohammed, while the white colour is associated with Hazrat Abu Bakr, the first Caliph, from whom Nizam ul Mulk deccended on the paternal side; the white round circle in the Center is the reflex of the moon (Qamar) from the name of the first Nizam, Qamruddin Khan.

According to a legend the stripes and dastar were added on the suggestion of Afsarul Mulk during the reign of Mir Mahbub Ali Khan Asaf Jah Sadas.

In order to maintain the memory of Saint Shah Inayat, Asaf Jah built a bazaar in the city of Hyderabad and named it Shah Inayat Ganj. The successors of Shah Inayat benefited from the income received from the shops in the bazaar.

About the Kulcha, Nawab Sarwar Jang has written in his autobiography that "The Kulchas given by Shah Inayat were preserved in the Royal Treasury and whenever Asaf Jah Sadas Mir Mahbub Ali Khan travelled these Kulchas were taken out."

D.F. Karaka's in his book

"The Fabulous Mughal" tells the story in a different vein: -

> "Once when Nizam ul Mulk was travelling on the road from Delhi he stopped in front of the house of a saint somewhere between Burhanpur and Khuldabad. At that time, he was quite young. The saint offered him whatever was ready to eat, which comprised only Kulchas and water. This was the only food which the saint could offer. The bread was very small which was called 'Kulcha'. Nizam ul Mulk was hungry at that time. He ate three or four Kulchas and feeling embarrassed for eating from the food of a saint, he apologized for his hunger. The saint told him "I have got more Kulchas in my house, my son, you

eat. It is all for you, you can eat as much as you can."

Nizam ul Mulk finished the fifth and then the sixth kulch a looked at the face of the holy man who nodded quietly and said 'my son eat more.' Nizam ul Mulk ate one more Kulcha. He was then satisfied. He then said 'Now I had enough' and put his hand on his chest, bowed his head and expressed his gratitude.

Again the saint urged him to eat more but Nizam ul Mulk could eat no more. Then the holy man said 'My son now you go, may the blessings of God be on you. His favours will shield you. 'Your dynasty will rule for seven generations'. His words came true. The family of Asaf Jah, ruled for seven generations. The flag of Asaf Jah flew in Hyderabad as the symbol of the Asaf Jahi dynasty till September 1948. Thereafter, till February 24, 1967 it was flown on the King Kothi Palace as the personal flag of Mir Osman Ali Khan. When he passed away the funeral proceeded with full military honours on the gun carriage towards his eternal abode and ten lakh people witnessed that his body was wrapped in the same Asaf Jahi flag.

ARMY

Nizamul Mulk Asaf Jah-I had maintained his army to safeguard the integrity and independence of the Deccan against the sneak attacks of the then Mughal Emperor and against the growing power of the French and the British East India Company. In 1799 the army led by Mir Alam and the British officers, fought a war against Tipu Sultan and defeated him. Later in 1811, this army was known, as the Hyderabad Contingent. The Nizam had to relinquish Berar to the British, in order to meet the expenses of this Contingent in 1854, and finally had to relinquish the Contingent itself in 1902.

In World War-I on August 4, 1914 Mir Osman Ali Khan

sent the first Hyderabad Imperial Service Troops to the war front. In 1934, the Nizam's heir Prince Azam Jah Bahadur, the Prince of Berar was appointed Commander-in-Chief of the Army.

In World War-II 1939, the Nizam placed his entire Imperial Service Force unit at the disposal of the British Government and made a generous grant of 4 crore pounds to the War Fund. When India became independent in 1947 the British departed from India leaving the Nizam to his fate.

With the integration of all Princely States into the Indian Union the political scenario underwent a basic transformation. The democratically elected Government replaced monarchy. The subjects of defence and foreign affairs come under the direct control of the Union Government. The Union list of subjects included railways, post and telegraphs, currency, coinage and legal tenders.

CURRENCY

With the exception of Hyderabad, in all other native States the Government of India currency was in circulation. In 1858 the British wanted the Nizam to remove the name of the Mughal Emperor from the coins and currency notes, after the fall of the Mughal Empire. Accordingly, on August 29, 1858 coins manufactured in Hyderabad were introduced as Hali Sikka. Coins were made of gold, silver and copper. The gold coins were called 'Ashrafis'. The new coins had the imprint of Charminar on one side and Nizam ul Mulk Asaf jah on the other. The initial letter of the Nizam's name was inscribed on every coin: 'M' for Mahboob 'O' for Osman.

Paper Currency Act was passed in 1918. The Government of India Printing Press at Nasik was utilised for the printing of notes. The special feature of the note design included Nizam's crest with crescent star. The denominations were written in five State languages namely Urdu, Marathi, Telugu, Kanarese and English both in figures and letters. 'Sarkar Ali' was inscribed in Urdu on the note.

Since Hyderabad was always in the fore front of reforms, a suggestion was made in 1942 for the issue of decimal coins which was accepted and implemented in 1945.

POST

The Nizam's postal system was in fact much better than that in the British India. Three local languages were adopted in all the stamps and stationery namely, Urdu, Marathi and Telugu besides English. Hyderabad was the first State in the world to release a stamp to commemorate victory in World War-II on December 6, 1945. Postcards and envelopes bore an embossed monogram of 'Sarkar-e-Asafia'. All the important sections of postal services like parcels, deposits, money orders, V.P.P. urgent delivery were run with the utmost efficiency. The postal department of the Government of Hyderabad was discontinued after the integration of the State with the Indian Union.

NIZAM STATE RAILWAY

In 1869 British India agreed to construct a Railway line which came to be called the Nizam State Railway. After Hyderabad's accession to the Indian Union there was an extraordinary expansion of the railway lines in the State.

PART – II

CIVILISATION AND CULTURE OF HYDERABAD

CHAPTER VIII

CIVILISATION AND CULTURE

The term civilisation comprehends both the material and the spiritual state of people. The material aspect, for instance, relates to the phenomenal transition from the civilisation of the caveman to that of the modern age.

The material is based upon the scientific and technological progress, communication revolution, the devices and the gadgets that have virtually transformed the conditions and the standards of living of the common man. The spiritual side relates to developments in education and knowledge and their impact on the moral and aesthetic sensibility of human beings. The material is represented in the external trappings of civilisation while the spiritual comprises the inner development of the human personality best expressed in the term 'Culture'–which is the refinement of sensibility that abhors violence hypocrisy and crudity and aspires to cherish the true, the good and the beautiful.

It is culture which promotes the qualities of compassion, sense of justice and respect for the worth and dignity of the individual irrespective of caste, class, race, religion and sex. If the material dominates over the spiritual, it breeds arrogance and greed that cause tension and conflict in human relations.

The uniqueness of the Deccani culture consists in

building the qualities of the spiritual on the base of material security and well-being. Poverty and ignorance are the adverse forces that degrade a person while wide spread prosperity backed by life affirming values transform refine and elevate his personality. It is here that the Asaf Jahi monarchy and the feudal system have been instrumental in developing the secular culture of Hyderabad.

The nobles of Hyderabad played a major role in the development of Deccani civilisation. If meticulously analysed, it becomes apparent that the cultural stream of Hyderabad emanated from a high degree of refinement, knowledge and basic values that characterized the nobility of the State. It is the fruit of age-old upbringing, learning, and imbibing of deep religiosity and humane ideas. Various factors such as geographical, historical, political and social constituted, so to say, the vital ingredients of Hyderabadi culture; its special feature being that it embraced the entire society in Hyderabad irrespective of community, caste or creed. A singular aspect was the evolution of peace, amity and harmony that in itself reflected the greatness of the culture of Hyderabad. The various features and traits of the pre-Islamic, Bahamani, Adil Shahi and Qutub Shahi times have been happily amalgamated and welded in this culture which blossomed during the Asaf Jahi period. The moral spirit of religion inducing human values and an aesthetic sensibility informing all spheres of activities stimulated its growth and development. Prosperity and public well-being were the bed rock of this cultural edifice. It is not possible for a poor nation with limited resources for livelihood to proceed beyond the preliminary stages of culture.

By the grace of God, the opulent nobles of Hyderabad cultivated without fanfare high cultural values that permeated every aspect of life and living. Three big cultural centres flourished in India: Firstly the centre in Delhi spearheaded the advancement that painters have immortalized in their works. This movement was not restricted to Delhi but its under currents spread in 18th century to Lucknow. It is common knowledge that the Lucknow culture was a source of inspiration to the rest of the country. In the 19th century, the cultural progress reached its pinnacle in Hyderabad putting into shade the other sub-cultures of the country.

Civilisation, in fact, is the reflection of imagination and action. As a man envisions his life and the world around him he would like to design life accordingly. The ideas which developed in the mind will apparently make their own images. But in order to realise these ideas, material prosperity and political peace are very essential. In a country devoid of econimic well-being, how can noble ideas find a fertile soil and flourish? They will only remain in the innermost recesses of the heart and will not blossom and fructify. If not nourished properly, noble sentiments will perish. Economic hardships and political instability will harm and hamper the forces of civilisation.

It is indeed a happy coincidence that Hyderabad was fortunate to possess, in a large measure the generosity of spirit and benevolence along with Nature's bounties. There was both wealth and political peace that brought about a real change in the life of the people. The manner in which the currents of water make their way on the surface of earth, similarly the proper use of wealth also creates its own beneficiaries. The wealth of Hyderabad was spent on holding 'mahfils', (assemblies) on designing and architecture of buildings, on preparing items of food, and on the art of tailoring and dress design.

CHAPTER IX

MODE OF LIVING

HOUSING

In the Deccan the old Hindu style houses had no courtyards and the roof was also not very high. There were square pillars of a special design. Later during the Mughal times there was a change in the construction style. The houses were divided into different and separate portions. "Zanana" was the portion meant for ladies and "mardana" was set apart for menfolk. The roofs of the houses were high, had wide courtyards and the pillars assumed a round shape.

In fact, in the Deccan, the Qutub Shahi period marks the beginning of the Deccani culture, because it was the cherished ideal of Qutub Shahi rulers to bring the Hindus and Muslims as one entity in every field of human endeavour and social life. As such an important change in fostering unity occurred in the mode of living and the construction of houses. A similar influence was apparent during the regime of the Asaf Jahi Government. There was no difference in the house of a Muslim Jagirdar from that of a rich Hindu, Raja or Jagirdar. The main gate of the palace used to be very impressive and so wide and high that even an elephant with amari could pass easily through it. Thereafter, came the architecture of the house, embellishments, gardens and decorations in and around the house. One side of the room would be covered with chandni or white cloth with masnad spread at different places and on the white cloth, large pillows were placed on the covered floor. On the other side, there used to be western style chairs, sofas, lanterns for light, wall lamps and chandeliers. The attendants appointed for service had singularity in their names and dresses. Chobdar (an usher), Shagir pesha (servants), Khasa bardar (a food carrier), Ab Khasa bardar (Water carrier), Khalamdan bardar (a treasure box carrier) and Huqqah Bardar (a servant who prepares the huqqah or smoking pipe) etc. were found at the palaces of both Hindus and Muslims and addressed by the same names. The turban and the belt were common and there was not the slightest discrimination between the Hindus and Muslims.

When western culture was introduced there was, however, a change in the style of the houses and its decoration. This style was adopted by both the Hindus and Muslims, and there was a blend of western motifs with Deccani culture and ethos.

If we scrutinize the tomb of Sultan Mohd. Quli, it will be clear that a successful attempt was made to amalgamate the Hindu and Muslim type of architecture. In recent times, the Osmania University presented a living embodiment of Deccani culture by combining different styles of architecture.

BUILDINGS

An important aspect of culture is the flowering of architectural concepts in the construction of buildings. Houses and buildings in a sense reflect the aesthetic taste of man. The spacious and imposing palaces, of the nobles were constructed during the 18th and 19th centuries, in which mediaeval influence is apparent. Some of the mansions had big verandahs with large rooms on either side which heightened the beauty of the building. In every deori balconies were constructed on both sides of dalan (veranadah) and its windows looked beautiful when opened out in the verandahs. Walls were usually painted white but doors and windows were coloured with 'banat' (a kind of cloth) with curtains on the doors. Wide courtyards were constructed along with the verandah. Just opposite the verandah in the centre of the courtyard there used to be a large cistern, always full of water, with running springs on both sides of the cistern. There were beautiful plants and excellent flower beds. The deories of the big nobles contained khanabagh with flowers and fruit-laden trees. In one corner of the garden, there was usually a horse stable and a shelter for elephants. Elephant was supposed to be a symbol of wealth. When people referred to opulence they always associated it with the possession of an elephant. In the verandahs and front verandahs a white cloth and charjama were laid.

Most of the buildings constructed during the 18th and 19th centuries had illuminated chandeliers and coloured lanterns that enhanced the beauty of the buildings at night. Mirdhangs were kept in which fish candles were lighted. White dastarkhwans were spread and a variety of sweet and savoury dishes of food were kept on them.

FOOD: DASTARKHWANS

There used to be several types of dishes on the dastarkhans of paigah and other nobles such as luqmi, samosa, varki samosa, and tootak which were eaten first and, thereafter roti biryani and pulav were served. Bread was also of different types such as roghni roti, naan, sheermal, phulka, paratha etc. Other dishes were mutbakh, mastaq and mutanjan. Delicious sweet dishes were prepared from grapes, bananas, pineapples, apricots and almonds besides vermicelli (sayviyan). In the big deories expert cooks were engaged for the preparation of such dishes. Some nobles appointed different cooks depending upon their expertise in preparing particular dishes. On these dastarkhans not only the host and members of his family enjoyed the dinner but their friends also joined. Even the servants ate food to their entire satisfaction.

BETEL LEAF: PANDAN

After the sumptuous fare served at feast and ceremonies, pan was also commonly offered in the Deccan. In Delhi particularly during the regime of the Mughals in Northern India the custom of pan was very popular. It still prevails. The Asafia Kingdom inherited from the Mughal rulers many traditions, and pan was one among them. It was a tradition to offer itr (perfume) and pan at the conclusion of the Darbar. At the time of the English Darbar the Nizam would offer itr and pan to the Resident and on the eve of the Mughalai Darbar, the Prime Minister or Peshkar would offer pan to the British in the order of rank and precedence. During 1904, it was directed by the British Government that 'Pan' should be presented by the Minister only to His Excellency the Viceroy's Private and Military Secretary, first Assistant to the Resident and to all the other British officials by the Peshkar and senior Moin-ul-Mahim, in the absence of the Peshkar. The practice whereby the Minister distributed pan and itr to all the British officers present, except those who received it from the Nizam was an old and well established one and no deviation from it could be permitted.(NAI, Simla Records, Foreign Department,

Secret-*, Procgs., May 1904, pp. 1-20). Like other customs in the Deccan the elegant style of pan and pandan continued.

Pan was used for medicinal purposes for thousands of years. To reduce the harmful chemical constituents in the betel leaf, catechu, lime, cloves and cardamom were used. Gradually pan, irrespective of its use in the household, was commonly offered at social functions. The general prosperity and contented life of the Deccan developed among the people the customs of pandan which had no parallel in the country. Among the nobles the chikni supari was prepared by boiling betelnuts in milk (the betel nut was cracked by a special kind of scissors called 'Sarota') to produce a special taste. Ordinary betelnut and chikni supari were imported into the Deccan from South India. In the last fifty years due to the high rise in the prices of betel nut, nirmoli is used as a nut. Nirmoli is a seed of a tree which is only found in the hilly region of Deccan. Those who use it only know that it gives a very good taste to pan.

In the manufacture of pandan, artistic workmanship of a high order was reflected in full measure. The manufacturers of pandan mostly belonged to Karimnagar. The custom of using copper and brass pandan was very rare. Mostly German silver, and silver pandans were manufactured. Pandan was an inevitable part of the marriage dowry. Together with pandan and khasdan (betel dish with cover) nagardan (box for keeping betel leaves), plates of various designs for presenting pan were also used by the middle class families.

Offering of triangular (samosa shaped) pan bira (betel leaf prepared and folded up) was the usual symbol of hospitality. From the point of view of taste the bira prepared with ripened betel leaf was supposed to be most satisfying. Bira or gillories were pierced with cloves of silver. On the occasion of marriage and other ceremonies presentation of pan wrapped in a thin silver leaf was supposed to be a sign of good taste. Pandan with all its requisites such as cardamom, betelnut, chikni, nutmeg, cloves catechu and betel leaves arranged in a tray was offered to the guests. With the passage of time there were many changes as a result of the rising prices of these requisites. Later, modifications were introduced in the form of kesarpoda i.e. small packets with all the pandan requisites. Trays with different compartments filled with these items, and later, boxes were introduced which were given according to the rank and position of a person. Some people adopted the English style. A small box with some cardamoms and betelnuts was distributed on such occasions.

DRESS

The standard of civilisation and culture of any country or nation stems from its ways of living embracing, language, food and dress. Dress plays a very important role in the shaping of a good personality. A well-known proverb runs thus: "Khaiye ap bhata (eat what you like): pahaniye jag bhata" (dress what pleases the world).

The dress of men for the most part consisted of sherwani, Turkish cap, pajama and boot or shoes and the women mostly wore sari and blouse. The old dress pattern of Hyderabad was different from the modern dresses. Wilfred S. Blaunt observes: "The people of Hyderabad have a well-fed look not commonly found in the inland towns. It could well be said that the people of the State are the best dressed people in India. There is something different in the bustle and cheerfulness of Hyderabad, a fearless attitude towards the Crown, which was in marked contrast to the submissive silence of the people in British India".

There was a marked change in the dress during the Asaf Jahi period. Nima jam and anqarkha were replaced by sherwani. Every type of silk, wool and cotton cloth was used for sherwanis. Gradually the custom of coloured silk sherwani stopped. The popularity which sherwani has acquired is not hidden from anyone. Because of its singularity the sherwani is regarded as the national dress of India and Sri Lanka. Along with sherwani, a shirt, muslin kurta and dohera pajama (or narrow sleeve pajama) reflect the Deccani mode of dress. The custom of wearing pagdi, dastar, different types of Turkish caps and saleem shahi shoes prevailed without distinction of caste and creed.

Good taste determined the choice of dress in accordance with the climate conditions. The nobles wore dastar on their head. Dastar was not only compulsory during the attendence of Darbar but also in functions and marriage ceremonies. Every rich man had to wear compulsorily the family dastar. Except for ulemas (the religious divines) no one was allowed to attend the Darbar without the dastar and bugloos. Ulemas were permitted with their amama (turban) and uba (cloak). There were three parts in the making of a dastar: A bini (nose) coiled on the forehead, the wall on the bini and its sides. The front wall is high, round and above the ears and low at the back of the neck. Dastars were of different colours—white, green, pink and red. Red is a strong colour and does not get soiled soon. The Turkish cap was introduced in Hyderabad during the closing decades of the 19th century. Nobles also wore Turkish cap besides the dastars. During the 20th century the fur cap was introduced. The black fur cap was designed by Moin-ud-Dowla whereas a cap narrow in front and broad at the back was designed by Salar Jung-III.

There was a distinction in the dress worn by women of the Qutub Shahi and Asaf Jahi periods. From the pictures of the Qutub Shahi period it appears that women wore narrow pajama and a broad jama. Sometimes the upper portion of the chest was open. The custom of applying mehndi, surmah (collyrium) and gaza (powder) etc. prevailed. Later the dress introduced among the Muslim women was totally different. Slightly narrow pajama choli, kurta on which gold and silver laces were stitched, and khadadupatta was used. Besides Muslims, this dress was prevalent among the families of Hindus of the upper class.

During the past 60 years the sari is commonly used, and with the impact of western culture, shirt or jacket was worn along with the sari in which varying types of frills were used. Later instead of the shirt and the jacket, only jumper and blouse remained. The sari is acclaimed to the most popular dress for women as it reflects dignity and elegance. Hyderabad is also famous for a wide range of saris suited for each occasion. The Venkatgiri, Pochampalli, Gadwal, Narayanpet, Dharmavaram, and Guntur saris were famous names of saris, which enjoyed an international reputation. These saris are durable, comfortable and economical in price. The Gadwal saris are a thing of beauty and a symbol of status. It is the ambition of every woman to have at least one Gadwal sari. The zari sari had a border of pure silver. They are costly but possess a classic charm. Though synthetic saris are cheap and easy to wear, silk and cotton saris are the most common traditional wear of the Hyderabadi woman.

A Chinese lady, who is the owner of the world's biggest firm of manufacturing dresses in Shanghai, considered thesari as the finest and most civilized dress in the world.

COSMETICS: BANGLES

No one knows the historical importance of bangles. According to some people, bangles are the sign of subordination for women. Some women with anindependent outlook desist from wearing bangles. In fact, bangles had no relation either with independence or slavery. This is a typical eastern custom which is associated with various beliefs and traditions. None can deny the antiquity of bangles.

Old photographs, statues and pictures of tribal women show their hands with bangles. Tribal women have their own culture and are not affected by the changing fashion of modern times. In Eastern civilisation, women have always attached importance to bangles in social life.

Women as a rule attach much importance for jewellery. However there are hundred of women whose economic conditions do not permit them to buy jewellery. Bangles bring pleasure and satisfaction to those who are not in a position to buy expensive jewellery.

In the lanes and bylanes, the familiar voice of sellers of cloth, sweets, chana (gram), chabina (parched grain), ice cream and ice fruit are very familiar. But the voice of "chodi bangdi goat" provided a thrill to the people in the street. The bangle-sellers would sit with an old tin box. Before he opens his box fully, many hands will eagerly move towards the box and then there will be a shower of praise. 'O God how delicate these bangles, what a lovely colour?" The vendors also try to cash in on the popularity of the latest movies. Accordingly, they would sell with gusto bangles bearing the name of Anarkali and Jahanara, Manjiri and Sarag. Within shouting distance of Charminar is the Lad bazaar. Shiny bangles with glittering semi-precious stones beckon even causal window shoppers. The lure of the bangles is enough to make one forget the heat and dust, the busy traffic and blaring horns in the narrow and congested lanes. There are bangles of different type such as lacquered, pearl, glass, enamel and metal. The vast range and variety make the choice a difficult exercise.

Though bangles are available in other cities, the lacquered stone-studded bangles are as unique as the Charminar. The bazar, which is centuries old, is a buyer's paradise.

JEWELLERY

Women attach great significance to jewellery. In the Deccan the prominent feature of gold and silver jewellery lies in its exquisiteness, beauty and durability. The goldsmiths of the Deccan had developed originality in the making of silver jewellery which was admired all over the world. Karimnagar was famous for fine silver filigree work. The goldsmiths displayed great skill in making items such as pandan, nagardan, itrdan, surmadani, arsi, betel box, cigarette pipes etc. They manufactured beautiful silver 'pazeb' (anklet) which was gold-plated and looked like real gold. There were items of jewellery for men also. Rulers presented jewellery to the nobles and other dignitaries besides conferring honours. In this connection, the munificence of the Asafia rulers had a proverbial mass appeal. After reading the daily diaries of the Asafia rulers one cannot but be impressed by the generosity with which they honoured nobles and courtiers with jewels and ornaments.

FLOWERS

Flowers were also used generally like pan. Holland is the only country in the world noted for planting a variety of flowers. Japan is famous for making paper flowers. The Dominion of Hyderabad had the privilege of using fresh and fragrant flowers. Flowers are commonly used in Hyderabad on auspicious occasions when garlands are offered to the guests after food is served. Specially, at the time of wedding, two garlands were offered to each guest, as offering of one garland was considered to be graceless. Flowers grow so abundantly in Hyderabad that any other name suggested for it would be 'phool ban'. Gulab (rose), chambeli (jasmin), motiya (Jasmin), Juhi (a kind of flower),

Batmogra (a kind of flower), Hasigar, (name of a flower tree) were grown in flowerbeds and were available in plenty in the gardens of middle class families. Flower jewels were unique and plentifully used at the time of marriage. Besides, the flower garlands, flower bracelets, (pahaunchi) karanphool (tossel), pankha (fan), phool sughni etc., were presented to the guests as a part of etiquette. Chameli and motiya flowers were sold on footpaths. Usually flower garlands were sold by the hawkers till late in the night.

PERFUMES

The nobles, apart from pan and flowers, used to present the guests with excellent itr (perfume) bottles at the time of their departure. Compared to scent and lavender, the local itr of Hyderabad was very famous. The imported perfumes from Khanouj were very much in demand. In Hyderabad mehndi (hena) and khas (sweet scented roots of grass) were available in plenty. The perfumes of gulab, chambeli, motiya, kewra (a kind of tree and its fragrant flowers), madanmast (a kind of flower) khas and hena were manufactured locally. An entire street was full of perfume manufacturers comprising mostly perfumers from Khanouj. The older the itr the more lasting is the fragrance. Some enthusiasts kept different itr bottles in beautiful scent boxes with the date of manufacture written on it. The scent box consisted of twelve and six bottles and the scent boxes were made of velvet.

KAJAL AND MISI (A KIND OF TOOTH POWDER) AND OTHER ARTICLES

Surmah (collyrium) kajal, misi, and mehndi were the commonly used cosmetics by ladies, as much as the present day lipsticks, cream and powder. Many kinds of incense were also used in plenty such as agarbatti (wood of aloes) Amber bati (Ambergris), Sandal bati and Barmaki. Hair and clothes were scented with perfumes. The sweet smell of incense gave a peculiar joy and freshness to life. The commercial centre for the sale of these items is still known as 'Laad Bazar' adjacent to Charminar which is the cosmetic centre for women.

SOCIAL LIFE OF HYDERABAD

As the Urdu language evolved out of happy association with the people of different communities speaking different languges, in much the same fashion, Hyderabad's social life and culture developed. This unique culture was a delightful blend of varying and varied influences for it felt the salutary impact of different cultures of different people who had made Hyderabad their home and, in turn, enriched Hyderabad culture while at the same time exuding the special Hyderabad flavour in all departments of life and living. It was a good blending of cultures and the people mixed freely with one another. Good taste, charming manners and graciousness were always in evidence.

Apart from the pomp and display of opulence on ceremonial occasions which was the hallmark of wealthy people, the surprising fact was that even a man of modest means had a certain graciousness of manner that had its own appeal. Even in the humblest home every thing was arranged tastefully. A small takht covered with a white chandni (white cloth) in the verandah would be an essential part of furnishing.

Dresses were carefully selected. Nobody would leave the house without wearing a sherwani and a cap. Welcoming a guest wearing kurta and pajama was considered impolite and against the established etiquette and norms of hospitality.

If there were children in the house, they would come out turn by turn, bowing low to present their 'adab' to the guests and return to their room. For children to sit in the company of elders, and listen to their conversation was considered bad manners. Sharbet (soft drinks), pan, and chikni supari were usually offered to visitors. On the occasion of Id, itr (perfume) was offered. If there was a feast, the sitting arrangements would be on the floor. Red coloured dastarkhwan was spread on a white sheet of cloth and tasty food was served in a very pleasant way.

The marriage customs and other social functions were a reminder of the gracious culture of Delhi and Lucknow. They blended with the culture of Hyderabad which had its own flavour.

CULTURE OF MEHFILS (SPECIAL GATHERINGS)

The mehfil of Hyderabad was unique in the observance of etiquette, in the respect and honour accorded by the host to the participants of the mehfil. First, lavish hospitality was a special feature of social life in Hyderabad. Each guest was gracefully honoured and made to feel at home by the host who stood by the side of the guest throughout the ceremonial mehfil. Every incoming guest would receive similar treatment. The manner of respect was usually the Hyderabadi salam. The respondent gracefully bowed the neck and head and moved his hand twice or thrice. If the guest happened to be an elderly person, the salam was said with a very low bow. Shaking the hand with salam was not the custom. An enquiry about one's health was replied with a salam or with folded hands. Even thanks were expressed by salam only.

CHAPTER X

PERFORMING ARTS

MUSIC

The famous intellectual Hazrat Tantavi Jouhri said that "this entire universe is musical". Music began with the origin of the universe. We can safely say that the history of music in the Deccan is as old as the land of the Deccan itself.

The Qutub Shahi rulers like the Adil Shahi rulers were fond of Taus (a musical instrument) and rubab (a kind of violin). Hence, during the reign of Mohd. Quli Qutub Shah and Sultan Abdulla Qutub Shah singing girls and musicians from Delhi, Lucknow, Agra, Banaras, Lahore, Kabul, Karnataka, Ahmedabad, Burhanpur etc. came and settled down near Golconda. Some localities and village sites were appropriated for them or were inhabited by them. Sultan Abdulla Qutub Shah himself was an expert in the art of music. Like Ibrahim Adil Shah, he also composed music for many songs. During the period of the last Qutub Shahi King, Abdul Hasan Tana Shah, there were grand festivals of music and dance. Two famous dancers, Taramati and Pemavati resided in their palaces in the environs of the Golconda Fort. It is said that Taramati, on a moonlit night, would go to the Golconda fort from her palace dancing on a strung rope to present mujra (professional dancing and singing) to the King.

Many members of the Tansen family came to the Deccan and settled in Hyderabad on hearing stories of the royal patronage of music.

In the Asaf Jahi period, during the reign of Nizam Ali Khan, the name of Mahlaqa Bai Chanda was prominent. Mahlaqa Bai was a poet and her pen name was 'Chanda'. She was the richest dancing girl of her time and possessed a jagir. Her daughter Hussainlaqa Bai like her mother, excelled in music.

During the Asaf Jahi period there was an office known as Dafter-I-Arbab-o-Nishat or Kanchan Kacheri supervised by mama sharifa, who held a high status in palace and society. She was one of the most influential persons at the Nizam's palace. She was assisted by a jamadar and four other subordinates. All the cases relating to dancing girls were presented to her. Most of these girls played a major role in the social life of the Nawabs and jagirdars and they received a monthly salary from the Nizams and the nobles. These girls were exempted from tax and payment of nazrana. They were given houses and on certain auspicious occasions jewellery, clothes and pandan were gifted to them. (APSA Records of Daftar-I-Arbab-o-Nishat).

During the period of Asaf Jah II Arastu Jah held the post of Prime Minister for nearly 32 years. His period as Prime Ministership is considered the golden period, for the munificent patronage of literature and the performing arts. During his period, along with arts and sciences, the art of music also made rapid strides. Many musicians from Northern India visited Hyderabad and salaries were fixed for them by the Government.

After the Arastu Jah period, many nobles and dignitaries also patronised music and raised its standard to a high level. Maharaja Kishan Pershad was fond of music and was himself well-versed in the art. It is said that he was an expert in playing the sitar and the harmonium.

During the later period, some of the more famous artists were Tetijan, Kalijan, Mahtab Begum, Shankari Bai Shamshad Begum and Vimla.

QAWWALI

The most popular form of music associated with Hyderabad is qawwali. It is said that this was the discovery of Amir Khusru. The qawwal sings the first line of a verse and then repeats the second line. At this stage, his two to three companions jointly repeat the same line a number of times. Most of the time, it happens that the qawwal presents, one or more than one couplet from a Naat (praising the Prophet) in modulation. Then in order to add more verses, on behalf of himself, he sings several couplets of other poets and then breaks the tune on the original stanza.

If the qawwal is an educated person and if he is presenting skillfully the poetic composition with correct diction then during the qawwali, any listener would be overwhelmed with the beauty of diction, its intonation and resonant melody in the voice of the qawwal.

An incident relating to the bewitching impact of poetry and music in qawwal is related below:

Once a man joined the qawwali party holding a crutch under his arms. As he was disabled, he sat in a corner where shoes are usually kept. After some time, when the qawwal reached the climax in rendering the Persian couplets the man was in sheer ecstasry and there was a glow on his face. Soon he started swinging and suddenly with the support of crutches he stood and presented himself in front of the qawwal and danced on one leg. He was in a trance and then fell unconscious on the ground. Luckily he did not fall on the petromax, which was kept nearby. He regained consciousness after a long time. When unconscious, the hair on his head and beard stood up.

Ali Bakhsh and Akramuddin were the famous qawwals of the Deccan. Ali Baksh qawwal was the disciple of Hazrat Sufi Abdul Qadar and he himself had disciples. He had thousands of disciples in the districts and villages of Hyderabad. He delivered profound sermons and sang inspired qawwali. Hazrat Sufi Abdul Qader gave Ali Baksh the title of 'Waiz Qawwal' (a teacher of Qawwals). He enjoyed great reputation throughout the length and breadth of India. Maharaja Kishen Pershad was also fond of qawalli. On the sixth day of every month there were qawwali programmes in his house called Aiwan-I-Shad.

The late Mulla Wahedi refers to an outstanding qawalli performance of Ali Baksh at the residence of Khwaja Hassan Nizami when Maulana Mohd. Ali Johar was also invited. After prayers at night, Ali Baksh started his Qawwali programme and on each verse of the first Naat, he sang many verses till the early hours of the morning. His singing covered verses of the Quran along with poetic verses. Maulana Mohd.Ali Johar was much impressed with his qawwali and he rewarded him amply.

FAMOUS SINGERS

Melody and voice are indeed the gifts of God and cannot be fully acquired by hard work. Every person cannot become a musician. Bu Ali Sena once said, "I found I could have mastery in arts and sciences but I confess my failure in mastering the art of music." In the Deccan, musicians who had mastery of this art were not one or two but numerous. Abdul Raof and Moiz uddin occupy the first position in the list. They were attached to the court of Prince Muazzam Jah. Raof was a graduate of the Osmania University and with his gifted voice, was fully conversant with all the nuances of the art of music. Blessed with a high sense of rhythm he sang in such an enchanting style that those privileged to listen to him enjoyed the feast of music. He had no match in ghazal singing. The tape records of his songs have been preserved as a valuable legacy by his admirers. Abdul Samad (badminton champion) and Abdul Qayoom (Superintendent Khazana-I-Amira) were also good singers.

Moizuddin was an excellent singer. He was a musician at the court of Prince Muazzam Jah. That was indeed a great honour. He learnt the basic musical ragas. Sand sang 'alap' and 'cheekh' according to rule with great skill and gusto and played the harmonium, tabla and sitar.

TABLA AND SITAR PLAYERS

Col. Faiz Jung earned a great name among tabla players. Most of his audience consisted of people who had a great taste and were themselves experts in the art of playing the tabla and the sitar. Abdul Qayyum Baqi, Professor of the Department of Urdu, Osmania University had dexterity in sitar playing and he was proud of his art. The late Binod Rao Pagdi a teacher in the All Saint's High School, was also a noted tabla player and was attached to the court of Prince Muazzam Jah.

The nobility patronized the arts of dance and music and parties of dancing girls were organised to teach children the culture of courtesy, social etiquette and the art of repartee.

Both for her appearance and voice Shamshad Begum was described thus:

Is qhirat-I-naheed ki har tan hai deepak
Shola sa lapak jaye hai awaz to dekho

"Every tune of this graceful and modest singer emited light and her voice blazed like flame."

Shankari Bai resembled Shamshad Begum but when she demonstrated her mastery in expressing emotions, the following words sprang to the lips:-

Ghazal usene chedi mujhe saaz dena
Zara umr-e-rafta ko awaz dena

"She has started reciting the ghazal, give me the musical instrument and recall the memories of an age gone by." Very few know, about the proficiency of Shankari Bai in the Persian language. She was deeply versed in Diwan-i-Ghalib.

DIFFERENT MUSICAL INSTRUMENTS

The musical instruments which were popular in the Deccan are listed below:

Pakhawaj (dhol Mirdhang), TashaMarfa, Tabla, Damdama daff, Dhera, Poongi (Tomari, Nafiri Shahnai, Naubat. These instruments were expressive of a happy religious and cultural harmony. Two musical instruments 'naubat' and 'roushan chowki' played by Muslims and Hindus respectively were part and parcel of every marriage ceremony and other such auspicious occasions. Bansari (Murali nai)–jhanj and (barbat) Sarangi, Nagara, Tantani, (anand lahri), Dotra, choutara, been, Tanbora, morbeen, Sitar, madham sitar, Taus, Sarod, Sarbath (an insrument resembling Taus), Dilruba, Timki were some of the musical instruments in vogue.

BOOKS ON MUSIC

Interestingly, the first book on the fundamentals and grammar of music in Persian was published only in Hyderabad. Later the following books in Urdu were published.

1. Ilhan Dilkash (Fundamentals of Music);
2. Tohfa-I-Moosiqi – Dule Rai;
3. Harmonium Guide – Kalidass.

PAINTING

It is on record that the first school of art, the first studio and the first picture gallery were established in Aurangabad Deccan. Each painter of the picture gallery was an art director himself. After seeing the coloured paintings of the Ajanta caves and the sculpture of the Ellora caves, one discerns a unique newness in them as they look fresh even today.

In the Ajanta caves, the greatest masterpiece is the picture of a queen. It is said that it is the image of the wife of Gautama Buddha. The prominent features of the other drawings of women are: thin and tall body, graceful limbs, thin waist line, fine elongated nose, thin lips, eyes resembling that of a deer and thin and long fingers. The beautiful painted figures have a life-like appearance and their limbs appear to be restless to move and lips are impatient to speak. It is strange that people were not aware of these masterpieces of paintings for centuries. They were discovered in Emperor Akbar's time. Akbar established the royal picture gallery, whose manager was Khwaja Abdul Samad, an expert painter. Akbar himself learnt painting from Kwhaja Samad.

In the book "Evolution of Indian Painting". It is stated: "when the royal photograph galleries of the capital city of Delhi were abandoned and artists were scattered in different parts of the country, a few painters, who came to Hyderabad and settled there, laid a foundation of a new style of Mughal painting which is known as Deccani Qalam (Deccan School)".

The history of painting in Hyderabad Deccan dates back to the period of Nizam-ul-Mulk Asaf Jah-I. The paintings of the period influenced the later Golconda paintings. Although influenced by the Mughal and Rajasthani Schools the Hyderabad style of painting had certain distinctive qualities.

Painting on glass became the fashion among Indian artists who were largely inspired by the British in the nineteenth century. Delhi, Patna, Banaras, Hyderabad, Lucknow, Murshidabad, Tanjore and Trichnapally were famous centres of painting on ivory and mica. Trichnapally was also known for glass painting since the nineteenth century. In Hyderabad, the earlier glass paintings were of superior quality and noted for their precision and bold lines. Keeping in view the difficulty involved in glass paintings, the Hyderabad paintings are perhaps the best known examples in India of this type of work.

During the nineteenth century, the Hindu Rajas of the Samasthans of Gadwal, Wanparty and Shorapur also engaged some painters and their patronage helped in the development of glass painting in Samasthans also.

During the period of Mir Osman Ali Khan there was, in Hyderabad Deccan an institution known as "School of Art" in which besides painting, training was imparted in sculpture. The Deccan saw the birth of outstanding painters and sculptors who in course of time attained great fame in making models of the human body. Abdul Qayyum, Fazalullah and Mohd. Turab head the list of such renowned artists. Several painters migrated after the integration of Hyderabad with the Indian Union. In almost all the advertising companies of Pakistan, the Hyderabad artists held a prominent place.

CALLIGRAPHY

The art of calligraphy is as old as the slate and the pen. There have been many renowned calligraphers in the world and Hyderabad Deccan did not lag behind in this art. During the Qutub Shahi period, with the progress of the performing arts, good calligraphy flourished. After the Qutub Shahi rulers, the Asaf Jahi rulers also patronised calligraphers. During the period of Mir Mahbub Ali Khan for the writing of Farmans. there were good calligraphers and fine penmen. During this period one of the pupils, Syed Mohd. Qudrat ullah Hussaini, teacher of Bahadur Shah Zafar and Hazrat Hafiz Syed Amiruddin bade farewell to Delhi in his youth and came to Aurangabad and settled there. Here Mufti Zia Yar Jung inducted him in the service of Mir Mahbub Ali Khan. As a result of the royal favours, Qudrat ullah Hussaini Intekhab Raqam, freed from tensions, displayed his skill in the art of calligraphy. During the period of Mir Osman Ali Khan, he made a mark as a well-established calligrapher. Hence, designing of currency notes, stamp paper, stamps, postcards, envelopes and documents is indebted to his art. The inscriptions engraved on the High Court building Osmania Exhibition Hall, Osmania Hospital, Public Garden Mosque, Khita Salaheen (land of pious persons) and Judi mosque are also the masterpieces of Qudrat ullah Intekhab Raqam. The other products of his creative art include monograms of the Osmania University and emblems etched on the palaces of the King and nobles.

Besides Intekhab Raqam, the other famous calligraphers were Imamuddin Aqiq, and the eminent tutor of Nawab Muzaffer uddin Imad Deccan in Khatt-e-Nastaliaq (plain round Persian writing), Mahmood Nawaz Moujiz Raqam, Hasmat Ali Aqder Raqam in Khitte-Naksh (A kind of Arabic handwriting), Syed Mustajab uddin Nehri Kamiyab Raqam and Peerzada Syed Shah Gulam Mahmood Khadri Mustajab Raqam who became famous. The last two were the pupils of Qudrat ullah. Mustejab Raqam came to Karachi after the accession of Hyderabad. On the occasion of the first Islamic Conference, in Karachi, the inscriptions displayed on the dais were the masterpieces from his pen. Mufti Azam Palestine Ameen ul Hussain was very much impressed by seeing these pieces and he presented him a copy of Quran Majid which he always kept with him and said "I have not seen even among the Arabs such a magnificent writer".

The inscriptions written by him at Masjid Armbagh Karachi, Mecca Masjid, Hyderabad, and Masjid Bhonq, Rais Ghazi Rahim yar Khan in the Punjab province still exist. Masjid Bhonq is situated at a distance of a few miles from the Sadqabad railway station. In this mosque, Mustejab Raqam had written the Kalimah Taiyyiabah in Khatt-e-Kufi (Kufic writing) 40 feet long and its breadth is more than four feet. On the outer arch of this mosque a long sentence of Suresh Buruj is written. This masterpiece is unique specimen of Kashikari (tilery) which is in blue and dust colour.

Imam uddin Aqiq was known as the Imam of calligraphy, throughout India. In 1896, he gave a present to the Emperor of Iran, Muzaffer uddin Shah Qachar. It was a picture drawn with a nail in seven different letters. Each letter technically was of a very high standard. Among his pupils, besides the nobles of the kingdom, Maharaja Kishen Pershad figures high on the list.

The monograms on the coins of Hyderabad Deccan, monogram of Ashrafi and specimens of some special seals of Government papers are attributed to Imam uddin Aqiq. He was rewarded with a mansab by Asaf Jah Sadas Mir Mahboob Ali Khan.

Mazhar uddin Mazhar, the grandson of Imam uddin Aqiq was the successor of his grandfather in the real sense of the term. At the age of six, when still a boy, he turned his full attention towards the art of calligraphy and, young as he was his expertise in each Khatt namely, Nastaliq, Salas, Nasq, Rehan and Shikasta (cursive writing) was impressive.

He wrote Bismillah-ir-Rehman-ir-Rahim, Sorah Ikhlas (verses from the Holy Koran) together on the gram dal, Kalimah taiyyiabah on the moong dal, the holy names of Panjathan Pak on one side of the til (Sesame seed) and

Allah Akbar on khashkhash (poppy seed). He was highly praised and received merit certificates from the Nizam and from the Industrial Exhibition Committee in Hyderabad. He was educated at the Madras School of Arts, in 1930, and received certificates, for his expertise and was called 'Taj ul Khattat'. He had a sharp eye on the huruf ki kurshi (seat of letters), the nishist, (setting) the dawair (circles, the shoshe (particle), the kashish (formation), the nukhte (points), the aarab (vowel) and noke palak.

The palace of culture glitters with the chandeliers lighted by Taj ul khattat. His innovative and unique monograms immediately attract much attention and viewers are enchanted by his superb workmanship.

The profound verses of the Koran, have in his calligraphy, been so impressive that it is as pleasing to the eye as it is ennobling to the spirit.

Perhaps one may rank him as the greatest calligraphist of his time. In the annals of calligraphy, he will always he remembered for his great contribution. The land of Deccan is proud of producing calligraphers of his calibre.

Regrettably, the art of calligraphy is now declining.

BINDING

The art of binding is as old as the descent of the divine book. It was by this method that books were preserved and it was called book-binding.

A prudent person has said that "when we throw a cursory glance on the creation of the universe, it will be clear that the body of all animals, is covered with skin, creepers cling to trees and plants, trees are wrapped with bark and the fruit with peel. The entire skeleton of human beings is preserved by their skin. This covering preserves the living creature against decay and book binding follows the same laws of nature."

Binding is also known as the art of Tajaleed (binding). Book is known as sahifa, binding is sahafi and the bookbinder is sahaf. The profession of most of the religious people is book-binding. One saint is famous as sahaf. Binding is an Islamic art, and it is connected with learning. Any book cannot be called a book unless it was bound. Before binding, a book is only a mere collection of dispersed leaves. During the golden period of Mir Osman Ali Khan in Hyderabad, this art flourished. Though there were hundred of workshops in the Deccan and thousands of book binders, one outstanding workshop which won fame was the Mahbubia Binding Workshop which was established in 1925. Its origin can be traced to Shaikh Mahbub Qureshi. A complete book could be written on the important work of this institution and its high standing. After the Police Action, this workshop shifted to Karachi. The following comments from experts on the greatness of Shaikh Mahbub Qureshi are given below:

"This workshop is in no way less efficient than the British workshop." (Maulana Abulali Maudodi).

"I am glad to see the work of this workshop. In fact the work done here is comparable to the best in Europe" (Nawab Nasir Nawaz ud Daula).

"The expert artists of Egypt, Germany and England express their surpise and appreciation of the excellence of the workshop" (Dr. Rahat ullah Khan).

"Shaikh Mahbub Qureshi had brought the East and the West together in the art of book binding by his single minded dedication to this art" (Nawab Ghous Yar Jung Bahadur).

"I have not seen any workshop in Europe in which book binding had reached such a high stage of perfection (Dr. Said Yamin Hashi).

"It must be accepted as an irrefutable fact that the bookbinders of Hyderabad possessed a high degree of skill" (Khari Mohd. Taiyyab Qasmi, Director Daru-ul-Uloom Deoband).

"As a result of the extraordinary competence of the bookbinders a modern touch was given to the art" (Dr. Zore).

"In reality this book-binding workshop can be termed as a performing art (Editor Dawn, Karachi).

"Till today, none has presented the Holy Quran with such splendour and beauty" (Editor Aafaq, Lahore).

BENEFICIAL REVELATION

Taj ul Khattat Mazhar Kamil revealed a scientific approach in the preservation of the cover pages of books. It is enough to write 'Kabikej' on the first and last page of the volume. He learnt this art from his grandfather, Imam uddin Aqiq, but he was unable to tell how he preserved these books from being eaten by white ants. He could only say that 'Kabikej' is the name of the king of insects who eats books. He preserved intact an 83-year old manuscript with his unique book preservation technique.

CHAPTER XI

URS (DEATH ANNIVERSARY OF SAINTS) FAIRS AND MUHARRAM

Urs of the great Sufi saints was held in high esteem by the believers. Attending the Urs was an article of faith with some of them. The devotees were afraid of the consequences in this life and in the hereafter if they absented themselves from the Urs.

Long before the date of the Urs, on one side the believers prepared themselves to attend the Urs and on the other side the officials of the shrine tried their best to make arrangements. Donations were collected from the followers. Letters were sent to outsiders asking for offerings for the Urs. Prepartions commenced with the plastering and coloring of dargah and other buildings attached to it, and Abdar Khanas (repositories for drinking water), were set up. There were make shift shops with roofs of leaves and straw. On the day of the sandal and during the Urs, temporary shops of sweets, chana, kabab, kulche, chakna, roti, food, pan, betelnut, toys etc. were set up, two to three days in advance. Entertainers also participated. Abdar khanas was a meeting place for friends and relatives. Musicians and qawwals also assembled there and Dastarkhans were arranged day and night. There was an atmosphere of cheer and gaiety. When the devotees visited dargah or a saint's mausoleum, they offered fateha [prayers]. The people used to wear their traditional family turban or a coloured cap after a bath. With rosary in their hands, they recited the prayers and offered salam. Sometime in the evening or late at night, sandal was brought in trays covered with golden covers and kept under the silver embroidered canopy. The army used to lead the sandal processions followed by a team of men who would recite the "darud sharif". The entire path was filled with the fragrance of agarbatties (scented sticks). In short, when the sandal reached the dargah then the old covers from the grave were removed and the grave was washed. There after, sandal paste was applied on it.

A new cover of zarbaft or kamkhawab (silk or satin with gold or silver embroidery) was placed on the grave. wreaths of flower were laid. Prayers and maulood khwani were held and qawwalli was arranged. Qawallis continued to enthrall the public. There were illuminations a day after the sandal. After the recitation of Quran Majid was completed, food was served. On all these occasions, the spiritual heads occupied the chairs of special honour.

Before the electric bulbs came into vogue, illuminations took the form of earthen lamps and glasses were placed on tatti (a frame work of bamboo for illumination) walls and its ridges. In darghas, the venue for singing and the location for water repositories, candles were lit in crystal glass chandeliers, lanterns, (hanging lamps) handi fanus, glass shade and a mirdang (a kind of glass drum). Glasses for illumination were specially made and were available on rent and were sold at the time of urs and coloured water was put in the tumblers and then oil to make the scene more exotic. White and coloured tumblers were fixed in tin baskets. In these boxes, the illuminated glasses were kept which emitted multi-coloured lights. These boxes were then placed on an elevated platform and tastefully displayed. On the day of illuminations, a general dastarkhan was organised for the visiting public and pilgrims and the wealthy people. The poor and the rich ate the same food and considered it as a source of grace and blessing.

At the time of the main Urs the hustle and bustle lasted for three to four days. People offered fans flowers and chader on the grave. Many made their petitions, other fulfilled their vows, some placed their son near the grave and prayers were recited. Fakirs and qalanders, nobles of the State, learned people and the poor made an assorted lot. There were people who visited the site only for entertainment, strolling along the bazaar watching the convoy of veiled women. Some gained spiritual solace, others felt happy to partake the bounties and others found pleasure in entertainment.

Some Urs were organised by the Government and by the spiritual head of the dargah. Such an Urs wase splendid because they had the backing of the Government officials and enjoyed Government patronage. Some of the noted uroos of Hyderabad were, the urs of Dawood Shah Sahib, Yousuf Sahib Sharif Sahib, Hazrat Khawaja Bandanawaz at Gulbarga and Moula Ali Pahadi Shareef.

LINGAMPALLY FAIR

After the urs of Koh Maula Ali and on the night of 18th Rajjab the road leading to Hyderabad was full of people. At the crack of dawn, the crowd increased in number and wended its way to the fair at Lingampally. It was not just confined to Lingampally. Right from Addikmet to Putli Baowli, a distance of four to five miles covering many localities, temporary shops would be erected selling fruits and sweets. Beside sports items, entertainment was also provided for the people. Roadside houses and gardens were well decorated. There were friendly crowds and an air of rejoicing prevailed. Those who could not attend the urs of Koh Sharif came later with children to enjoy themselves. There was heavy traffic and transport was arranged from the city to Koh Maula and from Koh Maula to the city. There were entry and exit points for thousands of elephants, horses, rath (an Indian chariot), Shakram (a kind of conveyance driven by bulls) and Jhatka (horse driven carriages). There used to be traffic jams and it would take hours to cross the road specially when His Highness the Late Mir Mahabub Ali Khan Asaf Jah Sadas visited the garden at Lingampally. He brought his queen to view the splendour of the fair. The camp of the city kotwal would be situated at a short distance from the royal garden, opposite the gardens of Mussalam Jang. Military guards were posted and elephants and horses of royal stable were kept on alert. While Arab soldiers enjoyed drinking coffee, a large crowd of men and women, servants, attendants, lancers, chobdars wearing silk sherwanis and coloured turbans went around. The royal kitchen, maze khana, abdarkhana, tambolkhana (betel leaf room) khahwa khana (coffee House) Mashal khana (room for keeping torches), toshak khana (a store room) and several such rooms kept the servants busy. Different types of "carts, some drawn by bullocks, mules or horses brought grain loads. Maids at the women's deori, maid servants, mama (a woman servant), kamatan, malan (a female gardener), mashalchin (a female torch bearer) wearing coloured saris, dupatta, silk blouse, knitted kurtani, adorned themselves with jewellery, with studded lacha, gold and silver trinkets, chand baliyan, ghantiyan, kade, kangniyan, pahunchiyan and metal added colour and grandeur to the spectacle.

Whenever the carriage (buggy) of ladies from the royal family arrived in a row, the crowd moved to one side of the road making way for them, an indication of great respect. Buggies had a look of grandeur with the fully decorated horses. The coachman (coach driver) wore yellow uniform with golden embroidery and two sais (horse keeper), who wore similar ornamental dress stood at the back of the buggy. Besides the coach driver, the mama of the peshi sat on the coach box wearing mashru (a kind of cloth) or satin pajama, kargah (a kind of cloth), kurti (blouse) covered with white sharbati muslin dupatta. They were decked with gold jewellery in the ears and around arms and necks, bangles and chandan. In front and on the rear side of the buggy there was a line of cavalry and on both sides an officer with a bare sword would accompany them. There was none in the crowds at the fair who was not delighted to see the splendour of their king.

The long road of four to five miles from Addikmat to Putlibowli was packed with people and the sea of humanity spilled over to the surrounding streets. Qutbiguda, Kachiguda, Narayanguda, Lingampaaly's entire fields where at present stands the Barkatpura market and where the houses of Aaraish Balda are located and along Khursheed Jahi gardens to Addikmat every open and shady place was full of men, women and carriages. Even in the remote corners of Nala and Kewraban, the poor people took shelter in shakram, jhatka, rath and bandi enjoying dishes of kabab, chakna and roti as the beating of drums rent the air. This common fair of the rich and the poor, soldiers, writers, Hindus, Muslims, men and women, old and young, boys and girls was enjoyed by all according to their taste. The fair concluded late in the night after large scale feasting. During this period, fruits, sweets and toys worth thousands of rupees were sold. The amusement of merry-go round, puppeteers, monkey and bear dancers, rope dancers, garodi, rented jahoke and shakram drivers, all earned well. The fair lasted for two to three days.

Many fairs were organised more or less in a similar manner. Celebrations of Nag Panchami Mela dates back to 1855. Till 1881 near the deori of Nawab Rasheed uddin

Khan Viqar ul Umara, the idol of snake was worshipped. After his death this mela started in the Baradari of Khursheed Jah in 1883 which is known as Nag Panchmi Mela. Annual jatras were organised in many temples, such as, Alwal jatra, Rambagh, Keshvgiri, Yadgirgutta, Yemul Wada, Kishen Bagh. Sitaram bagh, Phool bagh, Ramagundham, Eknath temple in Pattan (Aurangabad) Jain temple Kanchal Giri in Osmanabad.

Among all the Jatras the Alwal jatra had its own splendour. It was a day of rejoicing especially for the poor from the city and villages. This jatra was organised by Maharaja Sir Kishen Pershad. Special trains were run during this jatra. All the Government offices and the Residency staff were given a holiday. The Maharaja used to arrange a sumptuous 'At Home' for people. Without distinction of caste or class, rich and poor, intellectuals and laymen the members of the public participated amidst great joy and festivity.

MUHARRAM

Soon after sighting the moon of Muharram, alams were set up. The Badshahi Ashurkhana was in ruins after the decline of Qutub Shahi Kingdom. It was turned into a carriage shed. Nawazish Ali Khan presented a petition to Nizam-II for the resurrection of the alam. This was approved and the Ashur Khana was constructed again. Besides this, the King fixed a jagir of twelve thousand rupees for the expenses of the Ashurkhana. Every year he visited the Ashurkhana and attended the Majlis on 7th Muharram. Later this became a tradition for the Asaf Jahi rulers till the time of the last Nizam. During the reign of Nawab Mir Mabbub Ali Khan 40 seers of khichdi was distributed daily during the first ten days of Muharram. On 8th Muharram biryani was distributed. After the death of Nizam VI, this tradition was discontinued. Some members of the Shia sect wore black clothes, and some others green. Till the 10th Muharram, items such as Rot (a sweet roti) chonge, butti, khuboli (a kind of dish made of rice and gram dal), and sherbat (sweet drink) were prepared and distributed among the residents of the localities. The historical procession of Langer was taken out on the 5th day of the Muharram. The history of the Asaf Jahs is replete with instances of the complete tolerance and understanding between all the sections of people in Hyderabad. It is a known fact that in the erstwhile Hyderabad State both Hindus and Muslims shared equally in some of the most popular social activities, enjoying a common heritage of music and art, drawing inspiration from the same literature and philosophy as well as actively countributing to it by joining unreservedly in the same festivities and fairs and not infrequently, participating in the pujas and prayers. In spite of the diversities of race and religion, one generally gets an edifying picture of social amity and cooperation amongst the people of this cosmopolitan city which has been happily acclaimed as a bridge between the North and South of the country. The observance of Muharram festival even to this day truly reflects the composite character of the culture of the city, and stands out as an enduring monument of universal brotherhood.

Regarding the commencement of the "langer", it is well known that once Abdulla Qutub Shah riding on the elephant known as Murat went for recreation to the Musi river. On that day, the Musi river was in spate. The elephant was frightened by the waves of the river and turned towards the desert. The feel ban (elephant driver) was also thrown off his seat. For three days the elephant wandered in the forest. Hayat Bakshi Begum the mother of Qutub Shah, with motherly affection, arranged to hang tiffins on all the trees of the environs where the elephant was wandering, so that in case the errant elephant took shelter beneath the trees where tiffins were hanged, Qutub Shah would be able to eat. She also vowed that if Qutub Shah returned safely, she would make a gold chain and would distribute alms among all the beggars and poor. Her prayers were heard. The elephant entered directly in the fort and stood, and Abdulla Qutub Shah descended safely from the elephant. His mother was pleased. Immediately she got a gold chain made and putting it round the waist of Qutub Shah, sent him to Hussaini Alam along with 40 mounds of sugar syrup and eatables. Gold chain and all the eatables were distributed.

After this incident, every year, this langer was taken out with great pomp and ostentation in which, elephants, camels, horses and the troops joined, even after Hyderabad's accession to India.

There were three famous alwas (fire pits) in the city i.e. Khoni alawa, Hijraonka alawa and Musheerabad alawa. People gathered at these places. The following were the famous alams of the city:

Punjashah ka alam, Qadam Rasool ka alam, Imam Qasim ka alam, Naal sahib ka alam, Bibi ka alam and Hussaini Alam, Hazrath Abbas ka alam, Teqhe ka alam and Badshahi Ashur khan ka alam etc.

On the night of the last date of Muharram, opposite the police station of Musheerabad, wood was burnt in the alawa late in the nights. One Hindu goldsmith holding an alam would walk on the fire.

At different places different types of tazis were made and kept. Most of these tazias were marvellous specimens of artistic workmanship. Among these tazias, one tazia became famous, which was known as Haryali Tazia. It was kept near Charminar opposite Sardar Mahal. In this tazia, arches and towers were prepared with great skill.

In the houses of the Shia sect, marsiyah khwani (an elegy recited during the Muharram in commemoration of

Imam Hussain) and mourning was arranged. Among the Sunnis the Majils at Firoz Yar Jung Deori was famous. The majils (assemblies) of Baharam ud Daula and Tahur Jung among Shias attracted many Shia followers.

Among Hindus, Maharaja Kishen Pershad had great respect for Imam Hussain. He used to place tazias and alam in his house. He also appointed Marsiya Khwan and Nauha Khawan. He held majalis in his palace from 7th to 10th Muharram. On the 9th of Muharram the Maharaja, arranged Nazr-I-Niaz to the Naal Sahib and arranged a dinner on a large scale in which the Resident and British officials were also invited. The native officials also participated in the dinner. On the 10th Muharram, he came out personally from the palace and distributed alms to the poor. Raja Shiv Raj (Malwala Palace) also arranged abdarkhana, and illumination of bamboo frames during Muharram. In the Malwala Palace several images were erected. In front of these images, the artists entertained the audience. The Nizam Mir Mahbub Ali Khan paid his customary visit to Raja Sheo Raj Dharamwant at the time of Muharram and spent some time at the venue.

Raja Sheo Raj Dharamwant was incharge of the Revenue Department in the Nizam's Dominion. He erected Ashurkhanas near his palace for keeping alams and tazias during Muharram. These alams and tazias were taken from Ashurkhana on 8th, 9th and 10th Muharram. Majalis were also arranged. His family members distributed sweets, sharbat and food to the poor.

On the 9th Muharram the alam of Naal Sahib was taken out. On 10th Muharram, Bibi ka Alam was taken out which went around the city culminating at the Musi river in the evening. Large groups of people participated in the fair.

CHAPTER – XII

LULLABIES – HYMNS

Lori is a Hindi word. It is derived from the word lar i.e. lad. Lori consists harmonious and pleasing words which are sung in a gentle tune to cheer a child and put him to sleep. In lullabies and the hymns of chakki (grindstone), the poets dealt with life and living in a mystical vein. Such hymns have a prominent place in Urdu literature.

Nasir uddin Hashmi a learned historian has written that a Mukhtuta or a manuscript known as 'Lorinama' is available in the State Library, Hyderabad. This Mukhtuta is in a brittle condition. In this poem tenets of mystirism are explained in the form of lullabies. The Lorinama number is Maktuta 919 New State Library. Similarly the 'Chikkinama' of the great Sufi saint Hazrat Kamalullah Shah of Deccan is also very famous which is mentioned in his Muntakhab diwan 'Khirman-I-kamal.'

The topic 'Lullabies and hymns of Deccan' is so vast that it deserves detailed research and can be a fit subject for an academic dissertation. Some typical lullabies or hymns are set out below:

Alla bani ke jaon wari
Lallon se main ne Jhula sanwari
Payar se ankhon men aye khumari
Sadqe men tere surat hai pyari

A o suhagan jhula jhulane
Noor-I-nazar ko apne manene jhu jhu jhu
Utra Zamin per takht-I-Sulaiman
Naghma sara hain zahra jabinan
Jalwa numa hai mah-I-darakshan
Phonkji pad ker Ayat Qurani
Ao suhagan jhula jhulane

Jhula Jhulo rajdulare
Nindiya ayi so mere pyare
Aja ri nindiya ajari tu
jag rahe hain lal hamare
Kheo kudo jhula jhulo
Sadqe tumhare sadqe tumhare
Bale ki mere umar badi ho
Karti due hoon doman pasare
Tum per sadqe chand sitare
Ae meri dono ankon ke tare
Jhula jhulo rajdulare
Nindiya ai so mere pyare

JHULANAMA

Gahware men Salh Alla Jhulte the
Ke yạne Rasul-i-Khuda julte the
Khuda ko khushi jis ki thi jhulne ki
Khuda dekhta Mustafa jhulte the
Bana noor se jin ke alam ka jhula
Wahi pak noor-i-khuda jhulte the

The mushtaq is jhulne ke Nabiyan
Ke jab sarwar-I-Anbia jhulte thay
Gahware jhulate Malik adab se
Hamare Nabi Mustaga jhulte thay
Tasaduq bhi hota qamr asman se
Ke jis waqt badar udduja jhulte thay
Nigabhan o hafiz khuda jis ja dayam
Wahi shah har do sara jhulte thay

NAHIJI KI LORI

Amena bibi ke gulshan men hai taza bahar
Padhte hain Salh Allah Allay o salam aj dar o diwar
Nabi ji Allah Allah Allah ho la ila illa ho
Syed maki mah Madina payare Nabiji aye
Cheen liya dil man Mohan ne chand sa mukhda dikhaye
Nabi ji Allah Allah Allah ho la ila illa ho
Nanhe dil ka jhula banayi tar nazar
Sota hai is men mahi rasalat noor bhari har por
Nabi ji Allah Allah Allah ho la ila illa ho
Jibrail aye jhula jhulani lori de Rahman
So ja so ja rahmat alm main tere qurban
Nabi ji Allah Allah Allah ho la ila illa ho
Mohni surat nam Mohammad do jug ka sardar
Jan se payara rajdulara rahmat ki sarkan
Nabi ji Allah Allah Allah ho la ila illa ho
Dono jahn khoi gayi main ankh men ankh milye
Naina rasile is men kajal main to mer gayi hai
Nabi ji Allah Allah Allah ho la ila illa ho
'Amjad' ka dil mutthi men le kar sote ho kya anhan
nanhe qalm par sar rakh kar ho jaoon qurban
Nabi ji Allah Allah Allah ho la ila illa ho

MARRIAGE SONGS

Chowthi ceremony is performed on the second day of the marriage. In the night the samdhan (mother of bride-groom) comes to the house of bride for dinner and to play chowthi. No sooner the samdhans get down from the conveyence than they are welcomed by the following songs:

FIRST SONG

Dule ke na gadre log, ayyo ma dule ke na qadre log
Ye logan atyen bol ko main farash karai, sozni bichai,

Masnad lagai
Ayyo ma tataon po baithne ke log
Ayyo ma boriyon po baithne ke log
Ye toqan atyen bol ko main khasa pakai, dastarkhwan bichai, khasa chunai
Ayyo ma tukdon ke chabne ke log
Ayyo ma chippon men khane ke log
Ye logan atyen bol ko main palangan kasai, bister bichai, sej bichai
Ayyo ma bontaun po lotne ke log
Ayyo ma dule ke na gadre loq

When the samdhans are about to leave after the ceremony of chowthi they are persuaded to stay through these songs.

SECOND SONG

Samdhan javo nakkoji fajr gai katatiyun
Fajr gai katatiyun uska cham rangatiyun
Uska chmda rangatiyun tumna kurta silatiyun
Samdhan javo nakko ji fajr gai katatiyun
Us ki dum rangatiyun tumne hutla gunatiyun
Samdhan jayo nakko ji fajr gai katatiyun
Us ke singan katatiyun tumna singa lagatiyun
Samdhan javo nakko ji fajr gai kakatiyun
Is ki antariyan kakatiyun tumna naran pahanatiun
Samdhan javo nakko ji fajr gai kakatiyun

THIRD SONG

Banno po se kya kya waroona ma Banno po sek kya kya waroon ma
Hire bhi wari motiyan bhi wari nandan ko waroon ma bonno po se
Sona bhi wari chandi bhi wari Devran ko waroon ma bonno po se
Banno po se kya kya waroon ma

MISCELLANEOUS HYMNS

Song while bathing on the day of marriage:
In case of bride groom:-
Banna mera mal mal nahai ma
In case of bride:-
Banno meri mal mal nahaye
Song at the time of applying sandal and chiksa
Banna meri sandal lagaye ma Banno meri chiksa lagaye maaye ma
Song at the time of garlanding bride and bridegroom
For the bridegroom:-
Aya banna aya-hariyala banna aya lal dulara banna aya
For the bride:-
Ayi banno ayi hariyali banno ayi Allah Peer manayi
At the time of applying sandal:-
Sandal lagoa na meri hariyali banno

The song, while garlanding, at the time of jalwa ceremony.

1. Harori ma lalbanno ke gale Allah payari ke gale
2. Dalan men pahanaye har kya khushnuma laga ke
3. Mali ne laya dauna malan ne har kaya khushnuma laga ke

The babul (father) song is sung in a very touching

style at the time of rukhsati. The first line of the verse is as follows:-

Beti chali perdes babul beti chali perdes

DECCANI RIDDLES AND KAH MUKERNIYAN

The other names of riddles are chistan (puzzle) muamma (enigma) and buhjol. The central point is described in hints and that becomes famous as a proverb. Riddles are given below and it is for the readers to solve the riddles i.e. explain the meaning.

(A)

Am khai amrai men chilka sati bazaar men bo gai darbar men

Ilaichi (cardamom) phanas, kathal

Atasa batasa khane khan khajur-Mera masla nain bujhe to tumahare ammabawa mere mazdoor

Lock – key

Ek admi chalet chalet thak gaya, lao churi gala kato phir bhi chalne lag gaya.

Pencil

Lat pat sat gaon – teen mundi das paon.

(Cart)

Ek sandookh men bara thane, ek ek khane men tees dane,

Adhe kale adhe ujle.

Year month, day and night

Amma jhetri bawa datre, bach che nikle chand ke tukde

Pine apple

Itta sari ka nagan us men panch baigan

Palm and fingers

Upper dhaba nichche dhaba, beech men bathi kutni

khaba

Tongue

Itti sari ke betiya badshsh ko jhukai

A spittoon

Ekach dhan ghar bhar ko bhusa

A lamp

Aha ki thaili men uho ke dane

Chilli

Age khur piche kan mera masala nain bojhe to haiwan

Rabbit

Abrak ki madi men ghudrat ka pani – Badshah se kaho ati hai rani

Egg

Ek janawer (janwar) aisa tha jis ke dum per paisa tha

Peacock

Itti si bitya chutki jaisa pet, ujad pet po mati (mitti) pado kha gayi sara khet.

White – ant

Asalta masalta hath men liye to phisalta

Munjal (Fruit of the palmyra tree)

Ek jhad tha us ka nam shaikh madar tha – haddi haram thi shruwa (Shorba – Soup) halal tha.

Sugar cane

(B)

Bodke miyan baher nikle marte phako phak

chakki (A Millstone)

Badshah ke beti sej po leti jane wallon ko tarsa deti

Jalebi

Bin pani ke mahal banaya who karigar kaisa

White ant

(c)

Pani men ka pamda na hadi na chamda

Butter

Pahad po daranti

Imli ka bot

(D)

Teen pavan (paon) ka ghoda khata sau guna hagta so sona

Chulha

Teen pavan ki bill taqune khati gillian satti

Chulha

Tham main so mandva

Sky

(E)

Jangal men khade hain venkatram, sir po chatri ekach tang

Palm tree

(F)

Chalo sakhi ri hat ko jainge hamare sarika admi layenge

Mirror

Chand se chakla pan se patla

Papad

Chalo sakhi bzar ko jain ek shishi me do rang lain

Egg

Chalo behna bazr (bazaar) ko jain date nain so baingan lain

Egg

Char alang char palang char shamadani titer

batairladne lage murghiyan de loriyan

Pachchisi

(G)

Dastar p ki beti

Plate

Diwal (diwar) po baithe buzurg ate jate banttee tabairuk

Scorpion

(H)

Dhal maroon talwar maroon na kate who bail mera masla nain bojha so Hyderabd ka dher

Shadow

(I)

Resham ke raj men mali ke bagh men khate hen todte nein

Ole (hail)

(J)

Sone ki chidi (chidiya) dum se pani piti

Lamp

Subz masjid ujle khane beech men baithe siddi (negro) diwane

The custard Apple

(K)

Kanwal ke phool jhumke wali – maro nakko miyan main bachche wali

Garlic

Kala hai kavva nain sar bada hatti (hathi) nein kamar patli shiraz nein jhad chadta bander nein

A large ant

Kala jama hari pagdi

Brinjal

Kali mugi dum jawar ande deti hazar, ande pade tash men bibi padi ghash men

Phuljari (a kind of fire work)

(L)

Ghar hai darvaza hein pados hai bat nein

Grave

Gadhe ka pukara, unt ki gardan, hatti (hathi) ki baithak

Frog

Gumbad hai derwaza nein

Egg

Gawan (gaon) se mehmana aye kan kan (kahan kahan) ke akhbaran laye

Crown

(M)

lakh rupae ko seer

lakh

lakdi ka ghoda chmade ki lagham (lagam) mera masala nein bojhe to mere ghulam

Pattens

(N)

mitti ka ghar angrez ki topi us men haith ke hain Noor Mohammed

electric lamp

(O)

Neel ki chadder (chader) po chandi ke phool, mera masala nein bhujo to us ke mo men dhool

Sky and the stars

(P)

hale tak hili phir poch le ko chali

Pestle and mortor

Handyari (andheri) kothri men budda badbadatae (hai)

A smoking pipe

Hari thi gul bhari thi raja ke bagh men khadi thi
Rajane chadi mara to behosh padi thi

Coriander leaves

Hara sandokh, lal khane, us men baithe siddi diwane

A water melon

Hat phiri bat phiri phiri Hindustan aisa tamasha nadir dekhi

Phal ke mon men zaban

Pine apple

Hari masjid sufaid khane namaz padhthien siddi diwane

Custard apple

Every country and community has idioms and proverbs. There are more than five thousand Deccani idioms and proverbs. The idioms and proverbs which were prevalent in villages are mentioned here. They are satirical in nature having a reformation bent. There is expression of reality. The intellect and perception of the people of the village and their temperament and taste can be judged from these proverbs :

A. Anta ghafil, Adde ka bhoi, Etti ka bail, tatti toda
Adiyal tattu, Asman qira khajur me atka.

Aag laga ke pani ko daudi, apna bachha raj kunwar dosare

ka jangli suar.

apni ghai sab pe lai, ukli men sar diya to

musaloon se kya dar, apni chain men ande bachche dosere ki

dain men kudak, apna kah kar mamu ki bakriyan churana,

Attani aris ko dophar ka jalwa, Uth murde khur kha, Mamu unt se lambe

B. Bharam bhari pitara khali
Basi kadhi men ubal aya
Be painday ka lota

C. Tar ka patang

D. Chor ki bombdi chawdi tak
Che piddi che piddi ka shorba

E. Hisab ko ratti bakhshish ko hatti

F. Khwan bada, chaba bada khol ke dekhe to dahibada khugir ki bharti

G. Dambi ki handi phuti kette ki zar pahchani
Dil ki khushi dhan madi

H. Dand gafoor
Sahar ko uthi sahnak phutti roza mujhe ras nahin

I. Sare din gulgule id kay din kutkule
Sui ki jagah musal

J. Kam nain so kukdi kajal pakdi
Kam nein so hajjam billi ka sar mundaya
Kabab men haddi
Karamat ki billi haj ko chali

K. Girgut ki tarah rang badalna

L. Mehenti ko daliya, pakhandi ko pulay
Munh men niwala sar pe thola

M. Neki karo begi (jaldi) maro
Nani khasam kare nawasa dand bhare
Nam bada hath men kathil ka kada
Nasir Jang ka hela
Nathu ka bail

N. Wagat na sagat buddhi chadhe takhat

O. Hilte julte majnoon aye bail ganwa ke rassi la ayeh

P. Yun bhi sanam wah wun bhi sanam wah wah

CHAPTER – XIII

GAMES AND SPORTS

POLO

This game which is played by riders on horseback is chowgan or polo. This game calls for sturdy limbs and had origin in the Deccan. Polo was played for the first time in 1870 under the patronage of Nawab Mahir-ud-Daula. The photographs of tournament are not available concerning the competitions of this game from 1870-1886 for a period of sixteen years. Polo was one of the sports which the nobility had patronized. The Paigah nobles had their own polo team. During the Asaf Jahi period, there were seven polo fields. Among them the Golconda Polo field was the oldest one. Besides that there were the Fateh maidan, the Secunderabad parade ground, the Malakpet field, the Boinpally field, the Haslap polo ground and the field near Masahib Tank.

The first Golconda polo team was started in 1886. The credit for the formation of the team goes to Nawab Mahir-ud-Daula. In this team, there was one British officer whose name is not known. This team played until 1910. It is mentioned in Boostan-I-Asafia that Viqar ul Umara formed a polo team at his own expense. This team played well and won many trophies in tournaments. Also Nawab Fakhr ul-Mulk, had built two polo grounds in the compound of his palace.

In Hyderabad, polo was at its peak during 1911-1923, when the Third Golconda Team came into existence. The captain of the team was Shah Mirza Baig. A sports magazine published in Britian, recalls the history of the polo game and pays tributes to Shah Mirza Baig. It said:

"The world has hardly witnessed a player of the prowess of Shah Mirza Baig in the polo game".

He was among the first registered ten handicapped players in the world. This was the highest rating which can be achieved in polo. Till 1975, there were only three world class ten handicapped players. Later the strength went upto eight and the players hailed from Argentina.

The brother of Shah Mirza Baig who represented the team of Mahir-ud-Daula, displayed better performance than the Shah. There is no record today to prove his achievements. In 1929, there was a ladies' polo team, comprising of Hamidunnisa Begam, Begam Najam uddin Khan, Begam Asaf Ali Baig and Begam Abdul Ghani.

The Golconda team, played against other selected teams in India and was of a class all its own in the world. The Patiala team, the Maharaja of Alwar team and the India team comprised different regiments. These were the established teams of India and they enjoyed a wide reputation. The perfomance of Shah Mirza Baig was of a class apart as he was indeed the shining star of his time. In fact he was invited to play for Britain against America and Harlingham (England) in 1910, on the occasion of the coronation ceremony of King George V. Britain won in this competition.

The game of polo continued in Hyderabad from 1926 – 1954 but it was not that good in later years. Polo, as a game remained popular among the people. His Highness the Prince of Berar was a renowned and excellent player of polo. The Golconda team under his captaincy participated in many polo tournaments in the country and won great success.

In 1956, the stables at Golconda were disposed off. Because of the personal interest and efforts of Nawab Khusro Jang, the Andhra Pradesh Riding Club was formed; otherwise the sport, in Hyderabad would have come to an end. Polo is still played in the Deccan but on a subdued note in which the Indian Army and few local players participate.

In the Centenary Celebrations of Polo, the Andhra Pradesh Riding Club took active part in order to revive the game. The Centenary Celebrations were marked by important games for the His Highness Prince of Berar Memorial Cup, the Major General Nawab Khusro Jang Memorial Cup, the Vazir Sultan Tobacco Cup, the Andhra Pradesh Riding Club Cup, the Mounted Sports Hyderabad Polo Association Cup and for 22 trophies. The important Cup of the tournament Prince of Berar Memorial Cup was won by the Sultan's team which comprised Farooq Ali Lieutenant-Colonel K.G. Jalnawala, Lt. Ram Singh and Shah Ali.

Brigadier Masood Ali Baig needs no introduction in India and Pakistan for his prowess in polo. The renowned player Haskat Heugus of England, praised Brigadier Baig so much that instead of calling him Masood Ali Baig, he called him "Haski Baig".

Baig started his training in polo at the age of 14 under the world renowned Polo Player, Shah Mirza Baig. In 1936 Baig joined the Indian Cavalry and started his military career. He was the grandson of Sir Afsar-ul-Mulk, the Commander-in-Chief of the Asaf Jahi Forces.

Baig gained dexterity in polo besides other games. He had displayed his excellent skill in India, Egypt, England, America, Rome, Ireland and Argentina.

FOOTBALL

Like polo, Hyderabad also made a name in football. It is correct to say that this game progressed very much during the reign of Mir Osman Ali Khan. The first Football Club which was formed was known as "Unison Club". Later, the Deccan Club was started and then came the Hyderabad team, the Nizam Coronation, the Merry-go-round, and the Nawab Sahib Tarban football team. Football was considered a poor man's game. It found its way in Hyderabad through the British army stationed at Bolarum. Besides, the British army, Mr. Burnett, Principal, Nizam's College, and Father Garbelli of All Saint's High School played a major role in popularizing football. The first private club was formed by Vilayat Hussain, the Director of Posts in the Nizam's Government. He selected former students of Nizam's College for the club.

Merry-go-round earned a great name in football in India as well. The team matched its skill with the English soldiers' team. The first and second-games were drawn and there were six encounters but not a single match proved decisive. At the time of the seventh round, prayers were held in mosques for the victory of Merry-go-round team. The seventh game was held at the Petlaburj ground. No sooner did the Merry-go-round make the first goal, the spectators released thousands of birds in the air which they had brought with them. The birds which were released with joy were pigeons, parrots, mynahs, and cuckoos. At the end of the game the entire team was garlanded and went round the city in a procession with a band. The patron of this team was Walidad Khan Mondozi who arranged a grand celebration for his team's victory. After this grand success the Merry-go-round team was dissolved. Khader Khan was the goalkeeper of this team. He was a man of great abilities. He could guess from the eyes of the opposite player which side he was going to shoot the ball. Khader

Khan proved his mettle on the playing field. He pounced upon the ball like an eagle. Either he would hold down the ball or throw away in any direction with great alertness. He used to stop invariably the penalty kick. He did not even care for his life in stopping the dangerous hits by leaping in the air. He got injured but the ball never slipped from his hand.

CITY AFGHAN POLICE TEAM

This was the second renowned team which had established its name in the different cities of India. This team usually participated in the matches in Calcutta, Bombay, Madras, Bangalore and Bhopal. The only equally matched team was Mohammadan Sporting. The superiority of the football players could only be seen in these two teams.

The dawn of a new era for football began in the fifties. The Inspector-General of Police, Mr. Shiv Kumar Lal formed the famous Hyderabad City Police team. Late S.A. Rahim, the famous coach, was given charge of this team. The police team comprised of Aziz, Noor, Moiuddin, Laiq, Zulfiqar, Yusuf Khan, who later became Olympians. Anthony. Patrick, Jamal, Afzal, Susai, Eriah, Pentaiah all donned India's colours. They created a record by winning the Rovers Cup five times in a row. There was not a single All India tournament final in which the Hyderabad City Police team had not figured.

The Nawab of Tarban like Walidad Khan participated actively in the patronage of this game. His interest in football can be assessed from the fact that in those days he gave a scholarship of Rs.200 for a young player namely Abubaker. He maintained his own team, providing livelihood for poor players. In the British army, the canteen contractor, Lala Motiram, employed young men from Tirmulgherry, Bollaram and the surrounding places and formed a team mainly to play against the British soldiers. The local boys of this team gained skills and experience and later joined the State teams.

The annals of football remain incomplete without mention of the Physical Training College in Hyderabad. In this college, the instructors employed scientific methods of coaching and training. Abdul Rahim was also one of the trainees of this college. His entire life was dedicated to this game. The players, whom he taught the techniques of football, made a mark in the All India Football XI team. It is said that the team which went to Russia consisted mainly of players, who were elected members of All India Sport's Organising Committee. His book "Football" is the first book in Urdu language on this popular game.

The names of outstanding football players are as follows:-

Jaleel: He was the captain of the Hyderabad Team. The main feature of his game was that he never fell on the football ground.

Habib Ahmed: He was also a captain of the team. The chief feature of his game was that he used both his legs. He used to strike the penalty kick standing at one place instead of running to hit the ball.

Mahbub: He stopped every shot with his head.

Abdul Raheem: He was the brother of Dr.Abdul Ghani Secretary, Sanitation. No player could snatch the ball from him.

Sher Khan: He played in the position of full back for City Afghan Police team. He always took the ball in the air before the ball could fall on the ground.

Mohd Ali Dam: He played in the full back position. He was a deadly shot.

CRICKET

Hyderabad State played a prominent role in every field of sports. Cricket was the most popular game. In Hyderabad Deccan, the Government officials and the nobles promoted the game. Maharaja Kishen Pershad was very fond of cricket. He kept gold coins on the table and gave them to the person whose views about the possible score by a player came nearest to reality. In Colleges and High Schools the students showed keen interest in the game. The interest of students increased day-by-day and proved most fruitful. In Hyderabad Dominion, All India Cricket Tournaments were conducted on a large scale. The National Cricket Tournament like the Behram-ud-Daula Cricket Tournament had given the players and the people of Hyderabad an opportunity to see the performance of the renowned foreign players. Nawab Moin ud Daula of Hyderabad an eminent noble seeing the popularity of the game introduced the Moin ud Daula Gold Cup Cricket Tournament. The game of cricket is a gift to India by the British. There are early traces of cricket in Hyderabad dating back to the 18th century but the game took firm roots in 1920 when some British garrisons were stationed in Hyderabad. The noblemen of Hyderabad wholeheartedly patronized the game. It was between 1920 and 1930 that civilian teams and the regimental teams were also formed. The Secunderabad Club, the Residency Club, the Hyderabad Police Club and the Parsi Club played friendly matches mainly during the weekends. The game of cricket became popular because of Nawab Moin-u-daula. The matches in Secunderabad, attracted a large crowd and resembled a fair. A number of tents were erected all over the parade ground. These tents were erected by different Government Departments of Hyderabad or by different Associations. Entrance to these tents was either by pass or a ticket. A number of hotels were also set up at the parade ground.

Boarding facilities for players during these matches, were made available at Bashirbagh. They were entertained on a grand scale on behalf of Moin ud Daula Bahadur. After the match, the players were taken to places of entertainment and recreation. Music parties were arranged. In short, the cricket tournament was a celebration for the players. In 1962, the game of cricket was revived by the Hyderabad Cricket Association by inviting the country's top teams and even foreign teams were also invited to participate in the tournament. In 1938, Hyderabad won the Ranji Trophy Championship for the first time and Mr. Gulam Ahmed had the distinction of being the first Hyderabadi to play for India in an official test in 1948 against the West Indies in Bombay.

The renowned players which Hyderabad produced were Bahadur Shah, Syed Mohd. Hadi, Mohd. Hussain, Gulam Ahmed and Asif Iqbal.

HOCKEY

The game of hockey was very popular like cricket in Hyderabad. The team of Osmania University, Nizam's College, Warangal College, Gulbarga College, Aurangabad College were always at their best. Tournaments were held annually in which all these teams participated. Similarly, there were hockey teams in the high schools. At the time of the Annual District Conference a sports competition was held. On this occasion these teams toured different provinces and districts. Hockey was mainly played in Secunderabad. It was very popular at the school level. The Nizam's State Railway provided jobs for the players. During the fifties P.M. Reddy, Managaing Director of Deccan Airways ruled the scene. Raja Ramchandra Reddy, M.L.A. and President of the Andhra Pradesh Sports Council maintained a hockey ground and formed a team called

"Deccan Blues" which was one of the top teams in the South. Satyanarayana represented the State in the Rome Olympics in 1960 and later Mukesh Kumar.

TENNIS

Tennis was also played with great gusto and enthusiasm. The two players of international renown were S.M. Hadi and Captain Mohd. Hussain. Shivprakash Misra was a top class tennis player produced by Hyderabad, who not only dominated the local scene for two decades but was the only player to have represented India in the Davis Cup Championship.

In 1933, Nawab Mahdi Nawaz Jung constructed a stadium in the large compound of his deori where international tennis tournaments were held. The Y.M.C.A, 'Nizam's Club and Public Gardens tennis courts were well known. Nizam VII evinced keen interest in tennis and was present during the tennis tournament arranged at the Public Gardens.

SWIMMING

It is difficult to assess the number of swimmers in the Deccan. In the Hyderabad Dominions, where there were 26,000 tanks and ponds, there was a desire to swim from childhood. There were many top-class swimmers. In Taluqas, small towns and villages, small children wearing shorts, with tobni (dry pumpkin) or mudla (light wood) tied to their waist waded in the water capable of remaining in water for a long time or could jump in the water from a branch of a tree from a high platform. This type of diving was known as "Khan chidi marna". They also played games in the water. Gradually these games, gave way to high standards in swimming. Usually in the months of summer top-ranking persons and members of the public used to go for swimming in tanks, cisterns and big wells. There was a big concourse of people at the fountain of Chandulal Baradari. In the city of Hyderabad, there was a very good swimming pool, where swimming was taught for a small fee.

The high minded – youth who swam the English channel for the first time was a Hyderabadi called Shafi Ahmed.

Shafi Ahmed was a former student of the Osmania University. In 1928 he stood first in India for swimming in the Wellesly Square, Calcutta, continuously for 27 hours.

His Exalted Highness, the Nizam, gave Shafi Ahmed a costly prize on his achievement.

Some swimmers could even assume a sitting posture on the surface of the water as if they were on land. In the Mir Alam tank, one such person gave a demonstration by remaining under water for 48 hours. Thousands of spectators gathered to watch him perform this feat. He appeared on the surface of the water after ten or fifteen minutes and before coming out of the water, he performed many tricks, such as, swimming by folding both hands, swimming in the sleeping posture, sitting on the knees, sitting like a tiger and by fixing an open umbrella in his swimming shots.

OTHER OUTDOOR GAMES

Many outdoor games were played on a large scale and from 1930 arrangements for scientific training and coaching were organised at the college level. The names of the outdoor games are as follows:

Badminton, shuttlecock, basketball, baseball, jointball, tumbling, tennycoits, kabbadi, cycle polo etc.

MISCELLANEOUS GAMES

Besides these games there were other games which are listed below:

Lunpat	Chirkibilla	Sanakhor
Hingorcha	Ugal chanp	Chawa
Gillidandul	Jhad Bandar	Pather pasha
Miyanjani ki ghodi	Lattu	Talbam
Bhiduchupja	Bhidu itna	Kone ki billi

GAMES OF GIRLS

Ankh Micholi	Apdiki Cupdi	Andhi Pasha (hide and seek)
Erak Mirak	Hand Kulhiya	Gudiyon ki Shadi
Hapho Hariyapho	Chandni raat men	Sui purona

When we think of indoor games, chess, playing cards, pachchhisi (a game played with cowrishells instead of dice) and carrom-board come to our mind.

CHESS

The author of 'Ghuncha-I-Nishat' has called chess 'the king of all games'. Chess not only makes a man feel fresh but his wisdom is deepened, knowledge enlarged and perceptions developed. Some people believe that this game has ill-omens. But this is only an illusion. This game is played by only two persons. In chess there are 64 squares and 32 –pieces. The good player is called Shatir (a chess player) who keeps an eye on all the pieces of both sides and speedily decides his move in his alert mind long before his opponent can make a quick move.

The game of chess was very common in the Deccan. Both the poor and the rich played for entertainment. There were competitions among the good players and these competitions progressed so much that later it took the form of tournaments. People of all ages and all professios participated in this game. Some chess players were such experts that at a time they could compete with six or seven opponents on six or seven chessboards.

While playing hide and seek girls recited this couplet Ankh micholi kadwa tail – Billi pade wahi phulel.

In this game girls read this verse:

Apdi ki Tupdi ke pan

Pakdo mumani jogi ke kaan

However no one could match the superb Nawab Zia Yar Jang. Zia Yar Jang as chess player usually played without the horse on the board. Even leading chess experts of their time could not compete with him.

After the fall of Hyderabad, a chess player known as Abdul Gafoor earned a great name. His friends took him to every nook and corner of India and the players of Calcutta, Delhi, Bombay, Ahmedabad and Madras acknowledged his superiority. Abdul Ghafoor was also an expert in the art of binnot (club fighting).

ART OF 'BINNOT'

There were many experts in the art of club-fighting, (binnot). Maharaja Krishen Pershad, Prof. Abdul Qadir 'Hasrat', Head, Dept. of Diniyat (Osmania University) and Prof. Illiyas Birni were experts in this art. The teachers of this art were called 'ustad'. In the city of Hyderabad, there was a 'ustad', Mohd. Ramzan the perfume seller, whose shop was situated at Moti galli in Lad Bazar. The art of his club-fighting was such that he used to release two pigeons under the cot and he himself would lie on the cot and move the cudgel. The pigeons dared not escape out of the cot during his swift movements.

The pupil of ustad Mohd. Ramzan was Noor Mohd, who sold perfume and oil in the morning and in evening and at night would sell khulfi and after 11 o'clock in the night till the early hours, he would be busy with story telling. In spite of his busy schedule, he found the time to learn and teach binnot. In a demonstration he moved fast with the binnot tying two small tin boxes containing water on both sides of the binnot. When he stopped after five minutes, the water in the boxes was found to be intact.

Another outstanding person was Abdul Gafoor, whose name has been mentioned in connection with chess. In a demonstration, he tied cloth balls soaked in oil, on both the corners of the stick and lit them. After two three minutes he moved it so fast that a circle of fire was formed around his body by the fire balls. In appreciation of his art, the people applauded and he performed many startling feats while sitting and lying down. It would appear as if he was wearing a dress of flames. The description of binnot would remain incomplete if mention is not made of Maulana Syed Abdul Baqi Shattari, Ali Abbas Nawayath, Abdul Raof Khan and Ustad Gulam Khwaja. Ustad Gulam Khawaja attained the highest position in this art. Four people would throw stones from four directions and he could stop the stone with just a stick.

Abubakar alias Bakrmiyan was a strange individual. He is the same person whose mention has already been made in football. He was a renowned sportsman, an excellent swimmer, an expert in fencing with sword and stick, and a very good wrestler. He was indeed a master of every tricky art.

HUNTING

The total forest area in the Hyderabad Dominion was over 12,000 square miles. The forests were dense and vast and barring the elephant and the rhinoceros, almost all other animals were found. Among them, worth mentioning are tiger, borbachcha, panther, sambhar elk, nilgai (the white antelope), wild buffalo, stag, deer, tadas (a wolf like wild animal with a laughing cry) and wild goat.

As there were plenty of large and small rivers and tanks in the Dominion, many species of birds were also found abundantly. The hunting of tiger and other animals was popular in the forests of Nizamabad division, Warangal, Pakhal, Mulg, Medak and Narsapur. There were also hunting grounds in the forests of Pakhal, Etor, Nagaram and Pocharam.

In Atraf-I-Balda, the Sarrornagar hunting ground was known as Waliahad Bahadur's hunting grounds where deers, rabbits and titars (patridge) were in plenty. This hunting ground was very old. It was established under the supervision of Shams ul Mulk Abdul Fateh Khan during the reign of Nizam Ali Khan Asaf Jah II.

The hunting of wild animals was organised by the Government for the foreign visitors, Princes, Rajas, Viceroys of India besides important personalities and renowned hunters. The Rulers, Princes, Paigah chiefs, nobles had a flair for hunting and many of them achieved international fame.

The names worth mentioning are the renowned shot, Asaf Sadas Mir Mahbub Ali Khan, Mir Osman Ali Khan, Viqar ul Umara, Iqbal ud Daula, Nawab Moin ud Daula, Nawab Afsar ul Mulk, Qutb Yar Jang, Sana ullah tahsildar and Tahir Ali Khan. Nawab Viqar ul Mulk Iqbal ud Daula hardly missed a target. During his life time, he hunted nearly 100 tigers. Sher Mohd. Khan, retired officer from the Department of Army was a famous hunter of Parbhani who hunted the tiger alone. For hunting the tiger, a thorny fence would be erected and he usually hit the mark. Prof. Sultan Saif Bin Hussain, Department of Arabic, Osmania University never fired at a sleeping tiger. He woke the tiger, drew his attention towards him and then fired a shot.

HORSE RACING

The study of the historical books on the Deccan reveals the interest of the people in horse racing. Even hundred years ago Hyderabad had a long tradition of excellence in sports and games. The Asaf Jahi rulers and nobles of the State were not only avid lovers of literature, art and culture but also great promoters of sports. The first racing event took place in 1868 under the patronage of Nawab Mir Afzal ud Daula Nizam V, when lovers of horse racing came from Bombay. The famous historian Manik Rao Vitthal Rao, in his book, Boostan-i-Asafia has written about horse racing thus:

"Horse racing started at Malakpet in 1879 during the winter season but as early as 1876, a pavilion and a ground were prepared for racing but it later developed into organised racing. Annual horse racing event continued. During racing, the nobles, ministers, Europeans and His Highness visited the racing ground. For other spectators the sitting arrangements were made according to rank and tickets were sold. There used to be a lottery. To inform the people of places other than Hyderabad about the lottery, a temporary line of telegraph was set up. It was well patronized amidst din and bustle. After the outbreak of plague in 1898 racing was officially stopped. In 1892 horse racing was started at the Secunderabad ground. In 1901, horse racing started at Fateh Maidan and is still held there. In the long history of racing in Hyderabad September 10, 1978 proved to be an extremely important milestone, when the Malakpet Race ground attracted attention for the race lovers of India and those connected with this industry. Hyderabad, for the first time had the privilege of holding the important races of India Turf Invitation Cup 1978 in which horses from Bangalore, Madras, Calcutta, Bombay and Hyderabad participated. In view of the progress of the Hyderabad Racing Club it was given autonomous status in 1977. So far, all the races have been conducted according to the fixed rules of Madras Race Club. However, in April 1977, the Hyderabad Race Club became independent and introduced innovations such as State oriented classification of horses, which has been widely accepted by the racing fraternity.

WRESTLING

The art of wrestling centres on defeating the opponent with physical strength, energy and cleverness. In the city of Hyderabad, there were many wrestling arenas for physical exercise and training. The word dangal (wrestling arena) was sometimes used for competitons. The akhara (wrestling pit) was also named as talim. There were thousands of akharas in the city of Hyderabad and districts but two akharas of the city were very famous: Esa Pahalwan ka akhara and Mallad ki talim. Fifty years ago, there were a number of wrestling competitions. The wrestlers from the Punjab and Northern India participated in these competitions. There would be a bustle in these akharas from dawn and wrestling would continue till eight or nine o'clock in the morning. The inside scene of the akhara used to be very interesting. Some wrestlers wore breeches and some girded up their loins with a cloth. Some made gymnastic exercises and some performed baithaks (an exercise). Some were busy walking on the hands with the feet in the air, some moved the mallet and others moved a pair of mallets and moved them 500 times in a single breath. Some moved their hands like a boatman. One wrestler was seen lying with his face downward, another riding on him, dragging him and trying to put him flat on the back. Some wrestlers lifted the Santoola (Sangtola), while others were massaged. The Ustad standing in the corner instructed his pupils to use their energy properly. The following were the famous wrestlers of the Deccan.:

Ali Pahalwan, Esa Pahalwan, Raof Pahalwan, Feelban, Abdulla Pahalwan, Fakhruddin Jowhari, Ewaz Ali Mansabdar and Babiah Gowli.

Fifty years ago, the wrestling competitions were arranged in dangals with great skill and the people gathered in large numbers to witness the fights.

PALM FIGHTING

By inter-lacing the fingers, opponents endeavour to twist the hand or wrists. This is known as Panjakashi. The name of Abdul Latif Khan is associated with Panjakashi. Madhu Khan, Sarfaraz Khan and Peerbadshah of Mughalpura were reckoned best in the art of Panjakashi, but Abdul Khan and Ashraf Mian also come under this category. Once both tried their strength and the competition took a lot of time before their hands could be separated.

PART – III

ZAUQ-E-SUKHUN
LITERARY TASTE IN DECCAN

Chapter XIV

DECCAN MEIN ZAUQ – E – SUQHAN

Literary Taste in the Deccan
The Poetry of Nizam-VI and Nizam-VII

Mir Mahbub Ali Khan's diwan (collection of poems) has already been published. Ram Babu Saxena writes "His Highness the Nizam Mir Mahbub Ali Khan was an Urdu poet of considerable distinction and merit. His nom-de-plume was Asif and he belonged to the school of his Ustad Mirza Dagh. His ghazals are distinguished by a marked beauty of expression and delicacy of sentiments. His ghazals are excellent examples of spontaneous eloquence marked by piquancy, vigour and lyricism" (History of Urdu Literature, 1927, p. 199). The following verses are very famous.

Kabhi na dab ke mileinge hum unse ae'Asif'
Who shah-I-husan sahi shahryar hum bhi hain

"Asif will never stoop to met his beloved she might will be a queen of beauty, I too am the king of the land".

Lavo to qhatal nama zara main bhi dekh lun
Kis kis ki mohar hai sare mahzar lagi huwi

"Let me see my death warrant and the names of the signatories to the indictment."

A diwan (collection of poems) by Mir Mahboob Ali Khan has already been published. Two diwans of Mir Osman Ali Khan have also been published. The second diwan was published in 1974 after his death by the Nizam's Trust. The penname of Osman Ali Khan was "OSMAN'. He had mastered all the genres of poetry. His Persian compositions have an emotional appeal. In Naat (eulogy), he had a unique style. His compositions are published under the name 'Intekhab Kalam Asaf Sabe'. The preface is written by Prof. Rasheed Ahmed Siddiqui, Head of the Department of Urdu, Muslim University Aligarh, in which he writes:

> "The poetry of His Exalted Highness has to be understood keeping in mind the background of Urdu poetry which spreads over a period of 400 years. Urdu poetry had its beginning during the Bahmani period but it bore fruit during the Qutub Shahi and Adil Shahi period. In one respect the poetry of His Exalted Highness is a link in the chain of that historical heritage which contained the poetry of Mohd. Quli Qutub Shah, Wajih, Ghawasi, and Ibn Nishati. In the Deccan, the Urdu language and Urdu poetry came in two big waves. The fisrt wave of Urdu language and literature manifested itself in the old Urdu poetry already mentioned. The second wave came with the Asaf Jahi dynasty, during the first quarter of the 18th century. It is a strange coincidence that this was the time when 'Wali' reached Delhi with the lamp of Urdu poetry, which lit many a lamp in Delhi. Asaf Jah I's arrival in Aurangabad, opened the "gateway" of ancient Urdu in the "phraseology of Shahjahanabad". The history of the progress and development of literature in Urdu language dates back to the period of the Adil Shahi and Qutub Shahi rulers. It is a well known fact that Urdu poetry first blossomed in the courts of the Deccan under the rulers of Golconda

and Bijapur. These Rulers not only patronized literary men but were themselves writers of exquisite poetry both in Persian and Deccani language".

The Nizams were also distinguished patrons of arts and learning, and they kept alive the traditions of their predecessors. They never allowed the lamp of learning to be extinguished.

In fact they made Hyderabad a centre of scholoarly activities. They were not only distinguished partrons of art and learning but were also renowned poets. When Asaf Jah-I shifted from Delhi to Aurangabad and then to Hyderabad, many Persian scholars accompanied him, the foremost among them being Tajalli Ali Shah, and Lala Mansa Ram, son of Laxmi Narayan Shafeeq. Asaf Jah himself was a poet of distinction in Persian.

Though Sir Salar Jung-I was not a literary figure, he contributed much to the development of Persian literature, and patronized many poets and scholars. During the mid 19th century and later, there ware many renowned poets and writers who wrote several books in Persian and translated books from other language into Persian. One should not forget that in Hyderabad, Hindus contributed as much as Muslims towards the cultivation of Persian and Urdu language and literature.

The closing decades of the 19th century saw the advent of modern trends in administration. Persian was considered a foreign language and in 1884 Urdu was introduced as the official language. The period of Mir Mahbub Ali Khan (1869-1911) was a formative one, characterised by literary and cultural renaissance in the Urdu language, which had direct links with the North Indian literary developments. Deccani Urdu had lost its importance, for though it continued as a spoken language, it was confined only to the lower levels.

Urdu literature developed in Hyderabad under the patronage of Mir Mahboob Ali Khan, who was himself a distinguished poet Hyderabad became a centre for scholars and poets after they left Delhi, even before 1857. The scene shifted to Rampur where Nawab Kulb Ali Khan patronised the poets. His death shattered the hopes of poets and scholars, and as a result, they were attracted to the Deccan.

Those who flocked to Hyderabad from Rampur and Delhi, enjoyed favours at the court, hospitality and royal patronage. The royal magnanimity inspired literary activities in Hyderabad, and produced Hindu and Muslim scholars and poets of eminence. Thus, literary works in the South and the North were in great demand. By then, Urdu under Asaf Jahs was transformed and was different from the old Deccani Urdu. Hence with the rule of the Asaf Jahi dynasty and with Hyderabad as its capital, the transition from the ancient to modern Urdu began. The following is a specimen of the old Urdu from the poetry of the last ruler of Qutub Shahi dynasty, Abul Hasan Tana Shah.

Tuh muckh koi chander kate, koi suratein anwar kate
Koihusan ka mandir kate, koi kuch kate koi kutch kate

"some say you are the moon, some say you are radiant faced, some call you temple of beauty, while some others compare you with other things."

Abul Hasan Tana Shah the last ruler was a poet of the Deccani language. The culture which developed with the unity of Hindus and Muslims was glorious. Thousands of examples of Deccani culture can be seen during the period of Tana Shah where in every department of life, Hindus and Muslims served the State working shoulder to shoulder. He not only patronized Deccani as a spoken language and Telugu, but also used Persian as the official language.

Later, the Northern style of Urdu of Nizam ul Mulk Asaf Jah-I, appeared on the scene.

Gali n kaho koi mere dilber ko hasad se
Majh dil ke qale min ye duyae Yamani hai
"Do not abuse my beloved with jealousy as she is
a pearl of yamani to my heart".

The heir-apparent of Asaf Jah-I continued this accent and style in his compositions:

Chasma-i-bad dur dilbaran sare
Apne "Nasir" ko pyar karte hein

"May the evil eye stay away from all the beloved ones as they love their own "Nasir".

There were other literary patrons like Arastu Jah and Chandulal. Maharaja Chandulal was an administrator and Peshkar at the court of Nasir ud Daula Nizam-IV. He was a renowned poet of Persian and Urdu languages. His penname was Shadan and he made considerable contribution to the development of the Persian language. Shahdan was known for his generosity, which attracted poets not only from India but from places as far as Persia. It is said that about three hundred poets were connected with his house and the salaries received by them varied from Rs.100 to Rs. 1000. Shadan left two diwans in Persian and one in the Urdu language. Maharaja Kishen Pershad, Prime Minister of Hyderabad, belonged to one of the chief Hindu families established in the Deccan. He was a poet and scholar of repute and wrote with merit in Persian, Arabic and Urdu languages. As a prose writer, he earned reputation for producing works with singular ease, lucidity and charm. He wrote poetry under the nom de plume of 'Shad' and became a pupil of the Nizam Mir Mahbub Ali Khan who bestowed on him distinction of 'Shagird'-i-Khas Asaf Jah' (the special pupil of Asaf Jah). He also edited two journals entitled Dab-daba-i-Asafia and Mahbub-ul-Kalam.

A man of letters, the Maharaja patronized scholars, academicians, poets and writers. None of the gifted writers in India was a stranger to him. He helped everyone and everyone received bountiful patronage namely Iqbal, Josh, Dagh, Amir Minai, Ratan Nath Sarshar, Faani and a host of others. Chanda was the only woman singer, and a dancing girl. At the beginning Nawab Rukhud Daula patronised her family, to be followed by Nizam Ali Khan, Arastu Jah, Mir Alam and Chandulal. Though pious by nature, she was a cheerful woman and highly educated. She was proficient in music too. For this reason, the ruler was very kind to her. He bestowed on her jagirs, mansabs, titles, naubat and naqqara.

She was a poet and had a diwan. It is said that she arranged Mushairas at her residence. Appreciation of poetry and favours from the Rulers of Deccan attracted Shah Nasir Hafeez Dehelvi, Dagh, Amir and Jalil. Most of them are buried in Hyderabad.

As regards the progress of Urdu, the period of His Exalted Highness Nizam-VII is considered most fruitful. Urdu not only was fortunate to command respect at the official and educational levels but during the period of His Exalted Highness, Hyderabad became a big centre for Urdu poetry. Writers, poets and scholars flocked to Hydeabad in large numbers. In the Deccan both Hindus and Muslims strove equally for the progress of Persian and Urdu languages. When Asaf Jah-I shifted to the Deccan many writers accompanied him. Tajalli Ali Shah was the first among those who left his native place and accompanied Asaf Jah. He wrote Tuzuk-i-Asafia. The Peshkar of Asaf Jahi-I, Lala Mansa Ram's son Lachmi Narayan 'Shafeeq' was a writer and poet of Urdu and Persian languages. His book 'Chamanistani- Shuara' is reckoned as an important book. Among the Hindu poets, the most eminent at that time was Maharaja Chandulal whose court was famous for patronizing hundred of poets. Raja Makhanlal translated the rubaiyat of Umar Khayyam into Urdu. Premchand translated Shahnama in Urdu. Rai Gulab Chand 'Hamdam' Rai Bala Pershad ' rabt' Raja Girdhari Pershad Mahbub

Nawazwant were poets of great merit. 'Baqi' who translated the Rubaiyat of Khwaja Mir 'Dard' in Urdu was a poet of great merit. Raja Sital Pershad "Khuram" Behri Lal 'Ramz' are other prominent names. Among the Hindu scholars of Urdu, of course, the most eminent and prominent name is of Maharaj Sir Kishen Pershad who with his poetry, prose, epistles and other literary works enriched the Urdu language.

His Exalted Highness was not only an intellectual but also a distinguished poet. His Kulliyat (collection of poems) are a proof of his poetic talent. He was the guardian and sponsor of the great tradition of Urdu poetry. His poetry mirrors past traditions. In the poetry of His Exalted Highness the Nizam, echoes of renowned poets are found in respect of similies and metaphors, phrases, idioms, language and narratives. His erudition and insight are indicative of the fact that he could excel in each genre of poetry.

Ahon mein kuch kami na hui dag-i-ishkh mein
Tha ye ajab chirag ke roushan hawa men tha

"There was no paucity of signs in lover's suffering; it was a strange lamp which continued to burn even in winds"

ab us ada se app ka ana to dekhliya
tazeem ko khadi hai khayamat bhi rah mein

"Look at her seductive gait as she comes long even the Dooms day angel waits to pay obeisance to her".

Ilahi ho rahi hai id kaise aj makhtal mein
Koi bismil se milta hai koi khatil se milta hai

"Oh God why is the makhtal so festive today some are meeting the killed while some others the killer".

Jab hal-i-dil kaha hai mila hai yehi jawab
Kuch aur kahiye zikr ye sau bar ho gaya

"when I expressed the feelings of my heart, her stock reply was that I should talk of some thing else, as she has heard me say the same thing a hundred times."

Mahabbat Khuda jane kya rang laye
Suna hai thumen bhi khabar ho gai hai

"God only knows what will happen to my love. I heard that you too have come to know about it."

Maikasho aish uthalo ke bahar akhir hai
Jalwaye mai hai chirag-i-Sahri shishe mein

"Oh lovers of wine, enjoy yourselves, as it is the end of the spring season. The splendour of the wine in the glass in just like the lamp of dawn".

Kuch samaj mein nahin ata ye maama osman
Umar maloom nahin jati hai ya aati hai

"Oh Osman, I am at a loss to understand this riddle of life. It is not known whether age is going hence or coming thither". His Exalted Highness was quite successful at some places in adopting the style of 'Dagh'. Note the following couplets:

Ilahi khair ho badle huye hain yar ke taiwar
Sitam aya, ghazab aya, bala ai, khaza ai

"Oh God let all be well, my beloved's brows are knitted, in fierceness and fury; death and deluge appear imminent."

Hamari jan Gayi teri dil lagi tahri
Sikhaya kis ne ada ko teri khaza hona

"My dying is a thing of laughter for you, who has taught your beauty to become so fatal?"

RIYAYAT AND MUNASIBAT

Elegance and commendation of beauty are the essentials of poetry and fine arts. These are the essentials of civilised living.

Note the following verses:-

Afshan jama ke tum ne ye andher kardiya
Girnelage zamin per sitare naye naye

"By applying afshan (a kind of cosmetic applied on

the face) you have made every thing around you dark . New stars have started falling on the ground".

Kisne dast henai se ponch kar anso
Lagadi aag meri ashkbar ankhoan mein.

"Whose hands with henna (Mehndi) have wiped my tears, it has kindled fires into my tearful eyes".

HAMD, NAAT, AND MANQABAT

In these poetic forms the poet pays tribute to the feelings of faith in God, Prophet and Holy Imams.

HAMD (Praise of God)

Dil ko khuda ne apni mahabbat se bhar diya
Tasbih ko zaban di sajde ko sir diya
Nazan hain is ada pe gulaman-e-mustafa

Hum ko diya rasool to khair ul basher diya
Rutba baland ho gaya is musht-i-khak ka
Jab bar i-Ishq mere sir pe dhar diya
Kis munh se shukre ezidi ada karon
Na cheez the so is ko bi ek cheez kar diya
Har dard, her bala se bachane ke waste
Tasir di dua men dava men asar diya
Go main gunaghar tha lokin zahe nasib
Rahmat ne har gunah se mujhe pak kar diya
Osman ye us ka fazal hai tujh per ke be sawal
Niamat se apni damane maqsood bhar diya

"God has filled our hearts with His love. He gave us tongue to articulate the rosary they gave us head to prostrate (Sajdah) on the ground.

"The slaves of Mustafa are proud of this favour that

God has given them a Prophet to save mankind".

"The status of the clod of dust has been raised high, when He placed the load of love on my heart".

"How do I thank God, for making an insignificient thing so significant".

"In order to save us from troubles and ills, God has made prayers fruitful and medicines effective".

"Though I was a sinner, I am fortunate enough that God by His compassion and grace has redeemed me from all sins".

"Oh! Osman, it is the mercy of God on you that without asking He has fulfilled your desires with his graciousness".

NAAT SHARIF (Praise of Prophet)

Bana berpaye Ahmed sir ke yabi sad viqar inja
Zar enja gohar enja hashmat iftekhar enja
Ba taiyaba chon dar ayem ba hazaroun shoukh ber khwanam
Man enja zindagi enja a jal enja mazar enja
Za daghe ishq saroor sina gulzar Jina daram
Gul enja lal enja sunbul enja naubahar enja
Zahe masti ke bashed dar khayale saqi kausar
Khum enja jam enja mai enja saroor enja khumar enja
Nabashad jai man juz astan Mustafa Osman
Sir enja sajda enja bandagi enja Kharar enja

"Place your head at the feet of Ahmed (i.e. the Prophet) so that you may achieve and get respect in the world because prosperity as well as dignity and honour exist only in this world. When I enter the holy city of Madina, I may chant the holy verses with passionate love, as I wish to be buried here, on account of the pangs of love, my bosom is as good as a garden of heaven, because the roses, tulips, hyacinth as well as new spring is here. How pleasant is the ecstasy that I have thought of the cup bearer of the heavenly spring (Kausar) because the dream of mine is here, the cup is here, as well as intoxication and the after math of intoxication is here.

"Oh Osman, there is no place for you, except the threshold of the Prophet; with your head in prostration and obedience, you will realize that peace and rest are here only".

NAAT SHARIF

Khausin chun na goyom abroye Mustafa ra
Mazagh guft ye ezad an chanham haq numara
Us itaat ilahi didam jamale Ahmed
Waz hub Mustafai darya fatem Khudara
Har kas ke ghota zan shed dar Khulzum-i-mahabbat
Daram yakheen ke ya bad an durbe bahara
Uz majma karamat uz failz tu chan dur ast
Shah agar nawazi dervish be nawara
Gar abru tu Khwahi ai dil be sidiq niyat
Darbahre haq khuda fanashu yabi dure baqara
Gar asthana bosi garded nasib mara
Darya ye faiz saqi mishdah dabed bamistan
Girid saghar mai ya iha ulaskara
As Khusro-i-hasinan al shah nazneena
Roushan kun us tajali kashana gadara
Ae taje kajkalshan sultane deen panahan
Bar hale zar Osman chashme karam khudara

"Why should I not refer to the eyebrows of the Prophet as God Himself has said that eyes reveal the truth. By obeying God I saw the beauty of Prophet Mohammad and due to the grace of the Prophet I found God. Any one who drowns himself in the ocean of love will find priceless pearls. Oh you the great reservoir of generosity, I crave for your benediction, and pray for your favour on poor darvesh. Oh heart, if you seek honour with sincere intent, annual yourself in the pursuit of truth and you will then discover the portals of eternity. I will sacrifice my soul on your sacred mausoleum, if I be unlucky to kiss your threshold. The generous kindness of the saqi offers hope to the in toxicants. Oh, the Lord of Beauty and Compassion kindle the hermitage of the mendicant with divine light. Oh, Emperor of Emperors and protector of faith, be merciful on the miserable condition of Osman".

GHAZAL

Mahbbat men na dib baqi na tab o tawan baqi
Ahbi hissa men hain kya jane kya kaya sakhtiyan baqi
Gul o rihan o sumbul sab khizan men ho gaye rukusat
Magar bulbul ke lab pr rah gai ah o fughan baqi
Shabe dosheena ki bad mastiyan main kya kahoon saqi
Nikal aya hai din aur hai abhi khuwabe giran baqi
Zabane shama se sunta hun khisa souze ulfat ka
Shab akhir hogai lekin abhi hai dastan baqi
Khuda hi kashti-i-dil ka hai hafiz bahr ulfat mein
Na langer jis ka baqi hai na jiska badban baqi
Suragh akhir ko mil hi jaye ga yaran rafta ka
Ganimat hai jo ab tak hai nishan-i-karvan bagi
Slateen salf sab ho gaye nazre a jal Osman
Musalmano ka teri sltnat se hai nishan baqi

"I have neither the heart nor the power endurance to remain in love.

I do not know what more travails I am destined to suffer Although flowers have withered and fallen in autumn. Despair and melancholy are still resonant in bulbul's melodies.

'Need I talk about last night's revelries?
My eyes are heavy with sleep until late in the day
The flaming candle speaks of love that burns
The night is gone but love's ordeals remain
In the ocean of loves, only God is the saviour of the
Heartboat which has lost both its anchor and sails.
The clue to our lost companions is found finally
In the traces of the caravan that has passed by
Although emperors and dynasties have gone into oblivion, Osman
It's your kingship that keeps alive the true ethos of Muslims.

HINDU POETS WITH DIWAN

Hindu poets also displayed the talent and skill in poetry. There were many who had their diwan namely, Guru Saranbali 'Azad' Raja Rameshwar Rao 'Asghar' Dr. R.R. Saksena 'Ilham', Lala Mukund Lal Jowhri, Girdhari Pershad Mahabub Nawazwant Eaqi'Rai Bachulal 'Tamkeen', Raghavendra Rao 'Jazb', Balaji Trimbak Nath 'Zerra', Behari lal 'Ramz', Chattulal 'Shadan', Maharaja Kishan Pershad and Raja Narsing Raj Aali belonged to a family of scholars. Raja Nassing Raj's father Raja Girdhari Pershad Mahbub Nawazwant 'Baqi' alias Bansi Raja was in charge of the household affairs of the Nizam's palace, and was also a renowned poet. Narsing Raj was well versed in Persian and Urdu languages, a poet of distinction and a prolific writer. He was a man of learning and started a Kayasth pathshala. He was a great confidant and friend of Maharaja Kishen Pershad. His son, Rai Narhar Raj 'Saqi' was an Urdu poet of great merit.

CHAPTER – XV

DAGH-AMIR MINAI – JALEEL – AMJAD – FAANI

Hundred years ago, when poets gathered, the meetings were lively. In Hyderabad Deccan, poets received excellent treatment, and were held in high esteem by the people. As a result poets from the different regions of India were attracted to Hyderabad. 'Zauq' the tutor of Bahadur Shah Zafar was tempted to come to Hyderabad but could not reach due to some personal problems. He expressed the desire of his heart in these words:

Garche hai Mulk-i-Deccan men in dino Qadr-i-suqhan
Kaun jai zauq per Dilli ki galiyan chod kar

'Although there is taste and appreciation of poetry in Deccan these days, who will go there leaving the lanes of Delhi".

Ustad Zauq could not come but his pupil 'Dagh' reached Hyderabad on April 17, 1888 and became the tutor of the Nizam. He stayed here for one and quarter year and returned on July 12, 1889. The second time he came was on April 4, 1890. Mir Mahboob Ali Khan issued a Farman on October 14, 1891 to appoint 'Dagh' in State services and ordered payment of his salary with effect from the date of his arrival in Hyderabad. Thus 'Dagh' received three and half years' salary all at once. He became a court poet and stayed in Hyderabad for about 18 years and produced the best creations of his poetic mind. He attained honours, titles and privileges. His death in 1905 touched the Nizam Mir Mahbub Ali Khan so much that he ordered cancellation of the Darbar arranged on the occasion of Id. He sanctioned Rs.3000 for the burial of 'Dagh'. His last prayers were perfomed at Mecca Masjid under the orders of the Nizam. The funeral procession was carried under a silk canopy accompanied by thousands of people, even though it was on Id day. He was buried in the Dargah of Hazarat Yousufain.

In those days there were no currency notes but only coins. Money in bags was brought in carts from the Government treasury. When these bags were taken from the carts and the money heaped in front of 'Dagh', he was stunned with delight and had tears in his eyes. He said to himself"

"Imagine the condition of the man who spent his entire life on a salary of Rs.80 and is completely tied up with loans, spending a long time in great destitution and living on credit for three and half years". When by the grace of God a cartful of money reached, Taj Ali, the father of Tamkeen Kazmi wrote:

"I wish that ustad will not die as a result of great rejoicing".

AMIR MINAI

Amir Minai was a great poet of India. He was proficient in Arabic and had a remarkable knowledge of Persian. He was well versed in medicine, astrology and other sciences. He was a pupil of 'Aseer'. Gifted with an inborn genius for poetry and guided by his able preceptor he soon made a name for himself as a poet. He remained at Rampur for 43 years enjoying the favour of Nawab Yousuf Ali Khan and Kalb Ali Khan. In 1900, when Mir Mahbub Ali Khan was on his way back to Hyderabad from Calcutta and halted at Banaras, 'Amir' presented him an ode of welcome. Nizam was pleased and invited him to Hyderabad. Soon after reaching Hyderabad he fell sick and died after a brief illness. He expresses his unflinching faith in God in these beautiful words :

Is but ke jor khalic Akbar se kya kaheen
Apaski ched dawar-i-mahsher se kya kaheen
Kuch rahe ya na rahe per ye dua hai ke Amir
Naza kay waqt salamat mera iman rahe

'Who will speak of the tyranny of the beloved before the creator (God) or of mutual love play on the day of Reckoning. Whether anything remains or not, but oh, Amir, pray that faith must remain intact at the moment of my death.'

AMJAD

The poet philosopher, Ahmed Hussain Amjad, was the most famous poet of the Deccan in the genre of Rubai, although his poems and ghazals too are of enduring value. The collection of his poems has gone into several editions. He was a sufi and fakir.

Har cheez musabab se asbab se mango
Minnat se khushamad se adab se mango
Kyon gair ke age hat phailatay ho
Bande ho rub kay to rub se mango

"Be it anything ask with reason and modesty, with politeness and praise. Why extend your hand before others? If you are God's devotee, ask from the Heavenly Father himself".

SIDDIQ AHMED ASAR

He was the son of Fasahat Jung 'Jaleel', His compositions are very elegant and precise.

Teri nichi nichi nigahen salamat
Mujhe to koi bad gumani nahin hai

"I wish well of your modest and down cast eyes, I do not think ill of you."

HAKIM AZAD ANSARI

Ansari was a lively poet and his diwan was published. Here is a couplet from him:

A magar is qader kharib na aa
Kay tamasha mohal ho jaye

"Come to me, but not so close, that it become difficult for me to behold you."

ABDUL KALAM BADAR

He was a product of the Osmania University. He was a doctor by profession. Here is a specimen of his couplet:

Yek wajd ka alam hai ajab bekhabri hai
Phoolon ke ujale pe guman ay sahri hai

"It is a strange world of ecstasy and forgetfulness, the brightness of the flowers made me believe that it is dawn".

ABDUL QAYOOM 'BAQI'

He was a student and later Lecturer of Urdu in the Osmania University. He did a free translation in Urdu poetry of three thousand verses from 'Faust' by Goethe which was a masterpiece of his erudition. This translation has been published. Here is a couplet from a short poem entitled 'Zameen'.

Lutf is khak pe ho bada-ay-gum pine ka
Ibn adam ko milay kuch to sila jine ka

"There is a peculiar relish in drinking the wine of sorrow. The son of Adam deserves to gain this much from life".

BEGUM

His name is not known. He attended the poets' gatherings regularly at Maharaja Kishen Pershad's house. Covering his head with a dupatta, he recited the couplets with the voice of a woman. Here is an example:

Ari mama pani se bhar de lagan ko
Zara mein bhi dekhongi suraj gahan ko

"Oh mama fill the basin with water, so that I can also see the solar eclipse.

TAHSEEN SARWARI

His name was Kazim Ali. He was employed in Anjuman Tarrakhi Urdu. He died in 1977, but before his death he wrote a beautiful poem.

A gaye intezar tha jin ka
Darmiyan se hatao paimane

"He has come for whom I was waiting; remove the goblets that stand between us."

HAZRAT FASAHAT JUNG 'JALEEL'

He came to Hyderabad on September 5, 1900 from Manikpur. Mir Osman Ali Khan conferred on him the titles of 'Fasahat Jung' and 'Imam ul Fan'. He died in 1946. In one of the Mushairas he read a ghazal which includes these famous couplet:

Bat saqi ki na tali jaye gi

Kar ke tauba tor dali jayegi

The poet says "I will break my pretence if saqi offers me a peg of wine."

The pupil of Jaleel and the audience showered praises on the poet. Hazarat Bahdood Ali 'Safi' was also present. He repeated the verse making a slight change:

Bat saqi ki na tali jaye gi
Ki hai tauba tor dali jayegi

"The pretence has been broken, I will not evade the word of saqi."

With the correction of 'ki hai tauba' instead of 'kar ke tauba' by 'Safi' his pupils and audience praised him a good deal. Next day after the Mushaira, this incident was publicized in the lanes and bylanes of the city. When HEH the Nizam was informed about it, he issued a Farman informing the people that Jaleel was the tutor of the King and that he should not attend the 'Mushairas'. Since then nobody saw 'Jaleel' attending 'Mushairas' till his death. His ghazals were sent to the Mushairas of Maharaja Kishen Pershad. The Maharaja was an institution. His residence was a lighthouse of learning. Almost every month there were poets' gatherings (Mushairas) in his house. Every poet received his personal attention. Hospitality was unlimited and the Mushaira was held with great éclat. The Mushairas opened opportunities for some sort of liberal education. Idioms and language apart, it was the Mushaira culture that delighted one and all and had a cleansing effect.

After the death of the Maharaja, Raja Narshing Raj 'Ali', who was a great confidant and friend of the Maharaja, arranged a 'Tarhi Mushaira' every year in his memory at the deori. The first round of the Mushaira began with the compositions of Persian language poets. The Raja strictly complied with the norms prescribed for a Mushaira namely, the seating arrangements, list of the poets according to seniority and other details. Nawab Turab Yar Jung also participated in these Mushairas. Though Nawab Fasahat

Jung Jaleel, the ustad of Mir Osman Ali Khan Nizam VII, did not participate in the Mushaira, he sent his ghazal for recitation.

Nigah barkh nahin chehra aftaab nahin
Wuh admi hai magar dekhne ki tab nahin

"His glance, is no lightning flash nor his face the sun. He is just a human being but dazzles the eyes".

The compositions of Fasahat Jung Jaleel are an epitome of life's philosophy. His elegant diction, metaphors and incisive style are the qualities of verse that make him an outstanding poet of his time.

'HASRAT' TIRMAZI

His name was Syed Ahmed. He was employed in the Home Department. After Hyderabad's integration with India, he left for Karachi. He was reckoned among the first ranking poets. He never attended Mushairas in Karachi. In the following verse the word 'Koi' is repeated thrice to heighten the effect of pathos and desolation.

Koi nahin koi bi nahin koi bhi nahin
Ai shamay bekasi meri mahfil to dekhna

In the evening of my misery look at my company.! Oh candle.

There is none, there is no one, there is none at all".

He died on December 19, 1977.

SHOIB AHMED "HAZEEN"

He was an Osmanian and a poet of ideas. The following ghazal was popular at the Osmania Unviersity :

Ikhrar zulmkar lein aur phir bhi muskurain
Main sab samgh raha hun ji bhar ke azmayen
Wuh waqt dhundti hain phir ishq ki adayen

Main gesuon se khelon aur ap gungunain
Dil barq ashan hai asu bar jal chukka hai
Han ap muskurain bay khouf muskurain

"After admitting your tyranny, you still expect me to smile, I understand it all that I'll be continually tested until you are fully satisfied. You seek the moment to play the love game and when I frolic with your long hair, you would hum a song. My heart is well acquainted with the lightning that has burnt it a hundred times; you go ahead, smile and smile.

ABID ALI 'SAYEED

The main quality of his composition is simplicity and precision. He has employed small metres to great advantage. He has described in his poems intense feelings of the human heart.

Phoolon ki rut hai thandi hawain
Ab unki marzi ayay ya na aian

"It is the season of flowers and cool breeze now it is her wish, to come or not to come."

MUAZZAM JAH BAHADUR 'SHAJEEH'

Prince Muazzam Jah second son of Mir Osman Ali Khan was a poet who excelled in writing romantic poetry. His verses reflect his heart more than the mind. His three collections of poems Shamshir Shujaat, Dastoor Shujaat, Arz-o-Sana have already been published. The following verse is reckoned among his best.

Ab sirf be hisi pe madar-i-hayat hai
Jab se gaye hain ap na din hai na rat hai

"Since the time you have gone, there is no difference between day and night, life rests now on total lack of feeling.

SHAHID SIDDIQUI

He was connected with the Court of Prince Muazzam Jah. He used to write a humourous column for a newspaper. He was a poet of refined taste and mature sensibility. He was the author of Chiragh-i-Manzil, a collection of his poems. Here is one of his couplets:

Hum ko kiya ajal ke farishte ne jab salam
Walekum salam kaha aur mar gaye

"When the angel of death greeted me, I, too responded with 'may peace be on you' and died".

HAZRATH BAHBOOD ALI 'SAFI'

The play of language, phraseology, delicacy of ideas and humour are the essence of his poetry. He had a large circle of pupils in the Deccan. His compositions entitled 'Firdos-i-Khayal' has been published in Karachi.

Sau meharbaniyon ke iwaz muskura diya
Sarkar ne kamal kiya iktesar men
Acheh gun dekh achi shakal na dekh
Sunkhiya bhi sufaid hoti hai
Musa ke hosh udgaye kismat pahad ke
Kaisi sharab kisko pilai pachad ke
Jo fateha ko aye wuh likh jayay apni rai
Meri taraf se kuch na ho loh-i-mazar per

"For a hundred favours, she responded with just a smile. Your majesty has achieved wonders with such brevity. Look for good qualities not just a good looking face as, poison too is white in colour. Moses was stunned. Look at the luck of the mountain, who knows that wine was served to him that threw him down. Whosover comes to recite 'Fateha' should write his opinion but I, on my side do not want anything to be inscribed on the grave.

NAWAB MUZAFFAR UDDIN

His pen name was 'Sahib'. He was known as the poet of rubai. His collection of rubaiyat was published from the Deccan under the title "Suqhandar Suqhan". In his rubaiyat he has referred not only to ethical problems but to the nature of human passions in the following words: -

Bijli ko kadakne ki saza date ho
Tair ko phadkne ki saza dete ho
Fitrat ke takhazon se jhagarnay walo
Kya dil ko dhadakne ki saza dete ho

"You who punish the lightning for its thunder, and a bird for its fluttering, oh you, who quarrel with the processes of nature do you punish the heart too for its heart beats?

KHAZI MIR LUTF ALI 'ARIF'

He authored several books and was a thoughtful poet. At the time of Police Action he went to Bidar to bring his daughter and son-in-law to Hyderabad but was killed there.

Sajde yaron se shaikh ne sikhe
Wuh kahan tha namaz se waqif

"The Shaik has learnt prostration from his friends. Was he really conversant with prayers?"

AHSAN ALI 'ARSHI'

He was born at Shahbad, a small town in Oudh in 1901. He came to the Deccan in search of employment and made it his home town. Hazrat Zamin Kantori said at the first meeting, that 'Arshi' was a good poet. His best verse reads thus:

Agar tujh ko masroof gulgasht dekhen
Tarap jain kaliyan thaher Jaiye pani

"If they see you taking a stroll, the buds will become restive and the water remain static."

HAZRAT ALI 'AKHTER'

Niaz Fateh Puri accepts him as a major poet. Earlier, there was similarity in Akhter's thoughts with that of Niaz Fateh Puri. He wrote a poem entitled "Munkir Khuda se Khitab" which had a charm of its own. A prominent feature of his compositions is the stylistic use of Persian compositions. Here is one such verse:

In shookh nigahoon mein Akhter ab a hi chala tha rang-i-wafa.
Majboor hoon apni fitrat se khud mujh se takhaza ho nasaka.

"Oh Akhtar, in these flirtatious eyes the colour of faithfulness was about to come, but due to the constraints of my temperament I could not make proper overtures to her".

SHAUKAT ALI KHAN 'FANI' AND ABOUL HAFEEZ QATEEL

After passing his LLB examination from the Aligarh University in 1908, Fani practised law for sometime in Lucknow and then in Bareilly but the profession was not to his liking. He came to Hyderabad and joined the Education Department. He was also a Headmaster of a High School and owned a beautiful small house and a car. He was the court poet of Prince Muazzam Jah and enjoyed the patronage of Kishen Pershad. He invited trouble by disagreeing with the Director of Education. The efforts of well wishers to bring about a compromise hurt 'Fani's self respect. He expressed the rage of his heart in these terms:

'Fani hum to jete ji who maiyat hain be gor o kafan
Ghurbat jis ko ras na ayi aur watan bhi choot gaya'

"Fani is a living corpse without a grave and shroud. "He was out of tune with poverty and an exile from his own native place."

The fascinating atmosphere of the Deccan was a safe haven for poets who came from different parts of India. They made Hyderabad their second home town. The poet Allama Iqbal paid homage to the Deccan in the following poem:

Kya kahon is boostan e ghairat e firdous ki
Jis ke phoolon mein huva ai hum nawa mera guzar

Jis ke zare mehr alam tab ko saman e noor
Jis ki too afzaiyon per didaye musa nisar
Jis ke bulbul and alibe akhal kul ke hum safir
Jin ke ghunchon ke liye rukhsare hoor-i-nadar
Khita-i-innat fiza jis ki hai daman gir dil
Azmat derina Hindustan ki yadgar
Noor ke zaron se qudrat ne banai ye zamin
Aina tapke Deccan ki khat kar paye fisher

"What can I say about the simplicity of this heavenly garden oh, my friend, I happened to pass by the flowery way. Its minute particles are the source of illumination to the whole world. The light shed on Tur entranced Moses' eyes. Its bulbuls are Gabriel's campanions where buds mirror the rosy cheeks of heavenly virgins. This region of paradise is the heart of Hindustan and an enduring monument of her greatness".

Nature has woven the land with strips of divine light, which emit radiance from the fissures of the soil in Deccan.

CHAPTER – XVI

KHATEEL–MAQDOOM–NAZR–WAJD

Frustration and despair mark the poetry of 'Qateel' much like 'Fani'. It would appear that both have travelled together in the vale of tears that is this world 'Fani' and 'Qateel' both seemed to have been hurt with the unpredictability of fortune. In 1940, when 'Qateel' was introduced to 'Fani' at Mallepally, 'Fani' requested 'Qateel' to recite his ghazal. 'Qateel' took out one red coloured paper from his pocket which had an advertisement of a film, On the reverse side he had written his new composition. After listening to his ghazal 'Fani' requested him to recite another ghazal. This time Qateel took out a yellow coloured advertisement, on the back side of which he had written another ghazal. After listening to his compositions 'Fani' admired 'Qateel' as the best upcoming poet and wanted that his compositions be preserved.

Rasheed Ahmed had preserved twenty ghazals of 'Qateel'. Fani was surprised at the carelessness of Qateel. The two ghazals which Qateel recited were comparable to the theme and style of Fani.

The following is the ghazal of 'Fani'.

Wafa begana-i-rasam a beyah hai
Khamooshi ahel-i-dil ki dastan hai
Musali purshish–i-bimer lekin

Wuh shan-i-chara farmai kahan hai
Phir ab manzoor hai hangama-i-barq
Phir abkharad banaye ashiyan hai
Wuh dil ki ad men rahte hain 'Fani'
Tamanna mere un ke darmiyan hai

"Fidelity does not know the language of custom. Silence therefore is the story of the man of heart. It is good to enquire about the health of the sick but this is nothing when compared to affording curative treatment. Accept once again the revages of lightning and be ever prepared to build a new nest. She lives, Oh, 'Fani' under the cover of love. Desire is the only channel between her and me." The following is Qateel's composition :

Wuh betabi na wuh ah o fughan hai
Na ab dil hai na dil ki dastan hai
Wahan dil shaki ye taab-i-takallum
Khamoshi bhi jahan ek dastan hai
Sukut-i-hairat-i-nazara hai murg
Hyayat ek parda-e-husan-i-nihan hai
Nishat-i-wasal marg-i-jazba-i-shoukh
Nishat-i-yas se dad-i-sitam de
Qateel ab ah ki takhat kahan hai

(*Shair ki Duniyan*, p. 86)

"Neither is there a restless nor sigh and sob
There is now no heart nor any heart's story
Where the doubting heart cannot bear the pressure of speech
Where silence itself tells the story
While death is the scene of awesome stillness and silence
Life is a veil that covers beauty
Ecstasy of Union is the end of desire
Ecstasy of desire is a never ending intoxication
Looks of despair are the dividends of cruelty
'Qateel' has no strength left even to breathe a sigh".
Fazal tera shafeeh taat o zhad

Adal ai nawaz o isiyan posh

"God, thy benediction is on persons of piety and faith commending forgiveness from sins, while thy justice favours the sinner shielding him from sin."

That was a couplet from 'Fani'. The following is 'Qateel's couplet.

Yek majboor-i-masiyat aye
Bharam rakhle karim isiyanposh

The phrase "Majboor-i-masiyat" (helpless sinner) is strikingly original.

In this meeting, 'Fani' was requested to recite his ghazal. Hairat Badaiuni and Tabish Dehelvi also were present. After paying respects, Hairat inquired from Fani about his health. He replied, "People say 'Fani' is alive, you tell me, how I should refute this. I am a guest for a few months!" He said that he had composed a chronogram on his death which he wanted to recite. But the visitors refused to listen and told Fani Sahib that he should not talk about his death. They insisted that he should not recite the chronogram. But 'Fani' read the quatrain of the chronogram of his death:

Uwaz jahan guzisht ke akhir khuda na bood
O yin chuneen bazeest ke goy khuda na dast
Tughan-i-naz been ke be loh-mazar o
Sibt ast sal rahlat 'Fani' Khuda na dasht

"A voice resounds 'There is no God'. He lived in a manner that said 'there is no God'. The epitaph inscribed on the gravestone. 'Khuda-na-dasht' 'God does not exist' indicates the year of Fani's death as well as the pride of his rebellion. The value of letters (Khuda-na-dusht) comes to 1360 H. the year of Fani's death was correctly predicted by Fani. Fani died within a few months of its composition.

RAZI UDDIN HASAN KAIFI

He was a pupil of Dagh and was known as the successor of Dagh. In a beautiful poem, he said:

Addmi mein koi kamal to ho
Na ho Yousuf na ho Bilal to ho

"After all a man should be something special. If not Yousuf, he should be Bilal,"

MANZOOR HUSSAIN MAHER UL KHADRI

While writing the preface of the book 'Shair ki Duniya' 39 years ago, Maher wrote:

"Modern Hyderabad has rendered whatever service it could to Urdu literature. I can say with my own experience that the atmosphere of Hyderabad is well-suited for poetry and literature."

His lofty thoughts are reflected in the following verse:

"Khizan hai ghanimat bahar a na jaye
Nasheman banane ki fursat na hogi"

"Winter is good enough lest spring might arrive there will be no leisure to build the nest."

NAWAB MOIN UD DAULA BAHADUR 'MOIN'

He was a Paigah noble. A number of poets were associated with his Darbar. He himself was a good poet. His diwan has already been published.

Main aur tum se arz-i-tamanna majal kya
Payamber ki bat per itna malal kay

"I dare not express my desire to you. Why should you feel so sad at the words of the messenger."

MAZHAR UDDIN 'MAZHAR'

He is a poet of wit and sensibility. He resides in Karachi.

Ai ' na ru na dekh ai' na
Ched acchi nahin mukhabil se

"Oh you beautiful, don't look into the mirror. It is not good to tease your opponent."

Tera jadah, teri manzil, tere masken ka pata
Kis se puchain koi is rah se guzra bhi nahin

"Whom should I ask the address of your residence, the way and the destination, as no one has passed by this way."

MUJEEB AHMED 'MUJEEB' KHAIRABADI

He bade farewell to Khairabad in his childhood and went to the Deccan and made it his home town. Now Pakistan is his third home town. He is a thoughtful poet, melodious and eloquent. He is a king of both poems and ghazals.

Lutf-i-nazar se housla-i-ghum badha gaye
Mumnoon iltefat hon jina sikha gaye

"Your joyous presence has enhanced my capacity to suffer.

I am profoundly grateful to you for teaching me how to live."

Allah re tabassum rangeen o dilnawaz
Dushwariyan hayat ko asan bana gaye

"Oh God, her smile so colourful and heart warming, has made my difficult life easy."

MIRZA HADI 'RUSWA'

It appears his pen name is 'Ruswa' but his real name was 'Mirza'. He burst like a storm with spontaneous verses like these:

Haya ki shukiyon se uthte uthte jhuk gayen nazren
Meri khismat se in ke teer bhi aye Kaman hoker

"She raises and lowers her glances in playful modesty, to my good luck, the arrows of her eyes come slanted like bows (eye brows).

ABBAS ALI 'MOMIN' GULBARGAVI

He was a numberdar in the Excise Department. He attended Mushaira of Turab Yar Jung 'Turab' Zamin Kantori' and Kazim Ali 'Bagh' regularly.

Once there was a Mushaira at the residence of Zamin Kantori. Momin Gulbargavi was reciting his ghazal. 'Fani' Badaiuni was conversing with another poet. Momin stopped and addressed 'Fani' and told him that he was presenting a ghazal and said: "Listen carefully". Nobody could have dared to address 'Fani' the imam of the poets and respected tutor in this manner.

Momin Gulbargavi was quite flamboyant and stormy in presenting ghazal. His smallest ghazal contained no less than 250 verses. His long ghazal crossed 800 verses. Once he recited a ghazal which had 42 exordiums.

Zamin Kantori told Ali Akhtar in a mushaira that he could never compose lines which 'Momin' Gulbargavi wrote. He wrote one couplet on the mirror. Zamin Kantori considered this verse as the best of the verses written so far on the mirror :

Aina un ke mukhabil hai khuda khair kare
Ghar mein khatil ke bhi khatil hai khuda khair kare

"May God save us, there is an assassin in the house of an assassin. By God the mirror is opposite her."

MAQDOM MOHI UDDIN

Osmania Unviersity should be proud of this great poet of Hyderabad. His poetry was full of joy. This can be assessed from the titles of his poems. Such as, Piladoshala (yellow shawl). Intezar (the anxious wait) Jawani (youth) and Sagar ke kinare (on the banks of a lake) etc. Later certain incidents in his life made him change the themes of his the theme of his poetry. He wrote poems with revolutionary fervour. The following two verses indicate his passion for a better world :

Hayat le ke chalo kainat le ke chalo
Chalo to sare zamane ko sath le ke chalo

"Move on with life, Move on with the universe.
And in this onward march take the entire world with you".

Insan rah sake koi aisa jahan bhi hai
Is fitna zar mein koi asman bhi hai

"Is there any world worthy of human existence.
Has this querulous earth any sky."

Maqdoom with the ardour of a revolutionary yearned for a new era to dawn where there is no inequality and oppression where human beings live in freedom with discipline, dignity and harmony. Referring to the poet's role in the conflict between the oppressor and the oppressed he said:

Kya main is rizam ka khamoosh tamashai banu
Kya main jannath ko jahannum ke hawale kardun

"Should I remain a silent onlooker in this war.
Should I surrender heaven to hell?"

The great disparity between the haves and the have-nots leaves the poet restless, even in the rare moments of relaxation and pleasure in his personal life.

Khilwath-e-Rangeen mein bhi dusta hai youn duniya ka hall
Jaise peete waqt bhooke bal bachon ka khayal

"Even in my colourful solitude the condition of the world comes upon me with a serpent-like hiss and so afflicts me.

While drinking wine the thought of hungry and starving children haunts me. He depicts the state of the society wherein the oppressor is all powerful and the victim is in a condition of perpetual subjection and in suppressed anger.

Khaid hai khaid ki myad nahin
Jor hai jor ki pharyad nahin dad Nahin

"A prisoner serves an indefinite sentence, there is no complaint or cry".

Dil ke taikhanay men baroot bichi ho jaise
Ek ek sans pe dil hai ke sulga jayega

"The cellars of the heart are, as it were, filled with ammunition wherein each breath sparks the heart into flames".

SAHIBZADA MOHD. ALI KHAN 'MAIKASH"

He was another distingished poet from the Osmania University.

His first collection entitled 'Girya o Tabassum' has been published. He was a subtle prose writer. He had a restless heart with sparks of love. He died at a young age. He had a mastery over romantic type of ghazals.

Un ki ankhen hain maikada 'Maikash'
Jam ka intezar kaun kare

"Oh, 'Maikash' (drinks of wine), her eyes are the tavern of wine, who would now wait for the goblet?"

Roz marte hain roz jeete hein
Khwhish-i-marg teri umr daraz

"Every day we die, every day we live long live the desire for death."

UMRAO MIRZA 'NADAN'

He was the nephew of 'Dagh'. He had compiled a diwan but misplaced it. One of his following verses was recited by the late Umar Yafi in the presence of Baba-i-Urdu Maulvi Abdul Haq.

Wuh tur phur tabiyat wuh ghuse ka alam
Wuh shoal bhabuka si surat kisi ki

"With irritable temper and angry disposition
The face is all fire and flame".

Perhaps this verse is also composed by "Nadan".

Na mein samja na ap aye kahein se
Pasina ponchiye apni jabin se

"Neither have I understood, nor have you emerged from any where, better wipe out the sweat from your forehead".

JAVID AKHTAR 'NAZR'

He was famous as 'Nazr' Hyderabadi. When he commenced writing poetry he was a pupil of Ansari. He was acclaimed in the mushairas all over India. After reaching Pakistan, he was swarmed by writers. He was affable and friendly and met a premature death.

He wrote thus in his lyrical style:

Hagayagh jis qadr nazromen uriyan hote jate hein
Ye hastiaur mubham aur mubham hoti jati hai

"As truths become more and more revealing to the perceiving eye life becomes more and more unclear and uncertain".

SIKANDER ALI 'WAJD'

He was one of the most popular and creative poets of Hyderabad. In 1944 his first collection entitled 'Lahu Tarang' was published. His well-known poems Taj Mahal, Ajanta and Alisagar were written when he was only a student. A verse from Taj Mahal is very famous.

Jadu nigah-i-ishq ka patther pe chal gaya
Ulfat ka khwab khalib-i-marmar men dhal gaya

"The magic of love so affected the stone.
The lover's dream turned real in the marble mould.

The other couplet relates to the philosophy of living.

Weh kisi cheez ka mohtaj nahin
Jis ko jeena ka huner ata hai

"One who knows the art of living is never dependent on any thing".

POETS OF DECCANI LANGUAGE

The Deccani language means, the language spoken in the villages of the Deccan, which is quite intelligible compared to the "old Deccani language". Its construction and style are different. Its idioms and proverbs are distinct and the accent of words and pronunciation are different. As a result of its sweetness, delicacy and elegance, the language enjoys a special position in the genre of poetry.

It is said that the literature of a country reflects its times. This applies to Deccani poetry, which gives a true picture of society and environment of that period. The poetry of the Deccani language is very close to life. In it the ethical and the positive side of life is more prominent than just romance.

The poets of the Deccani language after a close

observation of living conditions and surroundings represented in their verses virtues and failings of society its weaknesses and strengths. They could be called poets of the masses in the real sense of the term through their satirical compositions. They made people realise their weaknesses. The folk songs are the best examples of Deccani poems.

'ALI' SAHIB MIYAN

His name was Gulam Ali, an old student of the Osmania University and a goalkeeper in the football team of Osmania Eleven. Though innocent looking, he was very mischievous. As a goal keeper in a football match, he felt that it was against his self respect to stop an easy ball. He remained in his position and the ball went inside the net. The crowds were surprised and the captain of the team came and asked him: "What is the matter? Gulam Ali replied innocentlv: "Why should I stop when the other ten players had left it, ". He also took part in dramas. He was a successful actor. His collection "Ghokru ke kante" has already been published. He was the first poet having a diwan among the poets of Deccani language. Following are some of the verses from his poem 'Shair':

Hat se kuch nain huwa to shari karne lage
Aashiqi to ghar ki kheti hai gire charne lage
Rat din pi kha ko tul rahna to un ki shan hai
Haur khuda se dur ho jana bada eman hai

Kai men bhi tang char men chouthe ka shouq
Zindagi "badbaghalon" ki muflisi gardan ka tauq
Gar hamen maktab huwahaur gar hamen mulla milien
Kar-i-tiflan sab tamam billiyanhaj ko chale

"People started writing poetry when they had nothing

else to do. Falling in love was their favourite hobby and they indulged in that pastime. They feel proud for being idle, spending day and night in enjoyment. Keeping themselves away from God is their faith. Interfering in other's affairs and forming their own groups are their hobby. Their life is just like that of a 'badbaghal' with poverty as a chain round their necks. Had we gone to a school and learnt from religious tutors (Mullas), we would have forsaken childish activities and undertaken Haj pilgrimage like the proverbial cat."

SARWAR KHAN 'DANDA'

He was a student of the Deccan Art School. His humour had a flavour all its own. A mushaira was organised under the sadarat (presidentship) of Chief Minister Sanjeeva Reddy in which Sarwar 'danda' recited the poem entitled 'Sanjeeva Reddy Mama' which became very popular. Two verses read thus:

Talim nahin so bachche niklenge kaise achche
Inko elam sikhana Sanjeeva Reddy Mama
'Dande' ki shairi men police ki diary men
stop hai na kama Sanjeeva Reddy Mama

"How do you expect the children to be good without education, Sanjeeva Reddy Mama, you have to educate them. Oh' Sanjeeva Reddy Mama, in the poetry of 'Danda' as in the diary of the police, there is neither a full stop nor a comma."

'RAHIM' SAHIB MIYAN

He was employed in the office of the Executive Council. In the beginning, he wrote serious verses. He had adequate command over prosody. His poem 'Chionti aur Insan' became famous. Later, he wrote humorous verses in Deccani. Later he started writing colloquial poetry.

Gup chup ako hallu se zanjeer khat khatian
Dil dhad gaya mera huwa khatka tabich mujhe

"When the door was quietly knocked, my heart pounded within me as I was afraid of this very moment."

NAZIR 'DAHQHANI'

His famous poems are Musa nadi ki kahani (story of Musa river), Watan ke liye (for country's sake), Mahbub ka sarapa (the profile of the beloved), Khairat (charity), Amir o gharib (Rich and poor). In his compositions, besides humour, there is sarcasm. His poetry is tape recorded and preserved by his admirers. A few years ago he visited Hyderabad Deccan. The fake news of his passing away was published in newspapers in Karachi. When he returned, it came to light that he got married in Hyderabad. He was reduced virtually to a skeleton but still was very cheerful and spirited.

Wuh ankhiyan men ankhiyan mila koch choray
Mere dil ke duniya hila koch choday
Main milne gaya to rula kuch choday
Mahabbat ki kahani suna koch choday
Bade ghag hans hans ko 'Dahgani' hazrat
Hateli men janat bata koch choday

She looked into my eyes and shook my heart. When I went to meet her, she made me cry by forcing her love story on me. She was so crafty that she smiled and smiled deluding 'Dahqani' with pipe dreams of paradise.

COMPOSITIONS OF WOMEN POETS
SARA BEGUM

She was a teacher in the Mahbubia Girls School.

"Yun sama jao meri nazroon mein
phir koi dusra sama na sake
"So fill my eyes with your presence so that none else can take your place."

LATIF UNISSA BEGUM

She wrote nazm, ghazal and rubaiyat.

Unchi hai har yek ouj se pasti apni
Aflak ke us par basti apni
Duniyan ne bahot hum ko sataya lekin
Utri na in turshiyon se masti apni

"My lowness is higher than every eminence. Beyond your skies is my habitat.

I have been troubled much by the world but no amount of pain has been able to lower my dignity and pride".

ANNESA HAROON BEGUM 'SHERWANI'

Be talab de to kya zarurat hai
Talab-i-muda' a kare koi

"Where is the need to supplicate when he gives us unasked."

JEHAN BANU BEGUM

Arzo o sama hai adna karishma karim ka
Kaun o makan hai jalwa Mohammed ka Meem ka
"Earth and sky are but small wonders of God's creation
The splendour of M or Mohammed pervades every nook and corner of universe."

NAUSHABA KHATOON

She is a poet who wrote a number of poem.

Following is the couplet from her ghazal:

Hai junnon tera naya paida naya virana kar
Waqf-i-jaulani khudara najd ka sahra na kar

"With your new mania create a new retreat. Enjoy the beatific solitude, but by God, don't turn a high land into a desert."

NOOR UNISA BEGUM 'NOOR'

Her compositions are mostly 'eulogies'. The following is an exquisite quatrain:

Ajab arzoo hai ajab justaju hai
Use yad karne ki is dil ko khu hai
Farishto hato guftagu Rab se hogi
Koi ba wazu ho ke ab khibla ru hai

"It is a strange desire and a wonderful search, my heart is ever attuned to remembering Him. I am ready to perform Namaz (prayer facing the kaba) after ablutions. Oh angels, keep away, now I will have a dialogue with Rab (God).

PART – IV

ARCHAEOLOGY MONUMENTS

CHAPTER – XVII

SALARJUNG MUSEUM

Nawab Mir Yusuf Ali Khan (Salar Jung III) was born in 1889 in the House of the Prime Minister of Hyderabad State. Zahir Ahmed observed "but for the timely birth of his son Nawab Yusuf Ali Khan in 1889, the sole relic left of the great Salar Jung family, the very name 'Salar Jung' would have been lost" (Life's Yesterdays, Thacker and Co. Ltd., Bombay, 1945 p. 162). When Salar Jung was only a year old, his mother died. Nawab Yousuf Ali Khan, to his misfortune, lost not only his father when he was a year old but also his uncle, Nawab Munir ul Mulk, guardian of the infant Salar Jung. The Salar Jung estate then was placed under the supervision of Zinath Unnisa Begum Sahiba, mother of Sir Salar Jung-I who died in 1895. Thereafter, the royal family supervised the management of the estate, as no adult member of the family survived. A Royal Firman was issued by the Nizam for the formation of a Committee, which comprised Raja Sheoraj, Nawab Imam Nawaz Jung and Capt. F. Dean, Later in 1890 by a Royal Firman, Mir Mahbub Ali Khan Nizam VI nominated Nawab Bahram u Daula, brother-in-law of Salar Jung II as the Chairman of the Committee.

As the Nizam was not satisfied with the Committee's management of the estate, he appointed a Commission consisting of Mr. A.J. Dunlop and Nawab Akbar Jung, to inquire into the finances of the estate. In 1894 Raja Lalta

Pershad was selected Director of the estate who worked under the direction of the Revenue Secretary, A.J. Dunlop. Raja Lalta Pershad worked hard to the entire satisfaction of the ruler.

Salar Jung III was appointed to the post of Prime Minister at the age of 23. As a Prime Minister, Salar Jung III worked with great zeal and sincerity and aspired to emulate the life and work of his renowned grand father. In 1913, Lord Harding, the Viceroy, visited Hyderabad. In raising the toast of the health of the Nizams, at a State banquet, the Viceroy said.

"I trust your new minister, the third Salar Jung, will maintain the high traditions of his family and that he will prove as strong a support and assistance to your Highness as his grand father, the famous Salar Jung" (Dharmendra Prasad, the Salar Jungs, 1896. p. 68). After three years, for personal reasons, Salar Jung III resigned from the post.

He died on March 2, 1949 without leaving any issue. In order to decide the cases relating to the inheritance of his jagirs and his wealth, a high level Committee was set up under the Chairmanship of Nawab Mehdi Nawaz Jung. Nawab Salarjung – III was a man of learning and a great patron of art. He gave Rs.1,00,000 to the Aligarh University as a grant. He patronized many Urdu magazines and was associated with many literary societies. The collection of rare objects was his most precious possession. To look after this valuable collection the 'Salar Jung Museum Board' was set up. Mehdi Nawaz Jung was appointed President. The Board decided that the life time collection of art objects and curios of the late Nawab Sahib should be handed over to the Government for the formation of a unique national museum. Hence, a large portion of the palace of Salar Jung with six acres of land was handed over to the Government of Andhra Pradesh to house the fabulous collection.

The Government also acquired additional four acres of land and gave a grant of Rs.5,00,000. The Government of India announced a grant of one million rupees. Thereafter, the planning of this magnificent museum commenced involving an outlay running into several crores.

The museum was established in the palace of Salar Jung and was opened to the public in 1951. On July 23, 1963 it was declared a National Institute when Pandit Jawaharlal Nehru the Prime Minister of India on the occasion of laying the foundation stone observed.

> "This museum in all respects is unique in itself. This is only one person's collection and the biggest art wealth in the world. It is reckoned among the most popular museums".

It was planned that on completion of the scheme the museum would be shifted to a suitable grand building under construction which would also be used as a training centre in the art of museology. Its library would be open for research particularly in the art of museology.

As a unique specimen of the civilization and culture of the Asafia Dominion, only a cursory sketch of the art collection can be given.

It was the sincere desire of the late Salar Jung that a new building of 300 rooms should be constructed in which all the rare pieces could be permanently exhibited but his ambition was not fulfilled in his lifetime. Salar Jung was very fond of collecting different art pieces. Nature had endowed Salar Jung with a genius to examine and differentiate between the original and the fake, between a inferior and a superior art object. He had prodigious memory as he remembered what he purchased and where, as well and the valuable antiques. Because of this burning passion he spent most of his time in travelling far and wide. Whenever he liked anything, he purchased it at the price demanded. Renowned traders with costly items from all over the world visited him to strike a bargain and went back happily. His fame as a collector of art objects had spread in the country and abroad. Any one, offering family heirlooms for sale in India, would be in touch with him and would first intimate him. Foreign art dealers like Christies and Sotheby of London knew him very well and frequently informed him about the availability of rare objects and dispatched their catalogues. While sitting in his palace, he would make a minute and detailed study with his magnifying glass and at times made purchases through telephone calls. His last consignment was a set of ivory chairs, said to be of Tipu Sultan of Mysore, which unfortunately he could not see since it was received after his sad demise. His style of purchasing articles was very unusual. Whenever, any trader came along, his companions and advisors closely inspected the goods and wrote the price on slips of paper. If the price was acceptable to the traders then the deal would be finalised promptly.

As Salar Jung had no issue, a Committee of trustees was appointed to look after his wealth and property. Some of the articles owned by him were preserved at Saroornagar and in the city palaces.

BIGGEST MUSEUM OF ASIA

A person cherishes the dream of a lifetime or ardently desires to realize it. The late Salar Jung was one of those fortunate persons whose dream was fulfilled in the form of the Salar Jung Museum which is now world famous and is regarded as the biggest museum in Asia today. The art of the East and the West and unique specimens of art and paintings which were collected from Iran, Turkey, Burma, China, Japan and from the different parts of India were arranged in a 200 year old palace, in one of its portions.

This palace consisted of big verandas and rooms. Coloured bulbs and beautiful lanterns lit up the rooms.

As one enters the palace, right in front, the eye cannot miss a big beautiful cistern in the centre of the large and ide courtyard, whose fountains lend enchantment to the scene. On all sides of the cistern, exquisite marble statues have been placed to highlight the artistic environment. In the veranda, two rooms are covered with mirrors. One room is called small glass house and the other the big glass house. The walls and even the roofs have large mirrors.

These big rooms house jade and glass items. In the verandas the marble statues seem to be so placed that they seem to welcome the visitors. One lifelike statue particularly stands out. It is a stone carving by an Italian sculptor. A lady after a bath is seen ready to cover herself with a sheet of cloth. At some places the sheet covering the body appears to be wet and gives the appearance of drops of water about to fall from her ringlets. The superb workmanship is indeed sovividly close to reality that the viewers are simply stunned by the sight.

The two statues made by the Italian sculptor are unique. One of these statues was purchased by the late Salar Jung to heighten the aesthetic content of his museum. Millions of rupees were offered to him for the sale of this particular statue but he refused to part with it. The other statue was made by Benzoni in 1876. A beautiful well-shaped woman is seen covering herself with a cloth and each fold of the cloth gives the impression of freshness and has a life like appearance.

In one of the backside verandas of the palace, a beautiful big clock, three feet wide and four feet long, still glitters like gold. Its beautiful embellishments heighten its beauty and in the center is a round dial. The scene on the upper portion of the dial is simply fascinating. On the left side, a beautiful small hut is seen with a tree in front of it. A small round piece of brass hangs over the branch of the tree. People flock to see the wonderful clock. No sooner the hand of the clock touches the figure twelve, the door of the hut opens and a man with a hammer slowly raises his foot and moves towards a tree and strikes a bell to announce the time and returns to the hut. The door of the hut gets shut. The crowds begin to disperse. They will again gather there just before the bell strikes.

Zuyo, the historian, has stated in the Urdu Digest of July 1968, that the rare clock is a testimony to the skill of Arabs. It was sent to the King of France as a gift by Caliph Haroon-ul-Rasheed. In 807 H. Haroon ul Rasheed sent a clock to the Catholic King, Charlemagne which was considered magical by his courtiers. Charlemagne and his companions were surprised to see the clock. In his court, nobody was capable of understanding the mechanism of the clock". An astonishing art was hidden in the clock of Haroon ul Rasheed. Exactly at one o'clock a rider emerged from the clock, at twelve o' clock, another rider at two o'clock, and so on at every hour. For every hour one rider was added.

No sooner does one enter the rooms than the finest artistic patterns emerge. The costly carpets and the beautiful colour combination of velvet add charm to the unmatched design one sees around the life size portraits of Salar Jung.

In 30 rooms and varandas innumerable art objects are exhibited namely, Irani carpets, specimens of Rajput and Deccani paintings, living examples of artistic skill of modern painters, masnads with gold embroidery, Kashmiri shawls, metal utensils of South India, beautiful printed designs of Malabar and Madurai, bidri work, ivory and decorative marble articles.

In one room, the memorials of the Mughal period are beautifully decorated and kept in almirahs. The diamond studded ring of Noor Jahan, costly daggers of Jahangir, Shah Jahan and Noor Jahan with their handles studded with rubies and diamonds dazzle the eyes. A twenty-four feet long golden cloth which is made of fine gold wires dazzles the eye. A carpet with the finest ivory work is a thing of beauty.

Another fancy item is the betel leaves box of Queen

Noor Jahan. One is astonished at the technique on the lid of the filigree work of the silver betel-box which is five inch in length and 3 ½ inch in breadth. There is another small lid in which tobacco was kept. When the small upper lid is opened, a grayish enamelled dove raising its head picks a grain and when the lid is closed, it quietly lies down.

One room is full of silver jewellery and accessories which adorned the horses and elephants at the time of the royal procession of Asafia rulers and princes. The big silver Pan-dans (a box in which betel leaves and its accessories are kept) reflect the elegance of the Asafia palaces. There is another betel dish which covers an engraved silver spittoon and beautiful filigree boxes in which pans were kept.

One room is reserved for jade items. On view is the 'goblet' of Jahangir, besides a variety of utensils, cups and saucers. There are utensils in which poisoned food could be immediately detected.

Salar Jung's range of interest embraced art and paintings. There are no less than ten rooms and verandas which display the finest masterpieces of distinguished artists.

Four special photographs with the traditional glimpse of the Mughal period from the album of Shah Jahan are unique. In some of these beautiful paintings one can see Mughal Princes on hunting expedition and a Mughal Princess is seen enjoying the fireworks scene. On one Mughal photograph "Atish Bazi", the signature of Emperor Jahangir is inscribed. The photograph of Emperor Aurangazeb on ivory is matchless for its unique artistry. Photograph of Nizam Ali Khan's procession of hunting can also be seen. These scenes of the 17th century are not unfamiliar. Along with the patterns of Rajput and Kangra art, there are many other rare paintings. The wide range covers painting in water colours and oil paintings. One painting focusses on a scene at a highway and on the other side, there is a splendid view of a magnificent building. One feels as he moves on that he is actually walking along the same road.

The photographs of G.P. Watt are vivid and lifelike. One section is devoted to masterpieces of paintings. As one gets along the staircase, ancient swords, shields, armoured garments of different periods are displayed, a reminder of the history of ancient traditional methods of warfare from the later Mughal period to Abdul Hasan Tanashah, Tipu Sultan and the Marathas. These garments seemed to be woven with chains that could withstand any attack by the swordsmen.

There are also specimens of western paintings. Among them, is that of a dog guarding the belongings of its master. This painting is indeed a work of art. The eyes have a particular attraction and from which ever side one sees, the eyes seem to be riveted on the viewer.

There are also beautiful paintings of:

Watts – Orpheus Eurydice
Theseus's – Ariadne Abandoned
Cooper's – Cattle in repose.

These attract those who are fond of Western paintings. They are all done in ancient and modern style. The finest masterpiece of oil paintings is "The Last Sacrament' in which the painter Mantannano had brightened the daylight and the light of the lamp by his expert touch.

Ten big rooms are decorated with the finest masterpieces of Japanese art and handicrafts. All these are studded with Nikko furniture, silk embroidered scenes, beautiful screen pagoda sculpture carved on ivory vases.

A day is not enough to see these wonderful pieces of art. Those who see it once, always regret for not having seen it in detail.

The exhibits of Indian woodwork are kept in a separate room. The 19th century memorials, the idols of the temples of Madurai, engraved tables and chairs and almirahs are well displayed. The finest furniture from all over the world is also on display. Handicrafts and art objects from different countries should not be missed. The selection of excellent furniture by Salar Jung III is considered one of the remarkable features of the museum. The European furniture of the 17th and 18th centuries, is placed side by side with excellent sofa sets, tables, chairs, dressing tables from India, China, Burma, Turkey, Egypt and Thailand. Excellent specimens of fine worksmanship of wooden furniture manufactured at Nirmal and Baiganpally are also on display. A rare piece of wooden work is a beautiful model of the Madurai temple in wood and a wooden fan manufactured in Madurai. The European furniture manufactured during the early period of Queen Anne and Queen Victoria attracts attention. Another rare piece of furniture is a set of four ivory chairs of Tipu Sultan matchless for their beauty and design. This was the last item to be purchased by Nawab Salar Jung.

The Louis XI furniture and the four ivory chairs were presented by Louis XI to Tipu Sultan as a gift. Brass and ivory idols of Chinese Gods and Goddesses, vases of various designs, the superior glass samples of ancient Chinese artistic skill can also be viewed. Two rooms and large verandas are decorated with numerous cut glass items.

The finest woodwork masterpiece is a rare statue done by an Italian artist. As soon as one enters the room, one can see a Mephistopheles standing in a dignified manner in his peculiar military dress. When viewed in a mirror behind it, one feels that Margaretta is standing at the back. In fact, these two statues are carved from one wooden piece. The aim of keeping life-size mirrors is to view both the sides of items, such as, jade, glass, wood and brass. Besides these beautiful vases, other innumerable decorative pieces are also on view. The great art connoisseur that Salar Jung was, his exquisite taste is reflected in the selection of various items of art and craft.

In one of the rooms, the royal dresses of the Mughal period with exquisite work of gold and silver laces are beautifully laid out. Among these constumes are Pishwaz (a type of gown) of NoorJahan, Salim Shahi slippers, angarkhas, dastars and Tipu Sultan's cap.

The library of this museum has a big collection of rare manuscripts and books. There are nearly 9650 books, out of which 2459 are in Arabic, 4146 in Persian, 1045 in Hindi and Urdu. Most of them are also rare manuscripts of the Holy Quran. An entire Quran has been written on one page or on gilded papers. There are 308 books in bulky volumes, on calligraphy, kitabat and religious sciences of ancient and modern times. The writings of the Holy Quran are either in the Arabic script, or in the form of verses. Some are in the Roman script.

There is a separate room for children, in which an entire army, train, dolls and toys of animals are decorated in glass cases. The museum is broadly divided in four parts: East, West, Library and children's section. In 1963, in an area of ten acres, Pandit Jawaharlal Nehru, the then Prime Minister of India, laid the foundation stone of the new building of the museum. The present building of SalarJung Museum is situated on the banks of the Musi. The museum was shifted to the new building in 1968. It is arranged on the principles of museology. It is equipped with modern lighting arrangements, a conservtion laboratory, with trained staff, artists, designers and guides. Electronic equipment has been installed to ensure security. TV cameras are also in use. It has an Education Section which holds seminars, lectures and exhibitions. The Engineering Section looks after the building and maintenance of the museum and electrical engineers attend to the generators and airconditioning.

The untiring efforts and refined taste of the late Salar Jung laid the foundation of the museum. It enjoys the status of a National Museum since 1959. It is certainly not only the biggest museum in Asia but also the finest memorial to the civilization and culture of Hyderabad.

CHAPTER – XVIII

ARCHAEOLOGY

THE BACKGROUND OF ARCHAEOLOGY IN DECCAN

It may be said that the Bahamani Kingdom started declining from 1481, when Mahmood Gawan was assassinated. The life of Mahmood Gawan was a puzzle for the historians. He was the only person, whom a group of historians considered a great martyr and benefactor of the kingdom, and the other group held him responsible for the decline of the Bahamani kingdom mainly due to his political policies. But the startling fact is that the death of Mahmood Gawan divided the large kingdom of the Bahmanies into five parts. There were five kingdoms in the Deccan namely, Imad Shahi (Berar), Nizam Shahi (Ahmednagar), Adil Shahi (Bijapur), Barid Shahi (Bidar) and Qutub Shahi (Golconda). Among these five, Nizam Shahi, Adil Shahi and Qutub Shahi kingdoms have great significance. The monuments of Nizam Shahi are bounded by Ahmednagar and Khadki (Aurangabad), while Golconda and Bidar come under the Nizam's territory. Since the Adil Shahi archaeological monuments are included in the Asaf Jahi kingdom, they merit study. Here we will deal only with the Nizam Shahi monuments.

The Nizam Shahi monuments can be divided into two periods. The first covers the period from Ahmed Nizam ul Mulk to Malik Amber. The second is the Ambari period. During the period of Ahmed Nizam ul Mulk, in Bir district, the excellent arrangements for the supply of water, construction of buildings, tombs and gardens are worth mentioning. Malik Amber made Khadki the capital of the Nizam Shahi Kingdom. He built the city and constructed the Ambari canals. Ghulam Ahmed Khan observes, "The most remarkable work of Malik Amber, for which his name has become a household word, is the ingenious system of water supply which he provided to the city. A canal, taken from a river about five miles from the city, consists of a series of a aqueducts with ventilating shafts of masonary. It serves the needs of the city even to the present day by the simple process of gravitation. 'The Rise and Decline of the city of Aurangabad, 1945, p. 221). Kali mosque and Bhadkal gate deserve special mention.

On the other hand, if we look at Bijapur, it is the treasure house of Deccani architecture. In 1484, Bijapur became the seat of the Adil Shahi rulers. Under Ibrahim Adil Shah, it attained a high watermark of progress and prosperity. The Sultan was a patron of learning and fine arts and he was passionately fond of music and singing. During his period many notable buildings including Gol Gumbaz were constructed. There are a number of buildings at Bijapur such as Gagan Mahal, Asar Mahal, Mahtar Mahal, grand wells, Jan baowli, Jama Masjid and numerous mosques and tombs. Ibrahim's Rouza, replica of the is a Taj Mahal, and among the world's tallest, is Bolti Gumbad, Arrangement of water supply and several other monuments bear the stamp of expert craftsmanship. The fort of Bijapur, which is a specimen of the finest Islamic architecture and its grand towers and the moat which cannot be crossed are in themselves outstanding monuments.

During the Barid Shahi period, the Bidar fort and high

rise domes of the Barid Shahi rulers are worth mentioning.

In the South, under the Qutub Shahi rule Golconda and Hyderabad, represent a special style of architecture.

The Golconda Fort is situated six miles west of Hyderabad, and has a history of more than 200 years. Also known as Mohammad Nagar it is built on a rocky edge 400 feet above the land. The fort is surrounded by strong crenellated stone walls, over three miles in circumfrence with 87 bastions at the angles. Some of these still contain large pieces of ordinances bearing Persian inscriptions. These buildings, though constructed of granite, have suffered from the ravages of time and the damage caused by the siege guns of Aurangzeb. Earlier the fort had eight doors. But now only four remain, Meca darwaza, Banjara darwaza, Jamali darwaza and Fateh Darwaza. These doors are made of teak wood with sharp pointed hooks, so that the elephants could not damage them in war.

The high rise Bala Hissar itself is a fort which had many offices. The renowned "Tana Shah Ki gadi", seat of Tanashah, is the two storeyed building situated on the highest peak of the hill, where Tahashah stayed during the last siege of Golconda.

Naginabagh was located on the right side of the Balahissar. There were very good arrangements for water supply. Water was supplied to each storey of the Royal palace. The ruins of the palaces are found just opposite the Nagina garden.

Between the Musa bridge and Fateh darwaza, there are ruins of a number of grand buildings. Among them, the palace of the Diwan still exists in good condition. Masjid Safa was constructed by the founder of the dynasty. The foundation of the new fort was laid during the period of Abdullah Qutub Shah.

The fort actually was an iron fort which could not be damaged by gun fire when the Mughal army of Aurangzeb attacked it. The Qutub Shahi monuments include Charminar, Jama Masjid, Mecca Masjid and Darul Shafa, number of palaces, such as, Dad Mahal, Gagan Mahal, Hussaini Mahal, Char Mahal, Gosha Mahal, Padshahi Ashurkhana and domes. A number of gardens were laid out around the city as a special feature. Also the Qutub Shahs constructed many tanks for the storage of water, such as, Hussain Sagar, Budwall and Ibrahimpatan.

THE POLITICAL AND CULTURAL RISE OF BAHMANI DYNASTY

The period of Ahmed Shah Wali Bahmani lasted till the tenure of Mohad. Shah Lashkari. Bidar was the cradle of civilization and culture till the fall of the Bahmani dynasty. This was a prominent centre of Islamic architecture, and art. The entire city was divided into four parts which is still remembered as Char Mahalle (four wards) or chowpal (a place for the public meeting of the village people), namely talim, minar talim, siddi talim and Noor Khan talim.

It should be remembered that education in those days meant in particular training in gymnasium the division of wards indicates its military character. In the South-West of the city, the Arak Fort was situated. Inside the fort there are royal palaces and four cabins. Besides the fortification of the fort, the entire city is surrounded by many strong towers and gates. The domes of the Bahmani rulers and the school of Mahmood Gawan are the two monuments which are worthy of special mention. These domes are situated outside the city in which, the most magnificent dome is that of Ahmed Shah Wali Bahmani. After Mohd. Shah Lashkari, the size of the domes became smaller. The dome of the last king, Kalim Ullah, was virtually a small circle. This decline reminds us of Iqbal's poetic line.

"Ye kabhi gauhar, kabhi shabnam, kabhi ansoo huwa"

This sometimes became a pearl, a dew and sometimes

a tear (becoming smaller and smaller).

The greatest cultural achievement of Bidar is the school of Mahmood Gawan. This school was the centre of sciences in its time and considered as important as the universities of Baghdad, Qahira and Khartba. Learned scholars from all over the world came here. The construction of the building was done on the lines of a residential university, which had three storeys, with classrooms and residential rooms for students. Mahmood Gawan constructed the school in two years nine months during the period of Mohd. Shah Lashkari. The year of construction is also interesting, which is adopted from a verse of the Holy Quran 'Rasna Taqabal Mana'. Through this, the year is assumed 876 H which meant 1469 A.D.

The area of the building, its grandeur and height were a matter of pride to the people. They wondered how such a huge building could be constructed in such a short period, and how it could have such embellishments. This building is situated from East to West. On the front side, there is a big arch which is the entrance gate. Inside the building is a courtyard and on all sides there is a three storeyed building. If the drawing of this building and its execution is examined carefully then it can clearly be surmised that the foundtion of Islamic style of construction was based on unity. In the front portion on both the sides of the schools there are towers, one of which had fallen due to lightning, another remained in its original condition and resembles the Chand Minar of Daulatabad. Apparently Chand Minar of Daulatabad is the victory tower of Allauddin II and the Mahmood Gawan school was constructed during the period of the third generation of the founder of Chand Minar. In the architecture of the tower, the special style of Bahmanis is found, which is not found anywhere else. Thre are two big Mihrabs (pulpits) on both sides of the school courtyard. In fact, this is the half portion of the incomplete dome. Similarly, one mihrab is situated right in front of the arch of the main door at the end of the courtyard. Even today an observer could easily make out from these mihrabs that these were the lecture halls of the school. The rooms made for the lodging of the students inside the school are complete in all respects for the convenience of the students. The front wall was decorated with glazed tiles on which Quranic verses were written.

This building is the best example of the Bahmani style of architecture. The 'Madrassa' was in a flourishing condition during the time of Farishta, staffed by professors and divines from distant courtries of Asia equipped with a library of 3000 manuscripts "(K.K. Mudiuraj, p.341).

THE DOME OF ALI BARID

Among the Barid Shahi domes, the dome of Ali Barid is worthy of praise. This dome is unique for its high elevation and extremely simple architecture. There is no apparent progress in the style of construction. From the cultural point of view, the interesting feature of this dome, is that the rubaiyat of Hazrath Shaikh Farid uddin Attar are written in Kashi Kari or with the help of glazed tiles. But since in Kashi Kari small tiles are placed and fixed, effort was made to bring them in a straight line and in a right angle. In this manner, we can easily judge that our usual mode of Persian writing, which is based on the beauty of curved letters, cannot be confined in the geometrical letters and angles of typing. This is the reason why the efforts of the usual Persian type practically proved unsuccessful.

Bidar was the centre of Islamic industries, and famous for the manufacture of arms, guns, textiles and for other cottage industries. Hence, even today the utensils of the Bidri industries with gold and silver work are famous. The chief feature of the Deccan is that the arts and crafts were in the hands of Hindus, whereas the himru of Aurangabad and paper industry was entirely in the hands of Muslims. Bidri work is still carried on in other places but with regard to technique, there is no equal to the Bidri work even today.

DEPARTMENT OF ARCHAEOLOGY – PROFESSIONAL EXCELLENCE

The Dominion of Hyderabad was rich in archaeological monuments. There are memorials from the Hijri era to the human civilization of every period. In the abundance of monuments, there is no State comparable to Hyderabad.

STANDARD OF WORKING OF THE DEPARTMENT

After a few years of the establishment of the Department of Archaeology, scholars and artists of the world desired to see the archaeological monuments, the manner in which these monuments were arranged. The excellent manner in which these monuments were preserved and cared merited attention and appreciation not only in India but also the world over. Percy Brown in his famous book "Indian Architecture" had quoted Justice Imle, of the Calcutta High Court thus:

"The smallest department of the Dominion of Hyderabad is perhaps Archaeology, but this Department appears to me the biggest among all the Departments. The preservation and care of monuments was done so methodically that it was not even done in British India. It will be a good idea if the Government of India entrusts the monument arrangements to be under the control of the Nizam's Government, because, the Department has adequate knowledge to keep the monuments in perfect condition." It was a practice in Hyderabad to send its officers for training to British India. The reputation of the Department of Archaeology was high and the grandeur of the annual reports of Archaeology was rare unlike the reports of other Departments. These reports were not merely abstracts of the annual performance of work, administration, statistics and receipts and disbursements, but there were separate books on archaeology, which contained useful material for the research students. The renowned authors and scholars of Europe had made references to these reports in their books.

Excavations were made by this Department at Muski, Kondapur, Hashmatpet and other places. In these excavations, objects like old coins, pots, jars clay idols, toys, seals teeth and horn jewellery, monuments of buildings, naval instruments, solid bricks and many other items were recovered. The stories of these monumental remains are self evident, which can be comprehended by intelligent people. These reports have been purchased in Europe and America, read and studied with great interest.

CHAPTER XIX

THE PAINTINGS OF AJANTA AND ELLORA

The ancient history is written on the rocks, stones and pillars. Hence, much has been written on the ancient civilization. If ancient civilization has to be seen then one has to go to the Ajanta caves. Ancient India breathes in these pictures. It is indeed a kaleidoscope of the fashion of the ancient people, their clothes, houses, food, utensils/ vessels, chair, stool, tools, lanes and alleys, marriage, customs, prayers, gatherings of dancing and singing, varied musical instruments, battlefield organization, the bustle of war elephants, war weapons, sea voyage, drawing of a ship, Darbars of the Rajas, adornment of women, their jewellery etc. There is nothing which is not presented here in vivid terms of the graphic world famous painting? The costumes represented in the paintings of Ajanta clearly indicate that the Hindus wore the very same dress which was the current fashion. The Greeks, who accompanied Alexander the Great to India, describing the dress stated that it consisted of two garments. —one was up to the middle of the leg, while another was folded around the shoulders.

A PIECE OF ONE SQUARE INCH IS ONE THOUSAND POUND

The Ajanta caves have seen thousands of seasons and cracks have developed in the roof from which water dripped inside and knee deep water damaged the walls and lower portions of the pillars. In fact, some pillars fell down and the pictures drawn on the walls, roofs and pillars were badly damaged. They were so badly damaged that even if one touched them they would break into pieces. At some places they fell as crust. Regrettably, no proper arrangements were made to look after them. Visitors wrote their names and carried pieces of these pictures by scratching on the walls. Captain Williams scratched one piece and took it to England. In London this one square inch piece was auctioned for one thousand pounds. This very piece is now kept in the Boston museum in America.

In short, the paintings of Ajanta were on the verge of extinction when the Government of Hyderabad thought of preserving them and incurred lavish expenditure for this purpose. It is impossible to find such an example in any other country.

Dr. Ghulam Yazdani, Director of Archaeology consulted Sir John Marshall Director-General of Archaeology of India and decided to invite experts from Italy for the preservation of these paintings. Lord Curzon also helped in this matter. Prof. Chakoni and Count Armeni were invited on a monthly salary of Rupees 12,000. Their expenses to and fro from Rome to Ajanta were borne by the Government of Hyderabad. Boarding and lodging arrangements for them were also made.

The following were the techniques used by the experts:

To apply material on the portions of paintings which were damaged from the surface.

To preserve the borders of the paintings which had developed cracks.

Mr. Garnith, who came to collect copies of the paintings in 1873 applied 'Copalwarnish' on these paintings, so that the impression could be seen clearly and preserved from moisture. This method later proved to be very expensive. In a period of few years, these paintings became dull and completely dark at some places. This varnish was washed with chemicals.

Insects which made holes in these paintings were destroyed.

The dung of bats which accumulated on these paintings for a long time was washed away.

Jogis (a scetics) and sanyasis (religious mendicants) once lived in these caves for long periods. As a result, the dust and the layer of smoke accumulated on the paintings was also removed.

The Italians spent two winter seasons in 1921 and 1922 and during this period they trained officials of the Archaeological Department. Since then the preservation work has continued which breathed a new life into these paintings.

Preservation of rock paintings for a period of 2,000 years is no ordinary matter. The surface was prepared in the manner in which rocks were made uneven and then they were filled with a solution. The solution was prepared with clay, cowdung, paddy husk and other plant fibres. A thin vacuum layer was fixed over the solution.

The colours at Ajanta, however, are still glittering. Specially the blue colour is bright and has a unique freshness about it. These ordinary colours and materials can be seen in Ajanta valley such as, chalk or white lead, soot (kajal) red chalk (Geru) yello clay, green clay and Har signar flowers. The American stone or azure is not found in India. This might have been brought from Sri Lanka or Iran. It could not be found in the mixture of colours in which glutinuous was used. In the old books on paintings, there is a mention of glue made out of Bel-giri (pulp of the bel) and animal fibre.

In the matter of research of preservation of ancient monuments the Asian region and to some extent, Europe, is indebted to the know how developed in the Nizam's Dominions. The Archaeological Department has taken great care and shown its expertise in the preservation of these all too rare and precious monuments. The preservation of the paintings of Ajanta was no easy task at the best of times.

THE BEAUTY OF STONE CARVINGS AT ELLORA

In the Nizam's Dominion, besides the temples of Ajanta, there are several Buddhist monuments, namely, the magnificent tombs of saints and places of worship at Ellora, Pital, Khore, Khatot Katch and Aurangabad. The beauty and the antiquity of stone carvings are of great importance and value. The places of worship is Pital khore and Khatot Katch were in a neglected condition. As a result, wild plants and mounds of clay made it impossible for entry into the temple. The stones of the pillars and stones above the pillars were weakened owing to the seepage of rainwater. There was every possibility of the stones falling down. These monuments now have been fully cleaned and, as a precautionary measure, new pillars have been erected. The Department had paid special attention to the Buddhist places of worship at Ellora and Aurangabad. The Department has concerned itself not only with repairs and cleanliness but has paid attention to the construction of pathways and stairs to facilitate easy communication.

KAILASH TEMPLE

The methodology used in the preservation of the Buddhist

monuments was similar to the methods adopted for the preservation of ancient monuments of other religions, whether Hindu or Jain temples or mosques, tombs and palaces. In Ellora the foremost is the Kailash temple carved in the famous Ellora caves. "Unlike any of the cave temples, Kailash is a great monolithic temple, isolated from the surrounding rocks, and has carving both outside and inside. It stands in a great court averaging 154 feet wide by 276 feet long at the level of the base, entirely cut out of solid rock, and with a scrap 107 feet high at the back. In front of this court a curtain has been left, carved on the outside with the awe inspiring forms of Lord Shiva and Vishnu and their consorts with rooms inside. It is pierced in the centre by an entrance passage, with rooms on each side. As the visitors pass their eyes are fixed on the large sculptures of Goddess Lakshmi over the lotus, with her attendant elephant. There are some letters and a date on the leaves of the lotus on which she sits, but are illegible; the temple probably belongs to the 15th century". (Archaeologial Survey Report of Western India, Vol. V). The upper portions of its door were in a very dilapidated condition and there was a possibility of its falling down. To strengthen them, iron beams have been installed but these were covered with plaster with identical cement colours, in such a way that the defects not visible. The monuments of the Brahmanical faith in Ellora have also been satisfactorily repaired and cleaned, such as, Ravan's Kai, Domarlina, Rameshwar and Dasavtar which were extremely soiled and in bad condition. They have been fully restored. The inside portions of these magnificent monuments which were made obscure and ugly by constructing weak walls were demolished and given an original touch.

CHAPTER – XX

ISLAMIC BUILDINGS : THE PLACES OF WORSHIP OF MEDIAEVAL PERIOD

The temple of Mahadeoji is situated in Jawatgi District. Raichur, the temple of Vishnav faith in Dechpalli, the Panch Ishwar temple of Pangal in Nalgonda District and the thousand pillar temple at Hanmakonda. Pratap Rudra Deva the Chalukaya ruler constructed the thousand pillar temple at Hanmankonda, which ranks, among the finest examples of Chalukyan architecture. This temple was dedicated to Lord Vishnu, Surya and Siva. A beautiful polished Linga is still seen in the temple. There also can be found splendid specimens of monolithic bulls (Nandies). The temples of Palampet are the monuments of Mediaeval Period. Large sums have been spent on the repairs and cleanliness of these valued treasures. The Palampet temple was damaged by heavy rain and by wild plants, due to a defect in the foundation. But with suitable timely planning, the roof, pillars and stone carvings have been saved. These temples are the finest specimens of the 12th century architecture of Deccan.

In the Ellora caves, among the Jain temples, the most illustrious are the carved temple of Indersabha, Jagannath Sabha and Parasnath. The Western portion of the

Indersabha was in a very precarious condition due to the fall of the rocks over a period of time. Preservation was no easy matter. One strong dyke was made taking into consideration all the technical aspects and the damaged portion of the temple has now been completely saved. The door of the temple, which was also in a weak condition, has also been repaired.

MOSQUES AND OTHER BUILDINGS

Among the other buildings, the mosque of Mubarak Khilji situated at Daulatabad Fort, Jama Masjid of Gulbarga, Masjid Bahmania known as Solah Khamb ki Masjid (Sixteen pillars Mosque) at Bidar Fort, Kali Mosque adjacent to railway station of Bidar, old Mosque of Mushirabad, and Toli Mosque near Karvansahu are fine examples of Islamic architecture. Besides repairs and maintenance of general cleanliness, efforts have been made to restore the ancient grandeur of these mosques. The roof of the Bahmani mosque of Bidar Fort had almost fallen and the flooring almost destroyed. In the courtyard of the mosque, new walls and new houses have been constructed. The magnificent memorial of the Bahmani period has been preserved for at least the next 200 years. The mosque of Mushirabad was in a similar condition and one of its towers remained tilted for quite a long period and finally it fell down. The tower was reconstructed according to the ancient style and, wherever the mortar embossing was damaged, efforts were made to restore it to its ancient glory and original condition. Since all these buildings are the finest specimens of Islamic architecture, preservation and repairs were carried out carefully and the ancient magnificence and singularities were maintained.

SEMI RELIGIOUS BUILDINGS

Among the semi religious buildings, the school of Mahmood Gawan of Bidar and Badshashi Ashurkhana of Hyderabad hold a prominent place. Badshahi Ashurkhana was built by Sultan Mohd. Quli Qutb Shah. The construction of that monument started in 1592 and was completed in 1596 at a cost of Rs.66,000. In this building the name of the then ruler is inscribed on the main arch and the monograms of his grandson, Sultan Abdulla Qutb Shah, are engraved. Karkashi has been done during the period of Sultan Abdulla Qutb Shah.

In terms of antiquity, this building is superior to the Imambaras of Calcutta and Lucknow and can be compared with the finest buildings of Lahore and Multan in conformity with the art of Chinikari (Karkashi). Perhaps these two buildings were constructed by the Irani artisans as the school of Mahmood Gawan is the only building of its style in entire India but its flat drawings and architectural style resemble the school of Isfahan (city of Central Persia). Similarly in the glass work of Badshahi Ashurkhana, the grandeur and decoration of the religious buildings of Iran and Iraq is found. The roof of the Ashurkhana which was completely destroyed was rebuilt. The weak walls and the portion of dilapidated building in the Mahmood Gawan school were repaired skillfully, which not only strengthened the building but restored its ancient elegance.

The other buildings, on which great attention was paid for their preservation are the Bahmani tombs of Gulbarga and Bidar the shrine of Adil Shahi Rulers at Gogi, the tombs of Barid Shahi Royal family of Bidar, and the Qutub Shahi tombs of Golconda.

Among these tombs, the tomb of Sultan Quli Qutub Shah, the founder of the dynasty, is very small and simple. The tomb of Sultan Jamshed Quli is two storeyed, octangular in shape and based on the Irani style. The tomb of Ibrahim Qutub Shah is comparatively bigger than the two and its dome is like a globe and its walls decorated with glazed tiles.

The tomb of Mohd. Quli Qutub Shah is more beautiful than all the other tombs of Hyderabad. The Muslim and Hindu styles of architecture have been adopted for the construction of this tomb. On the upper portion of the building there are beautiful paintings and bouquets on the gallery. The style of architecture in the tombs of Mohd. Qutub Shah, Hayat Bakshi Begum and Abdulla Qutub Shah is similar.

In the tombs, all the graves except that of Jamshed Quli Qutub Shah are in black stone. The structure of masonry work on the graves of the male members of the royal family is different from the graves of the female members of the family. The original graves are in a cellar. The passage to these cellars is closed excepting the cellar of the dome of Mohd. Quli Qutub Shah. In the construction of these graves, the Qutub Shahi style of architecture is the amalgamation of the Irani, Hindu and Pathan architecture. Each tomb has got a mosque. Salar Jung-I, during his Prime Ministership constructed an enclosure and repaired the tombs. There was a tank through which water was supplied to the fort and the garden through a canal. In 1952 this supply was discontinued.

The Qutub Shahi tombs and gardens were under the supervision of Sarf-e-khas till 1965. In 1958, celebrations of Quli Qutub Shah Day were started though the efforts of Dr. Mohi uddin Quadri Zore. It is still being celebrated regularly by Idara-i-Adabiyat Urdu. In 1965, the Department of Archaeology of the Government of Andhra Pradesh had taken over these tombs under its supervision. Apart from strengthening the structure, the preservation of the surroundings and land scape scenery were also kept in mind. Wherever the place was narrow or new construction appeared pompous, these places were made to look elegant in line with the monuments.

FORTS

Perhaps in no other territory of India are so many forts and of different types are found as in the dominion of the Nizam. The reason is that the plateau of the Deccan since the beginning remained a place of exercise for troops or horses of different conquering races. Besides this, the pecularities of the land in this region were suited for self defence. In the levelled plains, high hills are the natural forts for shelter. The monuments of the pre-historic age at the foot of the rocks of Moula Ali and Bhongir clearly indicate that the ancient inhabitants of the Deccan climbed these slippery smooth rocks when they sensed any danger. It is also not surprising that the tapering rocks of Daulatabad, centuries before the construction of a moat and city wall, may have been a place of refuge for the inhabitants of this region. Thereafter, a period might have come when the people dwelling in these plains, constructed earthen walls and forts for their safety. The ancient walls around the Warangal Fort and the clay towers of the villages of the Deccan which are known as 'bees' are memories of those days of war. Gradually, with the progress of science a period of construction of stony building commenced. In the beginning the shape and form was unskillful but later it was rectified. The main features of these constructions are the usage of magnificent stones. The appearance of the building was not dependent on the figures of Euclid. There was perfection in joining the joints of the stones. Their edges were connected in such a manner that there was no need to use mortar and the stones stands above each other because of their sheer weight.

DISCOVERY OF ANCIENT INSCRIPTION

Since ancient times to the present, the Department has discovered hundreds of new inscriptions. Out of which, three are those of King Ashoka, which are in the Brahamani script. The remaining inscriptions are in Sanskrit, Kannada, Telugu, Marathi, Arabic and Persian languages. A high standard been maintained in the research and accuracy of the interpretations of these inscriptions. These are either published in magazines or articles published in Epigraphia Indo Musalmica which is appropriated for Islamic Inscriptions. This magazine is published under the supervision of the Government of India.

So far twelve magazines have been published. The inscriptions published by the Department are included in the syllabus of the universities of Madras and Calcutta. The latest history compilations published by Cambridge and Oxford have references to the inscriptions discovered by the Department. It is a matter of pride to mention that the signs discovered by the Director of Archaeology on the utensils acquired from the prehistoric age tombs were accepted by some scholars as the source of the ancient Indian form of writing. Similar signs have been discovered recently in Mohenjodaro. But in 1917, the Director of Archaeology has proved the resemblance of these signs with some of the Brahmani letters and also with those primary letters which were prevalent in ancient times in the islands of the Mediterranean Sea, the adjoining countries and northern Africa.

MUSEUM

Besides higher literary research, the main motive of His Exalted Highness the was to impart latest knowledge to his beloved subjects. Accordingly, the Department suggested a scheme to set up a Museum in the City. The Nizam accepted the proposal and himself inaugurated the Museum. On this occasion His Exalted Highness delivered a historic speech in the following terms: -

> "I am glad to inaugurate the Hyderabad Museum and I hope in future, with the efflux of time it will progress and finally it will be reckoned among other famous and historic institutions of Hyderabad".

The expectations of His Royal Higness were largely fulfilled due to his interest in a few years. In a brief period the Museum of Hyderabad collected specimens in sculptures, paintings, armaments, ancient glassware, coins and Bidri wares which could be compared with the articles of those museums of India which were set up long ago. The treasures of ancient glassware of Hyderabad museum are comparable with the collection of glassware in any other museum in India. Similar is the case with the Bidri ware and the arms collection. The collection of coins in some respects is unique as the Department has discovered many mints in the Deccan. Through the kind courtesy of the Nizam, there is an addition in the rare collections from time to time. Some years ago, some gold coins were given to the museum by the Nizam. Among these coins was a coin of Muazzamabad. The gold coins of this mint are very rare.

MONUMENTS OF PRE-HISTORIC AGE

In the Nizam's Dominion, plenty of pre-historic memorials could be found. Hence, for their search and preservation, Khwaja Mohd. Ahmed; Director of Archaeology, was placed in charge of a special scheme. Thousands of implements made of stone were made available approximately from 70 places and they were preserved in the Hyderabad museum. These are stone axe, driller, saw and other instruments. Few such places were discovered where an industry for the manufacture of instruments made of stones existed during the pre-historic age.

In the village of Kalvar of Raichur District, instruments of the Branji period, such as, swords and axes were discovered. It was traced from the excavation that the industry existed in the village of Kalvar. Sir John Marshall was of the opinion that the Branji period did not exist in the Deccan but from the excavations of Kalvar, it was proved that the Branji period did exist in the Deccan.

The primary signs of the iron age were widely discovered. The iron goods of this period are mostly available from the tombs of the pre-historic age. In the Dominions of the Nizam, the burial grounds of the graves were discovered, which belonged to the pre-historic age. Among them, the graveyards of Banker, Agoli, Uppal, Lingsugur, and Tarkal are situated in large numbers near Hyderabad. In Maula Ali, Hashmatpet, Fatehnagar (near Allaudin Industrial Estate), Himayat Nagar, Gachchi Bawli near Mir Alam Tank, these burial grounds were discovered.

In Pattancharu in Medak district and Khet Reddy Palli in Mahbub Nagar District, a big grave of the pre-historic age was discovered. Efforts were made to the best of their ability to preserve these cemeteries, so that, in future, research scholars could work and investigate into the pre-historic period. The findings are presented in the form of a book. A magazine with photographs of the cemetery discovered at Janampet in Warangal district has been published.

Hazrat Shah Rajoo, the spiritual guide of Abul Hasan Qutb Shah and one of the family of Saint Banda Nawaz was buried in a magnificent dome in the south of the old city of Hyderabad. His eldest son, Akbar Shah, wrote a book in Telugu language, and himself translated it into Sanskrit. The book entitled 'Siranga Ramanjari' was published by the Department of Archaeology. Printing was completed in 1950 but the work had already been started in the Asafi period.

Permission was sought for the appointment of new staff and recruitment was made for the excavation work. Museums were set up in Panigiri in the Nalgonda district, Maski in Raichur district, and in Aurangabad. A building was acquired for the museum of Hashmatpet.

A special technical officer was appointed after the approval of the Nizam for the numismatic work. Simultaneously, additional staff was recruited for the scheme.

CHAPTER XXI

SOME HISTORICAL MONUMENTS OF THE CITY OF HYDERABAD

Bhagyanagar or the present city of Hyderabad was founded in 999 H. i.e. 1590 A.D. during the period of Sultan Mohd. Quli Qutub Shah. Near the present Shah Ali Banda locality, in the district of Chanchlam, Sultan Mohd. Quli's beloved Bhagmati resided. The present city was built after her name. After the death of Bhagmati, the city was named Hyderabad and after seven years of the construction of this city, the historical name of "Farkhundah Buniyad" 1006 H i.e. 1597 A.D. came into use in the Government offices. Some ancient legends are famous in connection with Char Minar, which have been popularised by some people who had faith in spiritual and religious beliefs. Some people are of the opinion that Char Minar is the abode of the Goddess of Wealth. This belief might be strengthened by the Char Minar was engraved on the former haali coin.

Some people believed that Char Minar is the dwelling of the Goddess of Fortune of Hyderabad. The reason for these strange traditions is that there is a memorial stone on the east of Char Minar on the roadside which is till worshipped. In the centre of the ceiling of Char Minar there is a room constructed in the style of a Hindu temple, which is known as Hindu Mandir. It was constructed by Qutub Shahi Kings along with a mosque. Irrespective of these strange traditions, Char Minar is the most magnificent and glorious memorial among all buildings of Hyderabad, which are associate with the joyous celebrations of love. It is a fact that neither time nor the changing customs have minimized the pleasant charm of this monument.

CHAR MINAR

When the foundation of the city was laid, Sultan Mohd. Quli in 999 H i.e. 1590 A.D. to invoke benediction and blessing first started the construction of Char Minar which is the portrait of a mosque and coffin (Tabut). The building was constructed out of stone and mortar exactly in the centre of the city. On its four sides, the propitious four arches were made, its every side is 40 feetwide and 42 feet high. The central building consists of four beautiful arched verandas. Its height is 24 feet and width is 40 feet. Opposite to these arches, there are four big public roads. There are many stairs for entry and exit. The upper portion is two-storeyed and its outer side is full of beautiful arches. On the four sides, there are four high towers, which are divided into compartments. Each tower is 80 feet in height. The entire building is built of stone and mortar, on which there is a carving of flowers. The height of these four towers from the surface is 160 feet. The French traveller, Mossio Theono, is of the opinion that "In the entire city, no other building is so beautiful from outside as Char Minar". It is true that Rupees 900,000 were spent. After the fall of the Qutb Shahi kingdom, during the Subedari of Bahadur Dil khan, the South-West tower of Char Minar fell down by lightning which was built during 1844, during the period of Nasir ud Daula with fine plastering of lime at an expense of Rs.100, 000.

On the roof of Char Minar, there is a beautiful mosque. On all its sides there is a mohantery and in its courtyard a cistern. Water flowed from the Jalpalli tank into the cistern. Jalpalli is situated in the environs of Falaknama palace (Saulat-i-osmania)

MECCA MASJID

Sultan Mohd. Qutb Shah started the construction of this magnificent mosque H i.e. 1617 A.D. under the supervision of Mir Faiz ullah Baiq alias Hunermand Khan Choudari. The construction continued until the period of Sultan Abdul Hasan Qutb Shah at a cost of Rs.8, 00,000. It was completed during the period of Aurangzeb. When Bad Shah Alamgir was asked for further decoration of this mosque, he said:-

Kar duniya kase tamam na kard
Har che girid muktasar girid

"Works of the world cannot be completed by a single person one should assign to oneself the little he is capable of".

An interested incident is connected with the foundation ceremony of this mosque. Sultan Mohd. Qutub Shah invited the learned and virtuous men and said that whosoever had not missed a single prayer, should lay the foundation stone of this mosque. None came forward among those present. On noticing this, the King said that from the age of 12 onwards, he never missed his prayers and sometimes he prayed even after midnight. The King himself laid the foundation stone of the mosque. In respect of its height and grandeur, it is such a big mosque in the Deccan that at a time 10,000 people can easily offer prayers. The building of the mosque is 225 feet tall, 180 feet wide and its height is 75 feet. The outside portion is rectangular in shape. Its platform is 360 square feet. Below the roof there are three rows of 15 arches each, and at the end of each row on North-South side there are two domes of hundred feet each. The mosque consists of three verandas in which there are 15 arches inside and five outside. The two towers in the front portion, and the sun dial clock in black stone in the court and the main gate are the memorials of the period of Alamgir. In the courtyard of the mosque, there is a cistern. Near this cistern two long stones of eight feet each are fixed on which 'musalli' (one who prays) sits there for ablution.

Sultan Mohamad Qutub Shah called this mosque by a nick-name given to the square shrine of Mecca. During the period of Aurangazeb, it assumed the name of Mecca Masjid. It was estimated to cost 30,00,000 Huns.

Mossio Theono said: "Since the last 50 years a mangnificent place of worship is under construction here. If it is fully built, it will be a big mosque in India. It is surprising to see the use of such big stones, specially the arch, where they perform prayers. More surprising is the fact that it is built on a single magnificent stone which was taken out from the mine by five or six hundred people who worked continuously for five years. To bring this stone to this place of worship it took more than five years. People narrated that it was pulled and brought by 1,400 bulls. (The Travelogue of J.B. Trevenier, French Trader, p. 25).

This historical mosque was named as 'Bait ul Aqiqh' 1023 H i.e. 1614 A.D. by Sultan Mohd. Qutub Shah. However during the reign of Aurangzeb it became famous as 'Mecca Masjid'. On the construction of the mosque 30 lakhs Huns were spent. In praise of Mecca Masjid a poet wrote thus:

Tawaf kaba ashraf maisarat garnist
Baya be kaba mulk Deccan ibadat kun

"If the pilgrimage of Holy Kaba is not attainable to thee, come and pray in the kaba of Deccan."

It is said that the reason for giving its name is that

Sultan Mohd. Qutub Shah arranged to get soil from Mecca. Bricks were made from this soil and are fixed in the central arch.

(History Massir-i-Deccan by Syed Ali Asghar Bilgrami).

DARUL SHAFA

Soon after the accession of Mohd. Quli Qutub Shah there was extraordinary cultural progress in the kingdom. During this period, a new city of Hyderabad was constructed in a wonderful manner. Charminar was built and Darul Shahfa was constructed. The author of 'Mahanama' had presented the glimpses of Darul Shafa and the lodging in this locality. Following is the translation of a Persian composition:

> "In the Darul Shafa there was an arrangement to accommodate nearly 4,000 sick. There was proper arrangement to supply food and the prescribed diet. Doctors treated them. There were 52 inns. People from far-off places like Turkery and Tajaki used to stay there. There was also arrangement to meet their requirements. Those in charge of the bathrooms were ordered that the poor who come for the bath, after having a hair cut from the Government barber should be taken to the bath and bathed free of charge. Hence those who were in charge of the bathrooms used to wait for an unknown number of guests, holding lungis in their hands. Even today the Darul Shafa building still remains on the same street of Darul Shafa and revives old memories. There is a square courtyard in this building. There are rooms on all the four sides which are the wards for the sick." ('History Mahnama' 102/B Asafia Library.)

TOLI MASJID

It is situated on the way from the Old Bridge to the Golconda Fort. This mosque was cosntructed 1082 H i.e. 1671 A.D. It appears that earlier there was a garden in its courtyard. On the North, South and Eastern sides stairs were built to climb the six feet high platforms. The building is divided into two verandas. There were five arches outside and three inside. There are 60 feet high towers on both the sides of the mosque. The Musa Tower of the Golconda Fort is named after Musa Khan. It is clear from the inscription that Musa Khan was the Commander and Minister of Adbullah Qutb Shah. The author of Gulzar-i-Asafia giving details of the name of 'Damdi Masjid' wrote that Musa Khan was appointed to the post of Superintendent of Mecca Masjid. He had granted one damri (the third part of a paise) per rupee as tahrir from the construction cost. Musa Khan constructed this mosque from the sum of this tahrir on the way to Mohammed Nagar Fort (Near Golconda Fort) near a locality called Karwan.

Musa Khan, played an important role in the accession of Abul Hasan after the death of Sultan Abdullah Qutb Shah.

MIYAN MUSHK MASJID

The mosque of Miyan Mushk is among the old and rare mosques. This is a small mosque. It was constructed in 1085 H. near Old Bridge. Miyan Mushk was the head of the army and was entrusted with the keys of an office during the period of Sultan Abul Hasan Qutb Shah. He died in 1092 H. His tomb is situated in the precincts of the mosque. On one side of this mosque there is a famous bathroom which is said to be constructed on the pattern of some ancient Turkish bathrooms. The technique of this bathroom is unusual. To enter this bathroom one has to pass through many passages in which the temperature rises gradually. The roof of the central part of the bathrooms is dome shaped. On all sides of the dome there are a number of cisterns filled with hot, semi-hot and water with ordinary temperatures as per requirements. The entire walls and the flooring and small arches are joined with a pipe which opens at a distance of several yards from the bathroom. At the end of the pipe there is an arrangement for burning the fuel. When the fuel is burnt then the hot wind passes through a pipe and reaches the vacuum of the floor of the bathroom. In this manner the bathroom got heated.

People were massaged by resting them on the floor which was continued usually for half an hour to 45 minutes. This work was performed by massage experts. After massage and bath one felt fresh and quite hungry.

Ancient kings, nobles and some admirers made use of the bathroom.

The contents of this chapter are taken from the following documents :

Historical background, By Syed Mohd. Akbar Wafa Khani. B.A.LL.B. (Osmania)

Article by Ghulam Rabani, Ex-Superintendent Archaeology, Rahnuma-i-Deccan, May 14, 1967.

Article by Ghulam Rabani, Ex-Superintendent Archaeology, Aaj Kal, Delhi.

Tohfa-i-Jashn Simin, Dr. Gulam Yazdani, Nazim Surrishta.

Article by Yusuf Uddin, Ex-Superintendent Government Department of Posts.

PART – V

ASSOCIATION OF CELEBRATED PERSONALITIES WITH HYDERABAD

CHAPTER – XXII

ASSOCIATION OF CELEBRATED PERSONALITIES WITH HYDERABAD

It is in the fitness of things to remember the names of famous Hyderabadis and celebrities who were invited from other parts of India and from abroad to contribute to the many-sided development of the State. However, we can only mention briefly the outstanding services of a few of them during the reign of His Exalted Highness Mir Osman Ali Khan.

(A) EXPERT ADMINISTRATORS

Nawab Chattari	Nawab Ali Yawar Jung
Sir Akbar Hydari	Khaja Sarwar Hussain
Sir Mirza Ismail	
Ghulam Mohammad	Sir Syed Ali Imam
	Sir Nizamat Jung

NAWAB CHATTARI

Nawab Chattari belonged to a noted Rajput family called Lalvani of Buland Shahar. He was among the leading nobles of the United Provinces Agra and Oudh. Born on December 12, 1888 in Kalanoor at Rohtak in the Punjab and educated at M.A.O. College Aligarh, he entered public life in 1910 and started taking interest in cultural, educational and political activities. He laid the foundation of Muslim Rajput School at Kalanoor in 1910 and was elected President of the Muslim Rajput Conference held at Kalanoor in 1923. He was elected unopposed from the Muslim constituency of Buland Shahar as Executive Council Member. In 1923 he was appointed Minister for Industries and Agriculture and in 1926 as Home Minister in the United Provinces. He was made Governor of the United Provinces twice. He participated in the Round Table Conference at London in 1930 and 1932.

He was a model of Muslim culture. Besides other subjects, he was educated in religion and had learnt the Holy Quran by heart at the Mohammdan College, Aligarh. He entered into active politics in 1920 and was appointed member of the Legislative Council. In 1926, he was appointed to the Ministry of Home and in 1928, Governor of the Suba. Later he became the Minister of Education in the Government of India.

In 1941, he was appointed to the post of Sadr-i-Azam in the Hyderabad Dominions and remained so for five years. Several reforms wre introduced during his premiership. He came to Hyderabad after serving in the fields of politics, education and administration in British India as an expert. The post of Prime Ministership was conferred upon him in a favourable environment. The Second World War was about to end and the British Government seemed ready to give India the rank of an independent Dominion.

During his tenure the Majlis Itehadul Musalmin became a new communal force. The activities of Itehad made Chattari realise that he could not survive long under such circumstances like Sir Akbar Hydari.

SIR AKBAR HYDARI

He belonged to a respectable family of Bombay. His father Sait Nazr Ali was a renowned businessman of Bombay. His native place was Kambat. He was born on November 8, 1869 in Bombay. He graduated with distinction from Xaviers College, Bombay, at the age of seventeen. He enrolled for a degree in Law but the Government of India selected him for training in the Finance Department. He completed the training with honours.

In 1888 he was appointed Accounts Officer in Nagpur. After one year he was appointed as Currency Officer at Lahore, and then brought to Calcutta. Three years later he was appointed Assistant Accountant General, Allahabad.

In 1893, he was transferred to Bombay and in 1900, appointed as Deputy Accountant General Madras. After a year he was entrusted with the auditing of the Government Press for India and Burma. In 1905 his services were obtained as Accountant General on a salary of 1950 rupees during the time of Sir George Casson Walker in Hyderabad. He was attached to the Home Office, High Court and Department of Education. Later he helped in fulfilling the plan for establishing the Osmania University, which had been under contemplation for a long time.

He retired from the State Service, but in 1921 when he was acting as Controller-General of Accounts at Bombay, he was called to Hyderbad and made the Finance Member of the Executive Council in place of Sir Glancy. He was known for his expertise in the administration of finance. He was the President of the Reception Committee to welcome His Royal Highness Prince Edward. In 1925-26 he presided over the Delhi-Inter Universities Committee. He was the Official Director Singareni Colleries Company Ltd. Chairman of Shahabad Cement Company Ltd., Industrial Finance Trust Ltd., Central Bank of India Ltd., Osman Shahi Mills, Azam Jahi Mills and Inter-Universities

Board. He was Sadrul-Maham for Co-operative Credit and Minerals Departments. The credit of purchasing the Nizam's State Railway and its nationalisation goes to him. He was sent to the Round Table Conference in London.

He was conferred Knighthood in 1928, and the title of Right Honourable in 1936. He was appointed Prime Minister in 1937 for a period of five years.

He was a man having great capacity for hard work and had uncommon pertinacity in carrying out his aims. He died in 1941.

SIR MIRZA ISMAIL

Native of Mysore Sir Mirza was the Diwan of Mysore for a long period. During the Osmania period, when he was appointed for the first time as Sadre Azam he rendered excellent service. He was again called to the Sadarat-i-uzma, (Presidentship) after returning to Mysore. This was the period when India got Independence and the partition of India took place.

Sir Mirza Ismail was one of the ablest Prime Ministers who served His Exalted Highness the Nizam and the State with ability and distinction. Sir Mirza was a seasoned administrator who had efficiently managed State administration in Mysore and Jaipur. From his reminiscences entitled 'My Public Life', it can be gathered that he had been requested several times to accept the reins of the Hyderabad administration. However, it was ordained that he should come in the first week of August, 1946, to Hyderabad. Hyderabad had the privilege of enjoying the fruits of the enlightened and wise administration of Sir Mirza Ismail for 10 months.

He was a veteran in the art of administration and knew perfectly the methods of avoiding delays and red-tapism. He was determined to see that the commonest citizen in the State should avail the benefits flowing from the State administration.

He made himself available to those people who were anxious to ventilate their grievances. Sir Mirza introduced the practice of conducting weekly inspections of localities and roads. He himself was a visionary in the field of art and architecture. He ordered the top-ranking executive officers of the Municipal Corporation, town planning and P.W.D. to accompany him on his inspections and took expeditious decisions in consultation with them. Matter s which were stuck in the office files moved briskly and concrete changes began to take place right before the eyes of the people.

Unfortunately, he found himself opposed at every turn by certain sections of the local Muslims who were set on a course which was suicidal to the State. This section was bent upon moving heaven and earth to see him out of Hyderabad. The silence of the Nizam and the subsequent intrigues and agitation forced Sir Ismail to ask for relief.

When Sir Mirza Ismail left Hyderabad for Bangalore, HEH The Nizam suspected that he might resign and would not return to Hyderabad. The Nizam ordered Hosh Bilgrami to go to Bangalore and persuade Mirza on behalf of the Nizam to pay a visit to Hyderabad at least for three or four days. Hosh went to Bangalore and enjoyed the hospitality of Mirza Ismail. He returned to Hyderabad and reported to the Nizam that the decision of Mirza in this matter was final and that he would send his resignation in a week. Thus the Hyderabad State and the Nizam lost the mature guidance of a sagacious administrator.

GHULAM MOHAMMAD (FORMER GOVERNOR GENERAL OF PAKISTAN)

He was a resident of the Punjab and graduated from the

Aligarh University. He was an expert in economics. He worked as a teacher in the Aligarh Muslim University for some time and was later appointed to high posts one after the other under the Government of India. He was appointed to the responsible post of auditing the accounts of military supplies. In this connection, he often toured Secunderabad.

On November 19, 1951, after the retirement of Nawab Fakhr Yar Jung, he was appointed as Finance Minister. His services were returned to the Government of India after two years.

ALI YAWAR JUNG

Nawab Ali Yawar Jung's services to the Osmania University as its Vice Chancellor are memorable. The University under his stewardship occupied a coveted position in the educational map of India. The Indian Government after independence appointed him as Ambassador to Egypt after the death of Dr. Syed Hussain. Later, he was appointed Vice- Chancellor, Aligarh Muslim University. In later years he was appointed as Governor of Bombay.

KHAJA SARWAR HUSSAIN

He was Secretary, Institute of International Affairs, Karachi. His father was Director, Buildings in Hyderabad. The magnificent and beautiful building of the High Court is a great masterpiece of architecture. According to Nawab Mushtaq Ahmed Khan, he spent his entire life in Hyderabad and had a strong affection for Hyderabad.

SIR SYED ALI IMAM

He was a renowned scholar in the Bihar Province. He earned fame as advocate, after graduating in English Literature and Law. He was appointed Member of the Viceroy's Executive Council, sometime after entering public life. During this period, when he went to Hyderabad he was honoured and received with great acclaim. After retirement from the services of the British Government in 1909, he entered the services of the Government of the Nizam. This was a time when the foundation of the Executive Council was laid and Sir Imam with the title of Moid-ul-Mulk was made the first Sadr-i-Azam of the Executive Council.

The Moidul-Mulk was known for his passion to serve the State and people. He left an indelible impact on administration with his efficiency and integrity.

SIR NIZAMAT JUNG

Nawab Sir Nizamat Jung (Nizamuddin Ahmed) was born in 1871. He was the second son of the late Nawab Rafat Yar Jung.

The ancestors of Nizamat Jung belonged to Arabia, who came to India during the seventeenth century. A part of the family came to Hyderabad along with Asaf Jah.

Nawab Nizamat Jung was educated at the Madrasa-i-Aizza and later proceeded to England in 1887 and joined Trinity College, Cambridge where he took the degree of B.A. LL.B (Honours) in 1891. He was the first Hyderabadi to achieve this distinction. Later on he became a Barrister-at-Law, being called to the Bar from the Inner Temple in 1895 during his second visit to England. In 1896 he returned to Hyderabad. In the same year he obtained his Master's

Degree. He was enrolled as an Advocate of the Madras High Court in 1896. He was appointed District Judge Parbhani in 1897 and subsequently Registrar of the High Court, and then became the Chief City Magistrate in 1899. In 1901 he was transferred to the Legislative Department as Under Secretary, because of his high legal qualifications. The Government of Mir Mahbub Ali Khan recognising his ability appointed him to officiate as Home Secretary and as Political Secretary on several occasions between 1901 and 1904. He was ultimately made Home Secretary during 1909-1910 and Political Secretary in 1918, having in the mean time served with distinction as a judge of the High Court for ten years and as Chief Justice for about two years.

He was appointed Political Minister in 1919. As a Political Minister his post was not a bed of roses. The nature of the work imposed on him great responsibility. Besides, maintaining cordiality and smooth interaction between the Darbar and the Residency, he was admitted to the inner circle of the Nizam's Councillors and had to perform this delicate, difficult and uneviable task.

The matter regarding the proper distribution of the water of the Krishna and Godavari rivers between Hyderabad and Madras Government which had been pending for more than 15 years, was at last satisfactorily settled by the able advocacy of Nizamat Jung together with the late Mackenzie, Chief Engineer and the late Habibuddin, Financial Secretary.

For his long, faithful and able service Nizamat Jung was honoured with a Knighthood by His Imperial Majesty the King Emperor, having already received the decorations O.B.E. in 1919 and C.I.E. in 1924.

He was also the Honorary Secretary of the City Improvement Board & Victoria Memorial Orphanage. Nizamat Jung was a man of wide sympathy and broad outlook and uncommonly tolerant disposition. He strongly disapproved communal dissensions as being fatal to progress. He was an accomplished scholar and a man of taste, known for his devotion to literary pursuits. He was passionately devoted to English poetry.

(B) EMINENT SCHOLARS, PROFESSORS AND POETS

ABDUL HALEEM SHARAR
MOULANA ALTAF HUSAIN HALI
MOULANA SHIBLI NOMANI
MOULANA SYED ABDULLA
MOULVI ABDUL HAQU
DR. MOHIUDDIN QUADRI ZOAR
SAROJINI NAIDU
FASHAT JUNG JALEEL
KHALIFA ABDUL HAKEEM
MOUDUDI ANWER IQBAL QUERSHI
ILYAS BARNI
DR. HAMIDULLAH
DR. RAZIUDDIN SIDDIQUI
DR. WALIUDDIN

ABDUL HALEEM SHARAR

Abdul Haleem Sharar not only held an important position as a novelist in Urdu literature, but was also a good historian and a capable journalist. Lucknow was his birthplace and his hometown, but he had extraordinary relations with Hyderabad. Hence, Nizami Badiuni has written in Khamoos-ul-Mushahir that he once again went to Hyderabad in 1891. Nawab Viqar-ul-Umara appointed him on a salary of 200 rupees. Besides this, for the draft of Tarikh-Hind he paid him 5,000 rupees as reward from the Government treasury. He went to England in 1893.

During his three years stay there, he gained good command over the French language. After returning to Hyderabad, he again started Dilgudaz from Hyderabad instead of from Lucknow. He went back to Lucknow in 1899, but he came back to Hyderabad again in 1904 and was appointed as Director, Education.

Abdul Halim Sharar belonged to a Kashmiri family. He began his career as a teacher. His literary activities especially his various articles trained him to become a distinguished journalist. He was also famous for his translation work. He was the founder and pioneer of modern novel writing in Urdu. In Hyderabad he edited the Dabdab-i-Asafia. In this magazine his novel 'Chanchal' was serialised. He was also the author of 'Gor-i-Ghariban' another novel which unfortunately could not get published. As a master of Urdu language, he developed his own distinctive style and was a brilliant humourist. He never craved for court support but always depended upon his own labour of love novel writing—to gain recognition.

MOULANA ALTAF HUSSAIN HALI

Moulana Hali needs no introduction. In 1305 H., 1887 AD, Sir Asman Jah, Madar-ul-Muham, Hyderabad State, while going to Simla, went to meet Sir Syed Ahmed Khan at Aligarh to inspect the Mohammadan College, where he met Moulana Hali. In those days the Moulana was a teacher in the Anglo Arabic School, Delhi. Moulana Altaf Hussain Hali was the renowned author of Musaddas-i-Hali.

MAULANA SHIBLI NOMANI

Moulvi Syed Ali Bilgrami called Maulana Shibli to Hyderabad insistently and appointed him to the post of

Director of Sciences. Shibli published books, such as, Alghazali, Sawaneh Romi, Ilmul Kalam and Mawazans Anee-o-Dabir from Hyderabad. He compiled Asif-ul-Lughat.

MOULANA SYED ABDULALA MOUDUDI

He was the founder of the Islamic Association and the founder of the Islamic Movement. He was born in Aurangabad where his father, Maulvi Ahmed Hussain was a pleader. He passed the Examination of Moulavi from Aurangabad.

After leaving Hyderabad he entered journalism. For sometime he was the editor of Aljamiyat of Ajamiyat-ul-Ulama-i-Hind, then he came back to Hyderabad and managed the editorship Tarjumanul-Quran and thus started his literary career. In the literary atmosphere of Hyderabad, Maulana compiled several books. Most of the texts written by him are used as reference books in the Universities. His Tafsir of Quran-i-Shareef and Tafhim-ul-Quran granted him everlasting fame. The book of Moududi about the Deccan, Deccan ki Siyasi Tarikh is the most valuable work on the causes of the decline of Muslim rule in India, and on the establishment of the Asafia kingdom.

DR. MOULVI ABDUL HAQU

His memory will remain alive as long as the Urdu language lives. Maulvi Abdul Haq was associated with Hyderabad for almost half a century. During this period, he worked as Principal, Aurangabad College and Head, Department of Urdu, Osmania University. He was a member of the Translation Bureau and the editor of 'Afsar', which a magazine on military affairs. His principal adhievement, however, was the establishment of 'Anjuman Taraqui Urdu' and its Secretariat. He spent his entire life in strengthening Anjuman-e-Taraqui-Urdu and in the propagation and progress of the Urdu language.

DR. MOHIUDDIN QUADRI ZOAR

Dr. Mohiuddin Quadri Zoar, was a staunch Hyderabadi. He championed the cause of the local Hyderabadis (mulkis), irrespective of their caste and creed. His love for every thing Deccani was very intense. In order to make known to the world the Deccan its contribution he took upon himself a gigantic task. He set up the Idara-i-Adabiyat-e-Urdu.

Dr. Zoar was the Head of the Department of Urdu in the Osmania University. A prolific writer, his writings based on careful research are a landmark in Urdu literature. Dr. Zoar compiled and edited the Deewan of Quli Qutub Shah and countered the theory that Wali was the first Urdu poet. He also undertook the task of publishing the literature produced during the Qutub Shahi and Adil Shahi periods to establish that much before Urdu was adopted by Delhi and Lucknow, Deccan was the centre of Urdu learning. He wrote detailed history of Urdu literature in Deccan. He edited a complete history of the Deccani poets and writers. He wrote a book entitled "The Diamonds of Golconda". His history of Hyderabad is an authentic document and he initiated work on the preparation of an Urdu Encyclopeadia but could not finish due to paucity of funds. Imbibing the Qutub Shahi culture and traditions, Dr. Zoar was the champion of commual harmony and of all that was true good and beautiful. He was an ardent lover of mankind, a reliable friend, and a writer of great perception. But for his untimely death, he would have risen to a very high position. He was held in high esteem for his scholarship and remembered with gratitude and affection for his personal qualities.

SAROJINI NAIDU

Sarojini Naidu was the daughter of Aghornath Chatopadhyay, an eminent scholar, scientist and expert educationist who was specially called to Hyderabad to ensure the progress and expansion of modern education. He was the first Principal of the Nizam College.

Sarojini Naidu was born in Hyderabad. Her childhood was spent in literary atmosphere. She passed her matriculation examination at the age of twelve from the Madras University. She then developed a taste for poetry and started composing good poems in English. Her taste developed to such an extent that she had no interest in college education. She kept herself busy day and night reading books of her choice and in writing poetry. When she was 16, the Government of Nizam awarded her a fellowship for higher studies in London in 1896. She got a scholarship of pounds 300 per annum for three years.

During her stay in London, she continued writing poems. Some of her friends introduced her to Professor Edmund Gosse who was a renowned writer and critic. After returning from England, she was married to Dr. Govind Rajulu Naidu who was the Principal Medical Officer of Hyderabad State. She dedicated most of the years of her young age to poetry. The first collection of her poems is known as "The Golden Threshold" which became extraordinarily popular in and outside India. Her house was known as "Golden Threshold". Her later publications were 'Bird of Time' and 'Broken Wings'. Sarojini Naidu was ranked number one among the Indians who wrote poetry in the English language at that time.

In 1905, she joined politics and her oratorial skills had

an electrifying impact on the people. After World War I, the first phase of the freedom struggle in India began in the form of non-co-operation movement of Gandhiji. She participated in the movement along with other Congress leaders. She endeared herself to the people by her leadership qualities. She won an abiding place in the Indian Hall of Fame. After Independence she became the first woman Governor and spent her last days at the Rajbhavan in Lucknow.

FASAHAT JUNG JALEEL

Hafiz Jaleel Hasan Jaleel belonged to Manikpur and was born in 1862. He had the distinction of becoming the ustad (tutor) of Mir Mahboob Ali Khan Nizam VI and Mir Osman Ali Khan Nizam VII. Before coming to Hyderabad, Jaleel was attached to the court of Rampur. He visited Hyderabad at the close of the nineteenth century. The tutor of Nizam VI, 'Dagh' had died in 1905 but 'Jaleel' secured this distinction after a long wait. He was appointed as successor to 'Dagh' as the royal tutor on a salary of five hundred rupees per month. Later, he was also appointed as royal companion. He was bestowed with the title of 'Fasahat Jung'.

During the reign of Mir Osman Ali Khan, 'Jaleel' continued as royal tutor, and he had to attend the Court daily with at least one poem. The duty assigned to him was to correct the compositions of the Nizam.

Jaleel's poetry was highly thoughtful and dealt with the philosophical issues of joy and sorrow, life and death. His style was simple, lucid and elegant. He was the master of Urdu language and composed in every genre of poetry. His death in 1946 was a great loss to the world of Urdu poetry.

(C) JOURNALISTS, POLITICIANS, ENGINEERS AND DOCTORS

ABID ALI KHAN
M. NARSING RAO
PANDIT VASUDEO RAO
ABDUL RAHMAN RAIS
MOHD. AKBER ALI
SYED AHMED MOHIUDDIN

ABID ALI KHAN

Abid Ali Khan, born in Hyderabad on March 19, 1920 was the son of Nawab Mir Mahmood Ali Khan. His grandfather Nawab Intekhab Jung was the tutor of Nizam VII. Abid Ali Khan belonged to a notable Jagirdar family. After matriculation from Aliya School, he completed his bachelor's degree in Philosophy from the Osmania University. He was fortunate enough to have a famous tutors like Khalifa Abdul Hakim, Prof. Shiv Mohan and Dr. Waliuddin. He actively participated in the literary and political movements along with the poet Maqdoom Mohiuddin. His relationship with Qazi Abdul Ghaffar developed in him a taste for journalism. He joined the famous team of Maqdoom, Mir Hasan, Sajjad Zahir and Kaifi Azami. His asociation with the intellectuals, writers and poets helped in the promotion of peace and progress. Later he became the Secretary of the Association of Progressive Writers in 1943. On the wishes of his father, he joined the services of Nizam's Government but was more fascinated by journalism than a mundane job.

His natural inclination towards journalism was the result of his interest which he showed in each department of journalism. He worked for the paper 'Payam' of Qazi Abdul Ghaffar and 'Raiyat' of Narsing Rao. His articles were published regularly, in 'Payam'. He also wrote for English newspapers.

He dedicated his life to journalism and decided to start a paper with the help of his close friend Mahboob Hussain Jigar. He purchased 'Wajahat Press' of Maulvi Abdul Halim. The first edition of 'Siasat' was published on 15th August 1947. At that time, the condition of Urdu jouunalism was at a very low ebb.

The sharp perceptions of Abid Ali Khan did not permit him to join politics. He was against illiteracy and conservatism. Initially he passed through a critical period. His enemies in the guise of friends always tried to harm him and his newspaper 'The Siasat Daily'. Sometimes he faced financial problems and was forced to think in terms of closing down his paper but his firm faith in God always helped him in times of difficulties.

He was honoured on a number of occasions. He won cash prizes for writing the best articles. In 1981 he was awarded 'Padmashree' by the Government of India in recognition of his services to journalism. 'The Ghalib Award' was presented to him by the former Prime Minister Smt. Indira Gandhi. Recognising his contributions in the field of journalism, literature, education and social service the Government of Andhra Pradesh awarded him the honorary degree of 'Doctor of Letters'.

He was a true symbol of Hyderabad; culture and nobility. He loved the culture and civilisation of Hyderabad noted for its human values, fraternity, tolerance and communal amity. He always raised his voice against mud-slinging against Hyderabad.

He was a seasoned journalist, a polished writer and a man of integrated and dignified personality.

He died in November, 1992.

POLITICIANS
BARRISTER AKBAR ALI KAHN
NAWAB BAHADUR-YAR JUNG
SIRAJUL HASAN TIRMAZI

BARRISTER AKBAR ALI KHAN

Akbar Ali Khan was a successful and popular lawyer of Hyderabad. He belonged to an affluent jagirdar family settled in Hyderabad.

Since his childhood, he was attracted towards politics. After completion of his matriculation from Hyderabad in 1917, he joined the Aligarh University and was associated with the Congress. His patriotic ideas led him into the non-co-operation movement of 1920 and he had to leave the University. With a few colleagues he started a camp under Gandhiji and Maulana Mohammed Ali. This association with Congress idealogy continued all through his life. He returned to Hyderabad and joined the Osmania University. In 1923 he completed his graduation. He went to England for further studies and tried to join Oxford and Cambridge; Ultimately he joined the London University. He took his LL.B. (Hons.) degree, studied for the Bar and started research for his LL.D but abandoned it and came back to Hyderabad.

He was a leading lawyer of Hyderabad State. His services were recognised by the Government and he was appointed as legal advisor to the Tungabhadra Project. He was also offered a Judgeship and the membership of the highest judicial tribunal which he did not accept. He was a senior advocate of the Supreme Court. He was a member of the Governing Body of the Osmania University on behalf of the Senate.

He also tried his best to do social service and public work. He started welfare activities for the people and ran a Cheap Grain Shop Association. In the old Hyderabad Assembly, he was elected to the Assembly from the lawyers's constituency. He was a City Father and the Vice-President of the Corporation for sometime. He was a member of the Executive Committee of Bhoomidan and an active worker of the Bharat Sewak Samaj. He was the General Secretary of All Hyderabad Lawyers Association and the President of the Revenue Bar Association. Akbar Ali Khan was an unofficial member of the Reforms Committee set up by Sir Akbar Hydari. He was a member of the committee which Sir Mirza Ismail appointed to look into communist activities. He served the Congress organization as the President of the Election Tribunal.

He was a member of Parliament for several years and was later appointed as Governor of Orissa.

ENGINEERS
NAWAB ALI NAWAZ JUNG
SIR VISHWESHWARAIAH
KHAJA AZEEMUDDIN
NAWAB KARAMATH JUNG
NAWAB AHSAN YAR JUNG

NAWAB ALI NAWAZ JUNG

Nawab Ali Nawaz Jung, F.C.H. Chief Engineer and Secretary P.W.D. and Member of the Legislative Council, was born in Hyderabad in 1877.

He was educated at the St. George's Grammar School and later joined Nizam College. In 1896, he was sent to England as a State scholar to study at the famous Engineering College of Coopers Hill. At London, as an engineering student he had an exceptionally brilliant career, topped the list of successful candidates and got many scholarships in various branches of engineering.

In 1889, he returned to Hyderabad and joined P.W.D. as an Assistant Engineer. He was Municipal Engineer in 1906, Auditor in 1906, Consulting Engineer and Superintending Engineer in 1910. He was promoted as Superintendent Engineer in 1912. In 1913, he was made Secretary to Government, P.W.D. and Telephones Department. He became Chief Engineer and Secretary in 1918 P.W.D. and all its allied Departments were placed under his charge in 1924. His charge also included duties as Engineer-in-Chief of HEH's Royal Palace works. The Bombay Government invited him in 1929 to collaborate with S.M. Vishveshwaraya on the financial and technical aspects of the Sukkur Barrage and his services were publicly acknowledged by His Excellency, The Governor-in-Council.

Ali Nawaz Jung was the first to hold the office of Chief Engineer since its institution in 1886. He conceived, launched and set-up large irrigation works. Flood abatement works were also designed for the protection of the city of Hyderabad. Many important buildings were built and a large number of major bridges such as those of the Godavari, Manjira etc., were constructed under his supervision.

The long awaited question of allocation of waters of the Tungabhadra and the Krishna between the Hyderabad and Madras Governments was settled at the joint conferences held in Madras in 1915 and again in Hyderabad in 1930 during which period amicable settlements were reached due to his efforts.

Hyderabadis owe to him the construction of the two reservoirs, Osman Sagar and Himayat Sagar. Extension of the telephone service to the districts was due to his initiative. A Department of District Power Schemes was created. The Wayra, the Palair, the Fatehnahar, Royanpally Projects were designed by him. Other works which contributed to the development of agriculture in the Dominions include the Nizam Sagar Project.

DOCTORS

DR. MALLANNA

DR. ABDUL HUSAN

DR. M.BAHADUR KHAN

DR. BANKAT CHANDRA

DR. MALLANNA

Dr. Mallanna was born in Mahowa in Madhya Pradesh where his father was working in the armed forces. His family moved to Hyderabad after the retirement of his father. Dr. Mallanna belonged to a backward class community known as Kurma. Dr. Lawrie spotted his talent when he was in Hyderabad Medical School and sent him to London in 1894, where he specialised in microbiology and tropical medicine. When he returned to Hyderabad he was made the Head of the Department of Pathology in Afzalgunj Hospital (Osmania Hospital). He was a boon to the medical fraternity in Hyderabad as he was the only pathologist with extraordinary skills. He went to Germany and worked under Robert Koch and brought in Hyderabad the latest knowledge in microbiology. He organised the Forensic Laboratory and acted as its Head.

CHAPTER XXIII

HYDERABAD'S CULTURAL TRADITIONS SOME NOTABLE COMMENDATIONS

Mohammed Ali Jinnah commended the glorious cultural traditions of Hyderabad Deccan. He praised the great legacy of the Asafia dynasty and in particular, the generous and liberal patronage of literature and learning, the wisdom and vision of the last ruler Mir Osman Ali Khan who tirelessly worked for the betterment and welfare of his subjects.

In 1916, the Annual Meeting of the All India Muslim League was held at Lucknow presided over by Mohd. Ali Jinnah. In his presidential address he specially praised the Asafia Dominion and its ruler His Exalted Highness the Nizam. He also said that the manner in which His Exalted Highness the Nizam worked is worthy of emulation by the British Government.

He said: -

"Some time back I saw in the Bombay Chronicle that His Exalted Highness the Nizam had decided the Hindu-Muslim dispute in his State in this manner:

> "There was a dispute between Hindus and Muslims in the Warangal region of the Nizam's Dominion, over the building of mosque which was

situated in the Hindu region. In spite of protests by the Hindu population, the other party continued the construction work. Hindus presented a petition to the Nizam who appointed a committee comprising of two Muslims and one Hindu to investigate into the affair. The report of the committee was in favour of the Hindus and a Farman was issued by the Nizam according to the report. The decision of His Exalted Highness the Nizam was indicated to the glorious tradition of the Asaf Jahi Dynasty. Why not we Hindus and Muslims in British India follow the same path and why should not we solve the disputes with these methods which were very successful in the Nizam's State"?

Allamma Iqbal was profoundly impressed by the great traditions set by the Nizam. He had the highest admiration and regard for Mir Osman Ali Khan and was instrumental in inviting him to Lahore under the auspices of Anjuman-i-Himayat Islam.

He said: -

"The Muslims of the Punjab had firm faith in His Exalted Highness Nizam in the capacity of a Muslim Ruler. He had relations not only with the children of Shahabuddin Shaharwardi but the Nawab of Chinwat (Punjab) Sadullah Khan, Prime Minister of Shah Jahan. On the basis of these special features, the Muslims of the Punjab should prove their firm belief in the form of a grand reception to His Exalted Highness. I had the privilege of an audience with His Exalted Highness the Nizam when I visited Hyderabad. During a personal conversation, I requested that the Muslims of the Punjab are desirous of and are impatiently expecting your visit for a long time, their expectations should be fulfilled."

The role that the State played in publicising Iqbal's work and message has no parallel elsewhere in India. This was done especially by Nawab Hasan Yar Jung through weekly lectures on Iqbal. The students of the Osmania University did so by adopting the ideology of Allamma Iqbal. Books and dissertations were written for elucidating his poetic vision and his universal message.

As a great patron of learning Moulana Shibli describes in detail the Nizam's benevolent patronage of literary societies and the Madrasas of learning.

The Nizam's birthday was an occasion of joy for the whole State once in a year. The people considered it their duty to express their unflinching faith and gratitude to their beloved ruler. The Birthday Celebrations would last for seven days.

Nadwat-ul-Ulema had the privilege of expressing its delight and faith on this occasion. Its greatest achievement was the Dar-ul-Uloom, whose foundation was laid by the Nizam.

The Royal Family played a leading role in the spread of oriental and western education. The Mohammadan Anglo-Oriental College was established at Aligarh. Hyderabad was the only munificent State to support this institution.

All the renowned authors who rendered literary services for the last 25 years were always encouraged and honoured by the Deccan and they enriched the Sate with their valuable works. Besides schools for Eastern and Western education, the khankhas (tombs of saints) of India were maintained by the graciousness of His Exalted Highness. The sustenance of hundreds of nobles and historically known families connected with the Nizam speaks of the generous royal patronage.

The establishment of the Osmania University with Urdu as its medium of instruction in all faculties of learning was a unique achievement.

The Nizam was God-fearing and attempted to arouse genuine religious awakening among the Muslims by praying with them in the mosques and forbidding them using liquor and wine.

The holy month of Ramzan was celebrated with great religious fervour and devotion.

A proposal was warmly approved by a committee of Ulemas to present the title of Mohiul Millath-e-Deen to His Exalted Highness on behalf of the Muslims of India.

Anjuman-e-Taraqui-e-Urdu was established by the All India Muslim Educational Conference in 1903 and Moulana Shibli Nomani, Maulvi Habib-ul-Rahman Khan Sherwani and Aziz Mirza were its Honorary Secretaries. In 1913, Maulvi Abdul Haq filled this post after the death of Aziz Mirza and remained as Honorary Secretary until his death till August 16, 1961.

The Anjuman shifted from U.P. to Hyderabad and flourished under the gracious patronage of the Nizam.

The Nizam himself assessed the worth of his rule in this couplet

"Salateen salaf sab hogaye nazr ajal Osman
Musalmanon ka Teri sultanat se hai nishan baqui"

All the preceding kings met with their destined end but Osman, the vestiges of the liberal Muslim rule will ever remain alive in your kingdom."

Moulana Abdul Hameed Badayani showered encomiums on the Nizam thus:

"His Exalted Highness Sultan-ul-Uloom Mir Osman Ali Khan, king of the Deccan following the foot steps of his ancestors had revived the old memories, whose eyes are set on the joys and miseries of his people and who is the best example of Islamic simplicity and equality, whose royal hands are ever active to constantly assist the deserving people and whose mind is free from prejudice.

The wealth of his State is spent on the welfare and progress of the people, not on pleasure and enjoyment and he is taking his State on the path of progress."

"The entire administrative machinery built up by the

celebrated Sir Salar Jung I was overhauled. The times awaited a statesman of exceptional grit, ability, tact and ability, tact and foresight, a leader who would not yield to circumstances but could force circumstances to yield to him. Fortunately for Hyderabad the hour produced the man in the person of Mir Osman Ali Khan, the maker of Modern Hyderabad" (vide Theo W. La Touche, Twenty Five Years as Ruler of Hyderabad, Excelsior Press, Secunderabad).

Apart from Muslim leaders and celebrities, the great non-Muslim intellectuals writers and artists, acknowledged the distinctive merit of the State government: its religious tolerance, administrative justice and educational policy.

Dr. Rabindranath Tagore, Dr. Rajagopalachari, Dr. B.C. Roy, Sir Tej Bahadur Sapru, Mahatma Gandhi and other experts and celebrities had specially congratulated the Nizam on the establishment of the Osmania University with the medium of instruction as Urdu and publicly recognized its importance.

The Nizam was liberal in giving grants to non-Muslims and to religious places of worship. In 1915, the Resident of Hyderabad wrote a letter to the Nizam informing him about the arrival of 'Swami of Kanchi Math' to Hyderabad on January 2nd, 1915. The Nizam made excellent arrangements for the Swamy's reception. He was duly honoured with typical Hyderabad hospitality.

While inaugurating the famous University College of Arts building, the Nizam saw his full size portrait adorning the dais. He affixed his signature on the portrait and wrote:

Quadim-e-Qaum

(Servant of the Nation/people) Can there be a better ideal of governance than this?

The famous editor and eminent leader of India, Pandit

Raj Narayan Dehlvi delivering his presidential speech at the Second Annual Convocation of the Sanatan Dharam of Hyderabad Deccan had openly acknowledged this fact: siad :-

"When I was proceeding towards Hyderabad, on the basis of the reports appearing in the news papers, I was under the impression that the condition of temples in Hyderabad State is unsatis-factory and the Government had absolutely not paid any attention to the temples of the Hindus. I decided that after reaching Hyderabad, I would draw the attention of the Government of the Nizam towards the temples but after reaching Hyderabad and on inquiring about this, I was glad to know that the reports of the newspapers were entirely misleading and prejudiced. All the temples are granted financial assistance from the Government of Nizam and compared to Muslim places of worship, the number of Hindu temples is more. Such an expression of magnanimity was made without distinction of caste creed or community in the best interest of a sovereign State.

The number of Muslim institutions maintained and promoted by the Nizam is smaller such as "Ashurkhana, Durgah and tombs of saints."

All are well aware of the fact that Hyderabad under the Asaf Jahi rule has been singularly free from religious begotry. Mr. T.H. Thorton, Secretary of State Government of India, said:

> "Having had the opportunity for generations to govern and conciliate a large and not unwarlike Hindu population, the ruling classes of Hyderabad are free from religious bigotry."

Henry George Briggs in his book entitled ' The Nizam (page 119 vol.I) wrote:

> "The Government had no hesitation or jealousy in employing the Hindus among its officers. Raja Pratapwant was the Prime Minister before Rukn-

ud-Dowla and there are other exceptions. The Principal Minister of trade and finance under the Ministry has always been a Hindu. The entire trade and finance are in the hands of the Hindus and as managers of revenue, there are as many Hindus as Mohammedans."

Persons of the eminence of Mrs. Sarojini Naidu and Rabindernath Tagore gave public expression to their firm conviction that Hyderabad is and has always been free from communal bias. Syed Abid Hasan (Whither Hyderabad, Hyderabad, 1935, pp. 59-60).

The sound of the conch was heard alongwith the sound of Azaan (the Muslim call to prayers) during the Nizam's reign.

A majority of Kayastas, Kshatrias, Brahmins, Telugu, Marathas, Reddys were admitted as Asaf Jahi nobles and were possessors of big Jagirs, samasthans and mansabs. Also a few names of Britishers, Parsis, French, Christians and Sikhs received mansabs for generations from the Nizam's Government.

The unbiased policy of the Asafia Dominion could be assessed from the fact the non-Muslim religious institutions which include temples, dharamshalas, goshalas jatras, processions of chariots, processions of Gods, purohits, astrologers, Brahmins, Bhikasthan, Churches, Fire-temples, Gurudwaras etc., were nearly 12,000 in number. Salary, daily allowance and grants. were fixed for them by the Government.

On the contrary, the number of Muslim institutions maintained and promoted by the Nizam was smaller Mosques, Ashurkhanas, Durgahs (Tombs), Khankhanas (Tombs of Saints), religious schools, Qazi (judge), Mufti (Muslim Jurist), Pir (holy man) received benefits like those of non-Muslims.

DEVELOPMENT OF URDU LANGUAGE AND SCIENCES

The famous humorous writer, Rasheed Ahmed Siddiqui, Head, Department of Urdu, Muslim University Aligarh has written an analytical preface on the compositions of His Exalted Highness Nizam VII :

> "When the Osmania University was established, education was imparted in the Indian language at the University level in each subject and the degrees were recognized by all the Indian Universities outside the State. It was a bright chapter for Indian languages and a magnificent impetus to Urdu language. Besides this, propagation and publicity of Islamic sciences by the highly researched Institution of Daratul Maarif, will not be forgotten in the history of Oriental Sciences."

Syed Altaf Hussain Barelvi who was attached to the Aligarh University for a long time wrote: -

> "The Madrasat-ul-Uloom Aligarh had the royal patronage of the State of Hyderabad Deccan ever since its establishment. At that time when the value of the rupee was higher, recurring and non-recurring grants of lakhs of rupees were granted. Grand buildings were constructed with the grants of Hyderabad, such as, "Salar Jung Manzil" with the grant from Sir Salar Jung Bahadur. "Asman Manzil" with the grant from Sir Asman Jah Bahadur, the magnificent two storeyed Osmania Hospital with the royal grant of His Exalted Highness Mir Osman Ali khan and finally during the Vice Chancellorship of Muslim University of Sir Syed Ras Masood, a valuable grant of 10 lakh rupees was given for the science college. Besides this, whenever His Exalted Higness attended the meeting of the University in the capacity of Chancellor, he would announce a grant of not less than 1 lakh rupees. A

permanent annual grant of 60,000 rupees was also sanctioned. Similarly, in 1886 an amount of 1,75,000 rupees was granted to the All India Muslim Education Conference formed by Sir Syed for setting up a reserve fund. The profits of this fund were used for the payment of salaries of staff. A delegation of lecturers and students of the Aligarh University visited Hyderabad during the summer vacation every year and they collected donations from generous people in large measure."

Besides monetary grants, great men like Nawab Mohsin-ul-Mulk, Nawab Viq ar-ul-Mulk, Nawab Imad-ul-Mulk Bahadur Aziz Mirza and Maulvi Chirag Ali, connected with Hyderabad were personal friends of Sir Syed. They actively participated in spreading Sir Syed's educational and reformation movement nationwide. A large number of Hyderabad students received higher education in Aligarh and after completing graduation, they returned to the Dominion and occupied high and responsible positions.

The literary, educational and cultural heritage of Aligarh and Hyderabad was similar like a confluence of two rivers. By means of this confluence, a general awakening was developed in the entire sub-continent.

CHAPTER – XXIV

A BUNCH OF POETIC TRIBUTES

Many poets from ancient times wrote in praise of Hyderabad Deccan and its rulers. Tributes of some renowned poets are given below:

MUNAJAT (HYMNS) PRAYER

The founder of Hyderabad Deccan and the first to writes a book of poems Mohd. Qutub Shah 'Maani' wrote:

"Munjat meri tu sun ya Samee
Munje khush tu rakh rat din ya Samee
Mera shahar logan sun mamur kar
rakha jun tu dariya men sin ya Samee
Maradat ka jam tarang de Qutub
Ai samarant de ainen ya Samee

"O God, listen to my prayers and bless me so that my days and nights should pass peacefully. Make my city as populated as thou has filled the ocean with fish. O Lord bless 'Qutb' to fulfill the multiple waves of desire and empower my vision."

Mulla Wajih, the Malik-ul-Shuara (poet Laureate) of

the period of Mohd. Quli Qutub Shah, author of 'Subras' and 'Qutub Mushtari' has written in praise of Hyderabad Deccan:

Dahkhan sa nahin thar (place) sansar mein
binj fazilan ka hai is thar mein
Dhkan mulk khan dhan ajab saj hai
ke sab mulk sir hour Dehkhan taj hai
Dkhan hai nagina nagothi hai jag
Angothi ko hurmat nagina hi lag

Wajih says, "there is no place like the Deccan in the world. It has produced great scholars. The Deccan is blessed with affluence and prosperity. The Deccan has an exalted position among all the countries of the world. The Deccan is the jewel fitted in the ring of the world. A ring looks magnificent only after it is studded with jewels."

Tabai was the poet during the reign of Abul Hasan Qutb Shah. He was the author of "Behram-o-Gul Andam." He wrote in praise of Hyderabad:

"Jo koi yead karta nai apna watan
o murda hai pairanan hai uska kafan
Agar koi ghurbat ein shahi kare
Agar mal hour mulk lakhan dahre
Deve khak tan ka watan ka nisha
Watan sab ko duniya mein pyara rahe".

"Whosoever does not remember his native place is dead, and his robe is a shroud. If anybody reigns even in poverty and offers the wealth of joy to many countries, one should look into oneself and consider the dust on his body as an exhilarating symbol of one's native land. The hometown is dear to all in the world."

GHALIB liked to visit Hyderabad after the freedom struggle of 1857. He sent a Qasida which extolled the rule of Nasir-ud-Dowla. (Refer Ghalib aur Hyderabad by Ziauddin Ahmed Shakeeb for details):

"Hyderabad Deccan roza rizwan shuda ast
Saz o bar tarb o aish farwan shuda ast

Hyderabad bahoot dur hai is mulk ke log
us taf ko nahin jate hain jo jante hain to kam
Hind mein hain ahel tasnun ki hain do sultanatein
Hyderabad Deccan rashk gulistan arm

Hyderabad Deccan has become a heaven. Here all things of happiness and joy are abundantly available. Hyderabad is very far off from North, hence people do not know about it. In India there are two kingdoms of Sunnies. Even heaven appears to envy Hyderabad.

MIR ANIS, the famous marsiyago (the master of elegy) visited Hyderabd Deccan in 1871. He read two rubaiyat spontaneously in a meeting at Hyderabad.

"Allah or rasul ki imdad rahe
Sarsabz ye shahar faiz buniyad rahe
Nawab Aisa Rai azam aise
Ya Rab Hyderabad rahe."

The city should remain fertile with the fountain of generosity blessed by God and the Prophet. O God may Hyderabad with such a magnanimous Ruler and noblemen always remain prosperous.

"Moujud hai jo kuch jise manzoor hai yan
Ilm o amal qata ka dstoor hai yan
Mukhtar-ul Mulk aur Bandagan-i-Ali
Rahmat Rahmat ye noor purnoor hai yan"

Whatever is available is accessible to all here. Benevolent governance and generous grants are the traditions of the dynasty. Mukhta-rul-Mulk, and Bandagan-i-Ali are extremely compassionate.

The Kulliyat (Complete works of a poet) of Moulana KHWAJA ALTAF HUSSAIN 'HALI' is full with verses on the literary patronage of Hyderabad and about its liberality.

"Asman Jah hai taqwiyat mulk Deccan
Aur hai muk-i-Deccan mulja –o-mawa-i-jahan
Ye makhola Hind mein mudat se hai zarb-ul-misal
Jo ke ja phoncha Deccan mein bas wahin ka ho raha
Parsi Hindu, Musalman ya Masihi ho koi

Hai Deccan ko har koi apni wilayat janta"

The strength of the Deccan and its great pillar is Asman Jah. Deccan is a safe sanctuary in the world. It has become a proverb in India that whosoever reaches Deccan remains there forever. Parsi, Hindu, Muslim, Catholic everybody considers the Deccan his own Dominion.

DAGH DEHELVI who was the tutor of Mir Mahboob Ali Khan Asaf Sadas, King of Deccan, came to Hyderabad and settled here. He had composed hundred of verses on the climate, environment, fruits, flowers and other prominent features of Hyderabad. A few from among them are given below:-

"Dilli mein phoolonki hai yek sair Dagh
Balde mein humne dekhli sair jahan ki sair
Nargis-i-bagh ko bhi hum ne na dekha bimar
Hyderabad ki kya ab-o-hava achchi hai
Shahar hai gulzar yuh khalq hai gulrang yar
Jaise Chaman dar chaman bagh mein phoole gulab
Balde ka yek yek makan is mein dar-ul-aman
Shahar yek yek gali jada-i-Rah-i-Sawab
Hyderabad hai jannat se siwa dar-ul-aman
Kha ke gandum na yahen se kabhi adam nikle
Kul jain ankhen dekhte hi is chaman ke phool
Rizwan ko ham dikhayen jo bagh-i-Deccan k phool
Nahin Hyderabad Paris se kuch kam
Yahan bhi saje hain makan kaise kaise
Na hai garmi, na kahin had se ziyadah sardi
Hyderabad mein hai fasal ka aisa alam"

Delhi is famous for 'Phoolwaloon ki Sair' but in this city of Hyderabad we saw, as it were, the most enjoyable and entertaining spots of the world. The climate is so pleasant that the flowers do not appear to fade or lose their fragrance. The city is full of rose gardens of every hue of people belonging to different castes and religions.

Every house in the city is safe and each and every road, every lane is secure from unsocial elements. Hyderabad is equal to paradise, a home of peace. Human beings who consume the wheat of Hyderabad would not like to go back. If we show the flowers of the Deccan to Rizwan (an angel guarding the gates of paradise) his eyes would remain open with wonder. Hyderabad is not less than Paris. The houses are decorated beautifully. Hyderabad is neither too hot not too cold because its seasons are moderate.

Allamma Sir Mohammad Iqbal came to Hyderabad Deccan in 1910. In memory of his visit he wrote two remarkable poems which were published in the magazine "Makhazan" of Lahore. A few verses from one of these poems are given below:

"Kuch to kah hum se bhi is waraftagi ka majra
Le gaya tujh ko khan tera dil be ikhtiyar
Kis tajal igah ne khincha tera daman-i-dil
Teri misht-i-khak ne kis des mein paya qarar
Kya kahon is bostan-i-gairat faridas ki
Jis ke pahloon mein huwa ai humnawa mera guzar
Jis ke zarree mehr alam tab ko saman-i-noor
Jis ke tur afzalyoon per didaye Musa nisar
Jis ke bulbul andalib akhal gul ke humsafar
Jis ke ghunchoon ke liye rkhsar hur ainadar
Khita janat fiza jis ki hai damman gir dil
Azmat derina Hindustan ki yadgar
Noor ke zarron se qudrat ne banaya ye zamin
Aina ban ke Deccan ki khak agar paye fishar

Dr Iqbal asks himself about the experience of his great beautitude when he was led away by his heart to reach the place which was resplendent with joy and peace. How should I describe the beauty of this garden of Paradise (Hyderabad)? When I pass through its flowery maze, its minute particles provide power to the sun to brighten the universe. The eyes of Moses get dazzled on its heights. Its nightingale is a companion of Gabriel and its buds reflect the cheeks of a virgin. The atmosphere is heavenly and this region is a veritable monument of the ancient grandeur that is India. Nature has created this land with particles of light. God has woven its earth with the strings of divine light which when pressed, will shine like mirror.

JOSH MALIHABADI

The poetry of revolutionary poet Josh blossomed in the literary atmosphere of Hyderabad Deccan. His heart was full of love for each and every particle of Hyderabad which he had expressed in a long poem. A few verses are as follows:

Hyderabad ai niqar gul badaman asalam
Assalam ai khisa mai ke unwan asalam
Tu ne ki thi roushni meri andheri rat mein
Mehr o mah khwabida hain ab bhi tere zarat mein
Mere qasr-i-zindagi per ai dayar-i-mohatrain
tu ne hi khola tha zauq-i-ilm ka zarin ilm
tu ne hi bande ko bakhshi thi kalid asrarki
tu ne hi zulfain sanwari thin mere afkar ki
tu hi mere rabaro yek an se par tol kar
Muskuraya tha mohabbat ka darioha khol kar
Walwalaon mein tere naghmaon ki rawani aiyi thi
Tere bhoan mein hawa kha kar jawani aiyi thi
Ai Deccan teri zamin ki rang raliyan dil mein hain
Pahle jo zai-i-qadam thin ab wuh galiyan dilmen hain
Aslam ai bazm yaran ai dayar-i-dostan
Asj atthara baras ke bad aye hoan yahan
Di hai rash-i-waqt ko gardon ne yek mudattmen er
Kal jawan ruqsat husa tha aj palta hoan edher
Lekin ai mere chaman meri jawani ke chaman
Ai Deccan nasrin Deccan sunbul Deccan susan Deccan

Tujh mein gultan hai mere dil ki kahani aj bhi

Pufishan tujh men hai meri naujawani aj bhi

Ab bhi hai Osman Sagar ki hawaon mein kharosh
Ab bhi at hai pahadaon se sada-i-josh josh

Is fiza mein hai qhayamat ka taranum aj bhi
Sibt hai yek dushman-i-jan ka tabassum aj bhi

Walwale nache the jo ghungro pahan ka paon men
Aaj bhi raqshan hai teri badlyaon ki chaon mein

Ao sine se mere luq jawo yaran-i-Deccan
Peshtar is ke ke rue josh ko dhanpe kafan

Josh Malihabadi sends his salutations to Hyderabad's beauty and gets nostalgic with sweet old memories. He says, "Hyderabad has brought light to him in his dismal days and he finds the light of the sun and the moon even in its particles. Deccan has given him a sense of freedom and developed in him a taste for knowledge and learning. It has granted him the key to mysteries and embellished his lofty thoughts. Hyderabad has opened the doors of love and affection to him. His life gets enriched because of its songs and his youth blossomed in its garden." He further said "O 'Deccan, the pleasure of your land is still fresh in my heart." Josh salutes the get-togethers in the houses of his friends, while on a visit to Hyderabad after eighteen years. The celestial sphere has spread the lustre of those days and will be long lasting. When he took leave from Hyderabad he was young and when he returned he found himself middle aged. But he adds, "O garden of my youth, hyacinth and lily of the Deccan, my heart is flooded with joy."

"The winds of Osman Sagar still blow and the voice coming from the mountains excites me and even to this day, the melodies and the dancer with bells on her ankles still surcharged the atmosphere. O, friends of the Deccan embrace thy friend before his frenzied joy is finally covered with a shroud."

SAROJINI NAIDU

The Nightingale of India expressing her feelings about the jewelled city wrote, "O coloured flower, house of pleasure, my native place, you are the Eden of my thoughts and imagination. Nobody would be aware of the storm of love which has arisen in my heart. My life has been created by the stream of beauty which nature has filled in your heart? Is my world not made up of your earth? Have your magical hills and deserts never sung a lullaby to me with bright ideas? Ah! Presently, I am in exile and roaming about in the grief of separation. Are you still not the adorable place of worship in my heart? Is not any search for you the aim of my soul?"

SIKANDER ALI WAJD

An outstanding product of the Osmania University he wrote a poem titled "Hyderabad Deccan".

Faza janifiza zara zara haseen hai
Haqiqat men mulk-i-Deccan gul zamin hai

Har yek naqsh tahzib jo dil nashin hai
Dil Hyderabad us ka amin ahi

Agar mehr o ulfat ki jannat kahin hai
To beshak yahin hai hahin hai hahin hai
Zamana dil agar hai bhi to kya gham
Mujhe tere dildariyanen ka yaqeen hai
Tere litf ka moujaza hai ke meri

Zaban gulfishan hai sukhan atashen ahi

Nafasat barasti hai diware dar se
Tei khak mein nikaht yasmeen hai

Banut khushuma shahr dekhe hain main he
Magar tera jadu kahin bhi nahin hai.

"Every particle of this land is pulsating with soulful joy.

In fact, the land of Deccan is fragrant with flowers. Its atmosphere is life giving and heavenly

The impress of civilization here is heart warming and worthy of cherishing. If there is any paradise of love and affection, it is here and here and here only. If the times are troublesome I am not grief-stricken because I derive comfort and strength from you; it is the magic of your affection that my language has turned poetic and fiery. The doors and walls are exquisitely pretty and your soil gives out the aroma of white jasmine. I have seen many beautiful cities but have not found your charm anywhere else."

KUNWAR MOHINDER SINGH BEDI 'SAHR'

a poem spontaneously Kunwar Singh Bedi read at 'Aiwan Urdu' in Hyderabad Deccan. Some verses of the poem are as follows:

Jahan fard apni jagah anjuman hai
Jahan har kali ak mahekta chaman hai

Jahan ki zamin rashk charkh-i-kihan hai
Jahan shukhiyan hain ada hai bhaban hai

Jahan sadagi mein bhi bankpan hai
Jahan raqhs farma hawa moujzan hai

Jahan shariyat hai jahan qadr-o-fan hai
    Jahan il-o-fan ke liye ek lagan hai

Jshan Hairat o Zoar ka bhi watan hai
    Jahan anjuman waqi anjuman hai

Jo such puchte ho sahr to wuh khita
    Deccan hai Deccan hai Deccan hai Deccan hai

Each individual is an institution in his place and each bud is a fragrant garden. Here the land is the pride of the ancient world, where there is fun, fascination and beauty. There is a gaiety in its simplicity and its breeze wafts joy. Here there is appreciation of poetry and art and a cultivated taste for the arts and sciences. This is the hometown of 'Hairat' and 'Zoar'. 'Sahr', if you genuinely ask about the magic of the region, it is the Deccan, Deccan and Deccan.

JAGNNATH AZAD

Dilli men yun zaban pe ayi Deccan ki bat
    Sahra men cher de koi jaise chaman ki bat

Liye har mouj men kaif gulistan-i-Deccan ayi
    Shamim gul ka bharkar roop buye pairahan ayi

Na tuta zindagi men silsila azadiyon ka
    Kabhi yad-i-watan ayi kabhiji yad-i-Deccan ayi

Bas itni bat hi sair Deccan ki aj baqi hai
Junoon mehman thahosh o kharma ki mehrbani thi

Ek husn Deccan tha ke nighoon se na chuta
    Har husn ko warna ba khuda chor gaye hum

'Azad' ab wuh sai MOSSORLE hi kyun na ho
Sairain tamam khatum hain sair-i-Deccan ke bad

"When a word about the Deccan was mentioned in Delhi it appeared as if somebody spoke about a garden in a desert. Each wave from the rose garden brought with it the intoxication of pervading perfume. Sometimes, I remembered the breeze of the Deccan, and sometimes the Deccan itself. By God, I have forgotten all other beauties with the beauty of Deccan engraved in my mind. O 'Azad' the tour of Musoorie is refreshing but nothing like the joy of recreation while travelling in the Deccan".

Ajkal hai Deccan men lutf suqan
Shair-i-khush bayan idhar ao

"The taste and flavour of poetry is in the Deccan these days. Poets of calibre are attracted to Hyderabad".

DR. SYED MOHIUDDIN QADRI 'ZOAR'

Shiraza bahar gul tar bikhar gaye
Ab kisko kya batayen ke zaib-i-chaman hai kaun?
Kashmir me koi to Karachi men hai koi
Ab 'Zoar' kis se puchte ahel-i-Deccan hai kaun

"The spring flowers are all scattered. What should one say, how does one define the beauty of this garden? Some of it is in Kashmir and some in Karachi. Oh 'Zoar' how does one identify a Deccani citizen?"

MAQDOOM MOHIUDDIN: MESSENGER OF REVOLUTION

Dayar-i-Hind ka wuh rahbar Telangana
Banaraha hai nai ek sahar Telangana

Bula rah a hai ba simt-i-digar Telangana
Wuh inqilab ka paighamber Telangana

Telangana is the guiding light of India and the her old of a new dawn. Telangana is attracting the people all over as the messenger of Revolution.

Dasht ki rat men barat yahin se nikli
Rag ki rang ki barsat yahin se nikli

Inqilabat ki har bat yehin se nikli
Gungunati hui har rat yahin se nikli

Shahr Baqi hai mhabat ka nishan baqi hai
Dilbari baqi hai dildar-i-jan baqi hai

Pyar se ank bhar ati hai kanwal khilte hain
"Jab kabhi lab pe tera nam wafa ata hai

A 'barat' (procession) starts on a lonely night from here with showers of colour and music. The song of revolution in each humming night starts from here. The city remains and the symbol of love remains, so also does its charm and fascination. Whenever your adorable name comes to my lips, the lotus blooms and my eyes are filled with tears of love."

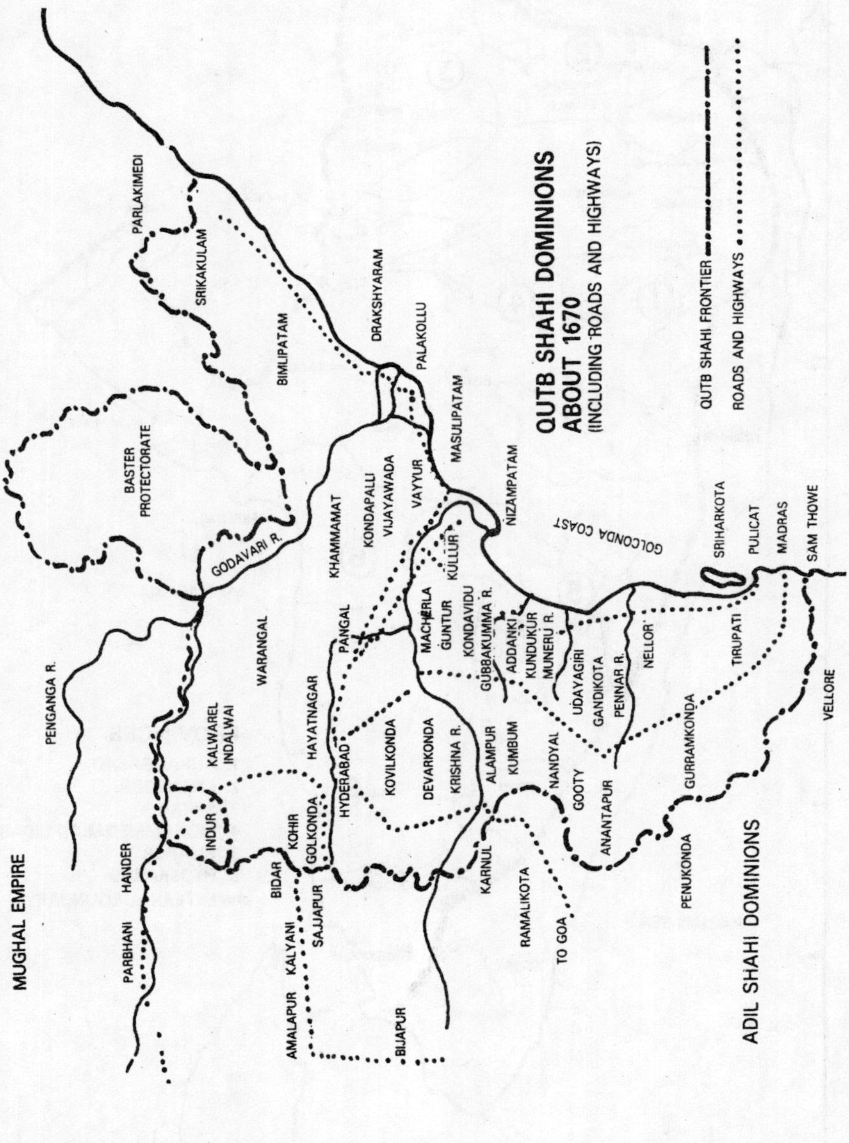

QUTB SHAHI DOMINIONS
ABOUT 1670
(INCLUDING ROADS AND HIGHWAYS)
QUTB SHAHI FRONTIER
ROADS AND HIGHWAYS
MUGHAL EMPIRE
ADIL SHAHI DOMINIONS
BASTER PROTECTORATE
GOLCONDA COAST
PARLAKIMEDI
SRIKAKULAM
BIMLIPATAM
DRAKSHYARAM
PALAKOLLU
MASULIPATAM
NIZAMPATAM
VAYYUR
VIJAYAWADA
KONDAPALLI
KHAMMAMAT
GODAVARI R.
PENGANGA R.
WARANGAL
KALWAREL
INDALWAI
HAYATNAGAR
PANGAL
HYDERABAD
GOLKONDA
KOHIR
INDUR
HANDER
PARBHANI
BIDAR
KALYANI
SAJJAPUR
AMALAPUR
BIJAPUR
KOVILKONDA
DEVARKONDA
KRISHNA R.
MACHERLA
GUNTUR
KONDAVIDU
KULLUR
GUBBAKUMMA R.
ADDANKI
KUNDUKUR
MUNERU R.
UDAYAGIRI
GANDIKOTA
PENNAR R.
NELLOR
ALAMPUR
KUMBUM
NANDYAL
GOOTY
ANANTAPUR
KARNUL
RAMALIKOTA
TO GOA
PENUKONDA
GURRAMKONDA
TIRUPATI
VELLORE
SRIHARKOTA
PULICAT
MADRAS
SAM THOWE

MUGHAL PROVINCE OF THE DECCAN UNDER NIZAM-UL-MULK ASAF JAH-I 1724 — 1748

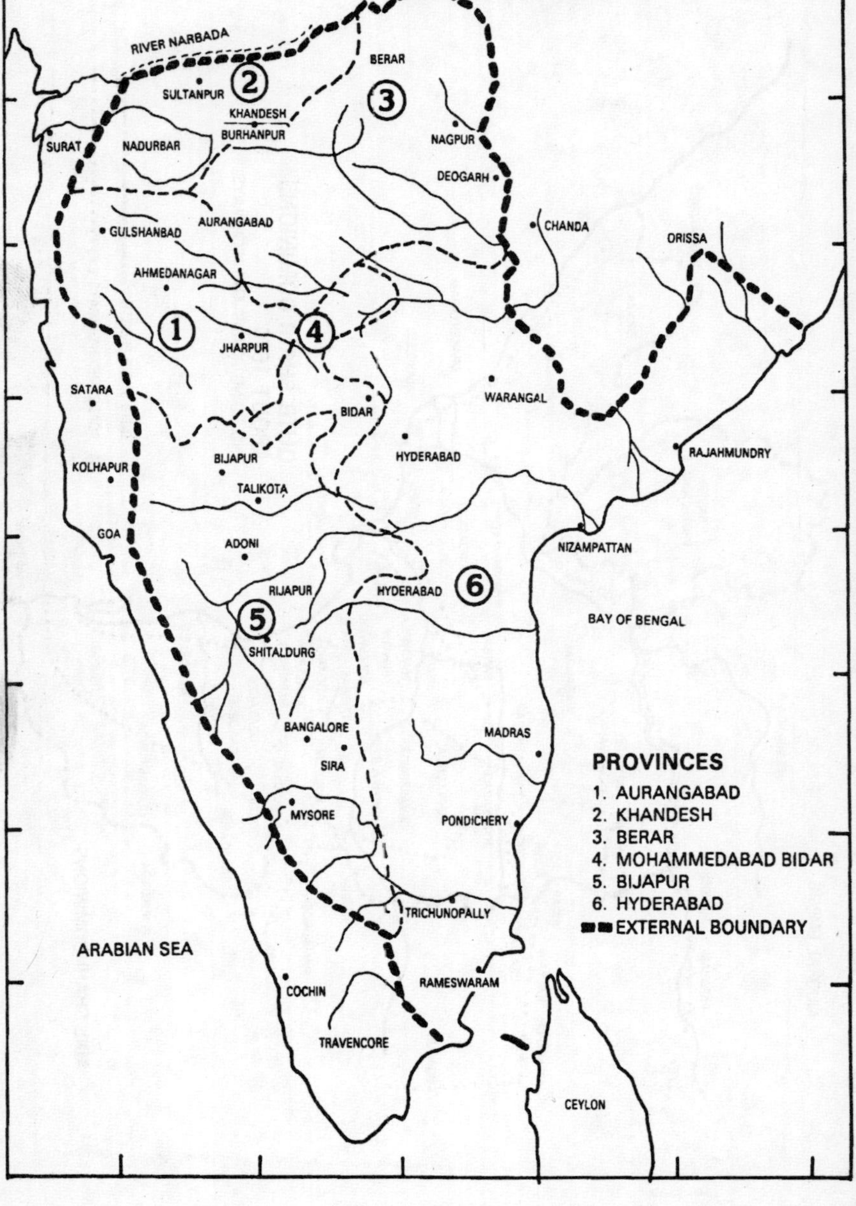

INDIA .. HYDERABAD STATE Pre-Independence (1947)

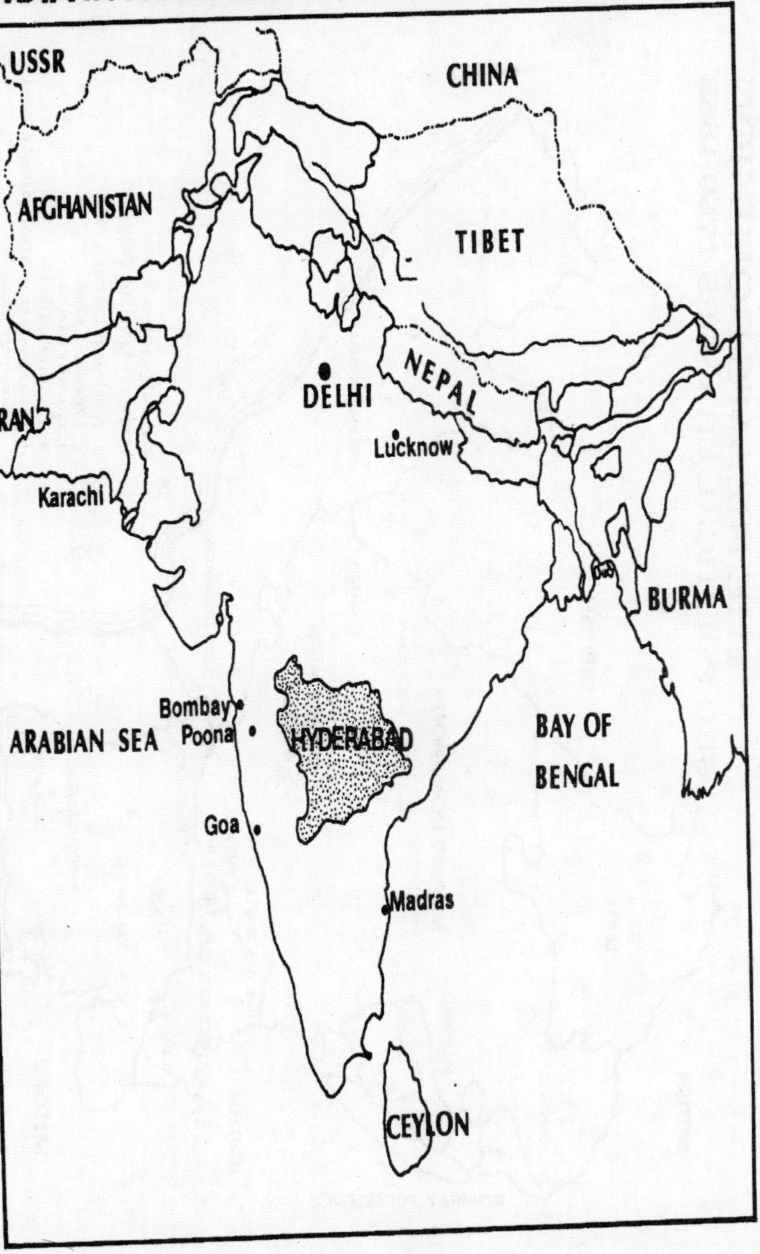

THE NIZAM'S DOMINION
GEO POLITICAL CHANGES 1759-1853

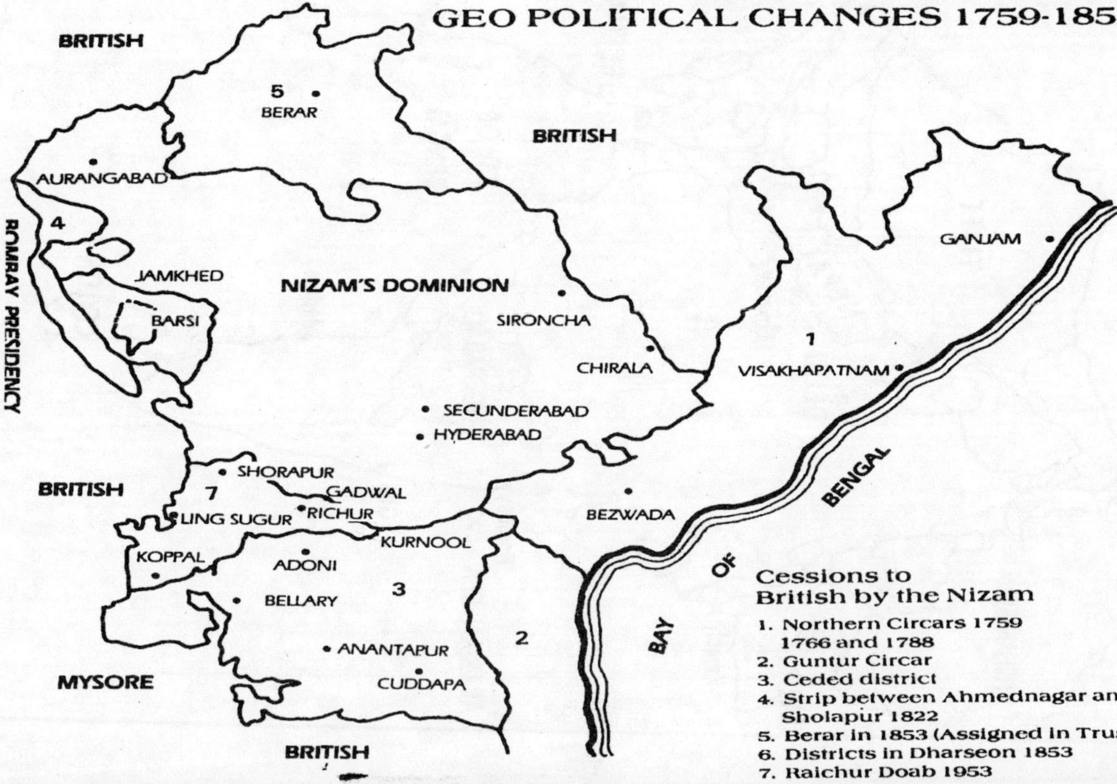

Cessions to
British by the Nizam

1. Northern Circars 1759
   1766 and 1788
2. Guntur Circar
3. Ceded district
4. Strip between Ahmednagar and
   Sholapur 1822
5. Berar in 1853 (Assigned in Trust)
6. Districts in Dharseon 1853
7. Raichur Doab 1953

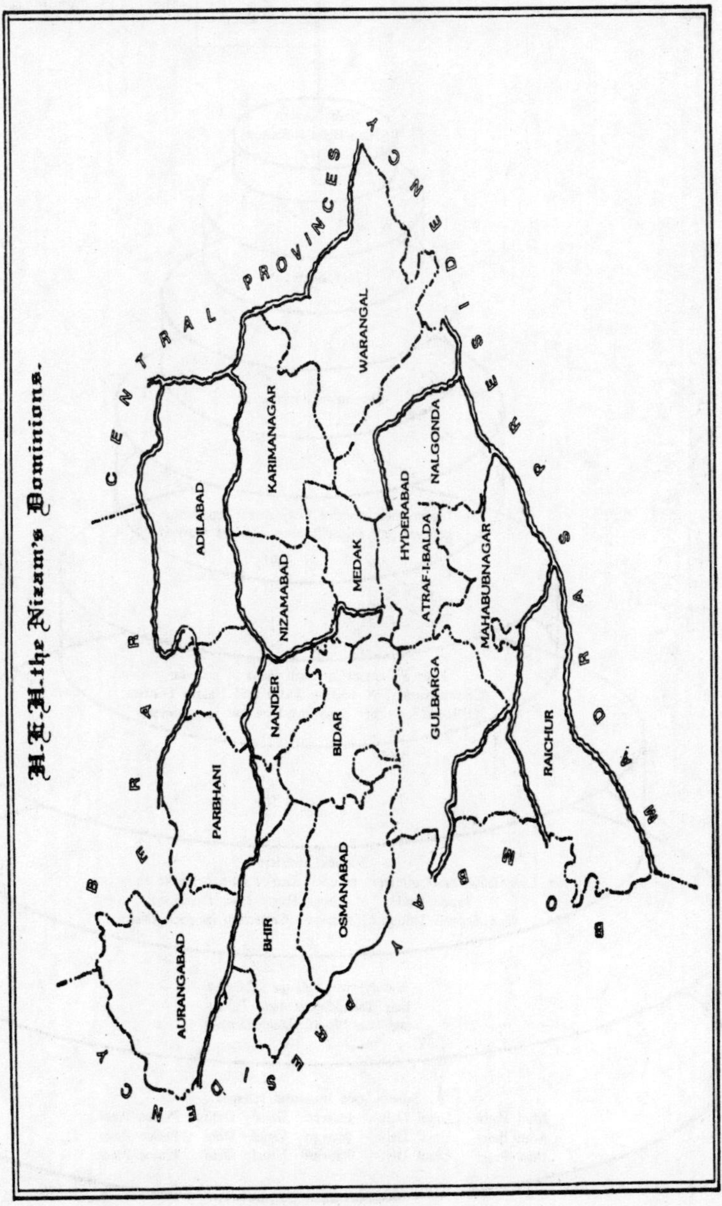

H.E.H. the Nizam's Dominions.

High Command Asafia Dominion

The Ten Ruler Administration At a glance.

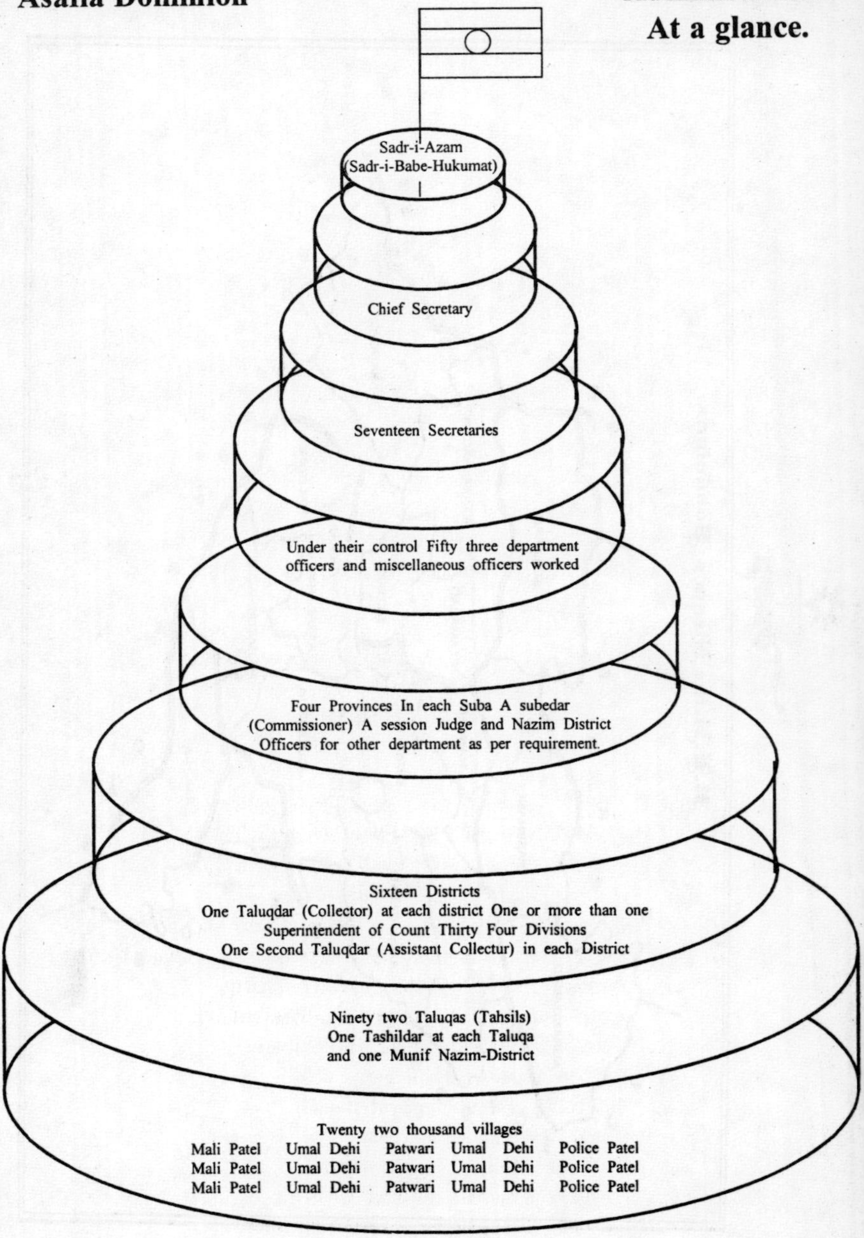

BIBLIOGRAPHY

BOOK REFERENCE

1. Armughan-i-Infani (Hayat-i-Osmani), Shaik Yaqoob Infani.
2. Inthekhab Kalam Asaf Sabe, 1975, Trust Hyderabad Deccan.
3. Intezam Kutb Khana, Mahbub Ali Qureshi.
4. Ikkishwin kul Hind Maashi, Confcrece, 1937, Hyderabad Deccan.
5. Boostan-i-Asafia vol.I-VIII, Manik Rao Vitthal Rao.
6. Basateen ul Salateen, (Tarikh Bijapur) Persian.
7. Be Tegh Sipahi, Nawab Siddiq Ali Khan.
8. Polo, Gesudaraz Khan.
9. Tassurat, Mulla Wahadi.
10. Tazkira Salateen Bahamani, Mutbua Hyderabad Deccan.
11. Tarikh Pak Hind, Matbua Karachi.
12. Tarikh Deccan Ahed – i – Halia, Dr. Yusuf Hussain Khan.
13. Tarikh Rasheed uddin Khani, Gulam Imam Khan Hijr.
14. Tarikh Adalat Asafi, Abdul Basit Khan.
15. Tarikh Farishta, Persian Mohd. Qasim Farishta.
16. Tarikh Golconda, Prof. Abdul Majeed Siddiqua.
17. Tarikh Adalat (Hakin-ul-Tawarikh) Mohd. Fateh Ullah.
18. Tariq Mukhtasar, Mutbua Hyderabad Deccan.
19. Tarikh Adab Hyderabad, Dr. Mohi Uddin Qadri 'Zore'.
20. Tohfah Jashan Simin, (Dept. of ARchaeology) Dr. Gulam Yazdani.
21. Tazkira Maashrat Hyderabad, Moid uddin Hasan.
22. Tazkira Maulvi Syed Qamar uddin, Dr. Basahrat Ali.
23. Jamal – i – Amjab, Hazrat Amjad Hyderabadi.
24. Chand Hamasar, Maulvi Abdul Haq.
25. Chuhne Huwe Phool, Col.Himayat Baiq.
26. Hayat Arstu Yar Jung, Ali Manzoor.
27. Hayat – i – Asaf, Mohd. Mahbub Junaidi.
28. Hayat – i – Fakr, Mushtaq Ahmed Khan.
39. Khirman – i – Kamal, Hazrat Kamal ulla Shah.
30. Dagh, Tamkeen kazmi.

31. Dabdaba – i – Nizam, Part – I, Abdul Raof.
32. Darbar – i – Durbar, Sidiq Jaisi.
33. Daftar Diwani-Mulki-o-Mal, 1357H, Nizamat Tabaat Sarkar Aali.
34. Deccan ki Siyasi Tarikh, Maulana Abulali Moudodi.
35. Deccan Culture, Nasir Uddin Hashmi.
36. Daulat – i – Asafia Aur.
37. Hukumat – i – Bartania, Maulana Abulali Maudodi.
38. Asar Qadima, 1935.
39. Report Sarishta Mazhabi.
40. Rukhat – i – Alamgiri.
41. Rahnuma – i – Tappa, 1909 -1940.
42. Suqhan dar Suqhan, Muzaffar uddin Khan 'Sahib'.
43. Sarquzasht Tappa, 1937, Mohd. Ahmed Nazim.
44. Safar Shahana, Maulvi Akbar Ali, Editor Sahifa.
45. Safarnama Mosio Theono, Safarnama Tavernir.
46. Sawaneh Maharaja Kishen Pershad, Mehdi Nawaz Jang.
47. Shair ki duniya, Mohd. Azeem uddin , 'Mahabbat'.
48. Saulat Osmania (Osmania), Khazi Abul Fateh Amir, Ullah.
49. Zabta – i – Tappa, Hukumat Hyderabad Deccan.
50. Ahed – i – Salaf, Maulvi Mohd. Murtuza.
51. Ghuncha – i – Nishat.
52. Fattoh ulbaldan, Persian, Maulana Asami.
53. Foot Ball, Abdul Rahim.
54. Faislah-i-Hindustan, Abdul Qudoos Hashmi.
55. Carvan – i – Hayat, Mushtaq Ahmed Khan.
56. Karnama – i – Sarwari, Sarwar Jung.
57. Kuliyat – i – Fani, Matbua Hyderabad Deccan.
58. Kalf – i – Suqhan, Dr. 'Zore'.
59. Gulgasht Deccan, Sibghat ullah Ansari.
60. Gulshan – i - Ajayab, Persian.
61. Gulzar – i – Asafia, Persian, Hakim Gulam HussainKhan.
62. Guzishta Lucknow.
63. Gazetteer Hyderabad Deccan, Mirza Mehdi Khan Koukab.
64. Lolinama, Matba Sultani Hyderabad.
65. Maasir ul Umara Vol II, Persian.
66. Maasir Deccan, Syed Ali Asgar Bilgrami.
67. Maasir Alamgiri, Persian, Mohd. Saqi.
68. Mahbub ul Zaman Vol II, Abdul Jabbar Malkapuri.
69. Muraqa – i – Deccan, Matbua Hyderabad Deccan.
70. Muraqa Jashan Osmani, Mohd. Fazil.
71. Mushahdat, Hosh Bilgrami.
72. Muntakhab ul lubab, Khafi Khan.

MAGAZINES AND NEWS PAPERS

73. Aajkal – Mahnama, Delhi, May 1965.
74. Urdu Digest, Lahore, July 1968.
75. Aiwan Mahnama, Hyderabad, October 1947, Deccan.
76. Haidri Jantri, Hyderabad Deccan, 1937.
77. Rahnuma-i-Deccan, Hyderabad Deccan, 1968.
78. Roznama Anjam, Karachi, Febraury 26 1967.
79. Roznama Aafakh, Lahore, March 18 1967.
80. Roznama Aghaz, July 21 1968.
81. Salnama Rahbar-i-Deccan, 1937.
82. Sabras Mahnama, 1939, Deccan Number.
83. Carvan Mahnama Hyderabad, Hyderabd Trust, Number, Karachi.
84. Roznama Jang, Karachi, February 28 1967.
85. Roznama Vafaq, Lahore, Febraury 28 1967.
86. Roznama Jang, Karachi, March 1 1967.
87. Roznama Nai Roushni, Karachi, February 28 1967.
88. Haft Roza Shahab, Lahore, March 5 1967.
89. Haft Roza Razakar, Lahore, March 1 1967.

SUBSIDIARY BOOKS

90. Asar Sanadeed Deccan, Humayun Mirza.
91. Arastu Jah, Prof. Abdul Majeed Siddiqui.
92. Asaf Jah Sani.
93. Star Directory, Calcutta.
94. Islam and Musiqi, Shah Mohd. Jafar Nadvi.
95. Anwar – i – Asafia, Syed Manzar Ali Ashar.
96. Paheliyan, Syed Maqdoom Alam.
97. Tarikh Asafi, Madbua Muradabad.
98. Tarikh Qutb Shahi, Qadar Khan.
99. Tarikh Khursheed Jahi, Gulam Imam Khan 'Hijr'.
100. Tarikh Riyasat Hyderabad, Mohd. Najm ul Gani.
101. Tarikh Hasan Waqiyat Deccan.
102. Tarikh Nizam, Mohd. Abdul Rahim.
103. Tarikh Birh, Mohd. Azmat Ullah.
104. Tarikh Rahat Afza, Mohd. Ali al Hussain.
105. Tarikh Deccan, Abdul Ghaffor Khan.
106. Tarikh Deccan, Nasrullah Khan.
107. Tarikh Qila udgir, Faramarz Jung.
108. Tarikh Kolas, Mohd. Amir Hamza.
109. Tarikh Aziz Deccan, Mohd. Abdul Aziz.

110. Tazkira Auliya-i-Deccan, 2 Vols., Abdul Jabbar Khan, Malkapuri.
111. Tazkira Salateen Deccan, 2 Vols., Abdul Jabbar Khan , Malkapuri.
112. Tuzak-i-Mahbubia, 2 Vols., Nasrullah Khan.
113. Tamadun Hind men Deccna ka Hissa, Abdullah Chuqtai.
114. Tarikh Zafra, Persian, Girdharilal Ahgar.
115. Hayat Mah Laga, Gulam Samdani Gouhar.
116. Darbar-i-Asaf, Gulam Samdani Gouhar.
117. Rusoom Hind, Pyare lal Ashoob.
118. Rusoom Delhi, Syed Ahmed.
119. Sir Salar Jang Azam, Faiz Mohd.
120. Silsila Sawaneh Salateen Asafia, Mir Murad Ali Tali.
121. Shikarnama Sher, Dwarka Pershad 'Ufaq'.
122. Shikar Sher, Maharaja Kishen Pershad.
123. Shadi Byah ki rusoom Hyderabad men, Safdar Ali Khan.
124. Shajra Asafia, Hakim Shama ulla Qadri.
125. Zia-i-Deccan, Mir Baqr Hussain.
126. Asar-i-Jadeed, Janki Pershad.
127. Ganjeena-i-Asafia, Syed Gulam Mohd.
128. Malik Amber, Shaikh Chand.
129. Mir Alam, Siraj uddin Talib.
130. Muraqia-i-Ibrat, (Swaneh Salar Jung ula), Syed Hussain Bilgrami.
131. Mazamen Mahfuz Ali, Anjuman Tarkhi Urdu.
132. Masjid O maqbara Mian Mushk, Mohd. Sardar Ali.
133. Hindustan Men Islami Tahzeeb, Dr. Aabul Latif.

ENGLISH BOOKS

134. Article of Gordon Rogers on Hyderabad Stamps.
135. A summary of Hyderabad's War Effort, 1939-43.
136. The Bulletin of Military Historical, Society London No 31 – 36.
137. The Choronology of Modern Hyderabad, Raja Trimbak Lal 1954.
138. The Days of the Beloved Mahboob, Lynton and Rajan 1974.
139. The Economic Life of Hyderabad.
140. The Fabulous Mogal, D. F. Karaka.
141. History of Legend in Hyderabad, 1953.
142. The Hyderabad (A Souvenir), 1944.
143. The Hyderabad Felatelist, Centenary issue, 1968.
144. The Hyderabad Mint Manual, H.CH. Armstead.
145. Ruler to Raj Permukh, Taraporewala.
146. Stanley Gibbon's Catalogue for 1967, Part I.
147. Song of India, Frank colone.

□□